The Amazing Aims and Claims of Jesus

What you didn't learn in church

Sir Anthony F. Buzzard, Bt., MA (Oxon.), MA Th

Restoration Fellowship
www.restorationfellowship.org

Atlanta Bible College
800-347-4261

ISBN 0-9673249-6-3

These chapters are dedicated to Barbara, my wife, constant companion in the faith of Jesus, to Sarah, my daughter, tireless and skilled worker for the cause of the Kingdom of God Gospel, and to all those who pray "Your Kingdom come"; in short, to all who long for the return of the Messiah Jesus, who was once here, to make everything right on earth, and to transform it into the Eden it was meant to be; and to all those who seek the pearl of great price.

"But I do not consider my life of any account as dear to myself, so that I may finish my course and the ministry which I received from the Lord Jesus, to testify solemnly of the Gospel of the grace of God. And now, behold, I know that all of you, among whom I went about preaching the Kingdom, will no longer see my face. Therefore, I testify to you this day that I am innocent of the blood of all men" (Paul in Acts 20:24-26).

"Make them holy in the truth. Your word is truth" (Jesus in John 17:17).

"God avails Himself of human thought and speech to make Himself known and His speech intelligible" ("Revelation," *New Schaff-Herzog Encyclopedia of Religious Knowledge*).

"The official line taken by Christianity...was not directly tied to the actual words and deeds of the historical Jesus" (Bart. D. Ehrman, *Jesus: Apocalyptic Prophet of the New Millennium*).

"Compared to the dynamic religion of Jesus, fully evolved Christianity seems to belong to another world" (Geza Vermes, *The Authentic Gospel of Jesus*).

"Polytheism entered the Church camouflaged" (Prof. Friederich Loofs, *History of Dogma*; Paul Schrodt, *The Problem of the Beginning of Dogma in Recent Theology*).

Table of Contents

Introduction

The first nine chapters of this book are designed to give readers who have no special training in the Bible a clear idea of God's grand program for every one of us. God's design for you and for humanity is to grant immortality to those who love and obey Him. God's program is for all who pay attention to what He has said. In the Scriptures, God spoke through a variety of different prophets and finally in His uniquely born Son, Jesus (see Heb. 1:1-2). God intends to grant endless life to believers in Jesus, the Messiah, and the coming Kingdom. I believe that the Kingdom of God is the answer to the great puzzle of life. It was the core of everything Jesus taught. It is the Christian Gospel. Jesus preached the Kingdom as Gospel, always. In fact, all of the Bible is concentrated on one major theme, the coming Kingdom. The Bible is a single drama in two parts, the Old Testament and the New.

The Christian Gospel is called the **Gospel (Good News) about the Kingdom of God**. I am going to have to repeat this basic fact many times, because the public seems not to know what Jesus preached about. Ask your friends "What is the Gospel?" and see if they mention the Kingdom of God. If they do not, ask them how the Gospel can have any other foundation than the Gospel preached by Jesus.

You can verify the facts about the Christian Gospel for yourself very easily by reading the New Testament, starting of course with the teaching of Jesus in Matthew, Mark, Luke (John uses other language to say the same thing). And there is lots of background information about the Gospel of the Kingdom in the Old Testament. Paul said that the Gospel is based on the promises in the Old Testament (Rom. 1:1-2). Any translation of the Bible available to you will give you the necessary information on what the Gospel is. But don't make the mistake of not starting with Jesus!

The Bible contains a thrilling story, an amazing drama, and it promises a wonderful outcome for our world. At the same time it threatens those who do not pay attention to Jesus and his aims and claims, with a tragic future. God expects us to listen to what He has to say to us through His agent, His Son Jesus. He gives us a choice. The Son laid before us two possible destinies — life forever or death, extinction. The Gospel is both a promise and a menace, a threat.

Everything hinges on our willing response to the Gospel of the Kingdom as announced by Jesus and later by the Apostles.

The first nine chapters of this book refer to or quote a number of fundamentally important Bible verses. You would not need to have your own Bible to follow what I have written. If you do have a Bible any version will confirm the story unfolded here. The Revised Standard Version or New Revised Standard Version or New American Standard Bible are generally reliable and easy to read versions. I would suggest not reading the King James Version, unless that is all you have. My reason is that you do not speak English the way the King James Version is translated (in 1611). Though it was in its time an accurate translation, its language puts up a kind of barrier between you and the vitally important words of Scripture. But if the King James is your favorite Bible that is fine. The Gospel of the Kingdom is clear even when it comes to you in old English. You should treat yourself to a modern translation also, if possible.

It is essential for the reader to know that I am inventing no new teachings here. Everything I have written has appeared in scholarly literature, in commentary on the Bible. But the public knows little about that literature. And some scholars have a poor record of actually believing what they know the Bible says. They often report well what they find, but they do not get very excited about us actually believing it! Or proclaiming it to others as essential information for learning the meaning of life.

I am asking you to think hard about what you may have learned about "the Gospel." Have you accepted without careful thinking and analysis a Gospel which is missing vital ingredients?

Do you realize that Jesus is the one we must listen to above all and his teaching is summarized in the caption "Kingdom of God"?

That last statement is so obvious in our Christian documents, the New Testament and its background in the Old, that a child with a basic reading ability could discover it easily.

What I am suggesting is that churches do not do a good job of relaying the Gospel as Jesus preached it — the Gospel about the Kingdom of God. I have attempted to explain those areas in which what we learn in church departs radically from some of the plainest and most emphasized teachings of Jesus and his Apostles. I can only ask the reader to read with an open mind.

These first nine chapters are written in fairly simple English. The sentences are generally not long or complicated. Part two of the book contains seven guide lessons on the Kingdom of God. In these seven lessons, there is a deliberate overlap and repetition of material in the first nine easier chapters. The guide lessons add more confirmation from outside authorities and more biblical detail about the Kingdom of God Gospel as preached by Jesus. They are a supplement to the first nine chapters. There is frequent repetition of basic Bible verses. The style is deliberately a little more complex but well within the reach of the average reader.

The guide lessons offer more evidence about the Gospel for the inquiring reader. They will help you to understand God's gracious offer of immortality for all believers in the Gospel of His Son, Jesus. They will assist you to develop your own presentation of the Gospel of the Kingdom. Readers will have opportunities for passing on what they learn in different settings — formal or less formal.

Yes, the message of Jesus explains how each of us can achieve immortality. That is why the Bible is by far the most precious document in the world. It is a priceless treasure. It has often been terribly obscured by church tradition.

Finally I have added some appendices with a list of biblical texts about death and resurrection and further confirmation from many experts of some of the main foundations of the Kingdom Gospel of Jesus as I am convinced he meant it to be understood and acted on.

Readers are asked to read thoughtfully, analytically and prayerfully. The Berean approach (Acts 17:11) is always the right one. Ask questions of others, read with a passion to get at the truth of Scripture, and be prepared to share with others what you find, once you are certain of it.

Quotations of the Bible are from various translations and I have translated the Greek and Hebrew myself occasionally. On the whole there is nothing controversial at stake here. Many modern translations convey the central concerns of Jesus quite well. But beware of some of the modern paraphrase versions of the Bible which can be quite misleading in *some* passages.[1]

Churches have inherited much of what they believe from early post-biblical "church fathers" and not from the Bible. Since the Protestant Reformation in 1517 Protestants seem to follow Luther and Calvin as new "church fathers." Luther's approach to the Gospel is strangely unbiblical since he did not think that the historical Jesus preached the Gospel! He did not start with Jesus' own preaching of the Gospel in Matthew, Mark, and Luke. He also thought that there was nothing Christian about the book of Revelation since "Christ is not taught in it." Luther called the book of James "a straw epistle." James, the half-brother of Jesus, disagreed with Luther's understanding about how to be right with God. Luther's idea was that the Gospel is found in Romans and Galatians and 1 Peter, but not primarily in the gospel accounts of Jesus' preaching. He thought that Matthew, Mark, Luke and John were relatively unimportant as far as the Gospel is concerned!

Calvin's God is so cruel that He predestined some human beings, even before they were born, to be tortured in hell forever. Calvin, who was well read in the Bible, also authorized the burning at the stake of a distinguished Bible scholar who challenged him on an important doctrine.[2] Killing others for any reason is utterly unlike anything advocated by Jesus. And killing another believer over a doctrine is really just murder, which the Bible forbids.

Roman Catholics believe that the Pope is the current representative of Jesus and what the Pope says officially, "from the chair" of his claimed divine authority, cannot be wrong. He claims for himself infallibility. The Pope claims to be the unique and only genuine successor to the New Testament Apostles. Church tradition can replace the Bible's teachings according to Roman Catholics. For instance Catholics state that Mary, the mother of Jesus, was taken bodily to heaven. The Bible certainly never says any such thing about Mary.

---

[1] For example the opening words of John's Gospel in the Living New Testament.

[2] Michael Servetus was burned at the stake in 1553. For a moving account of this terrible event read *Out of the Flames* by Lawrence and Nancy Goldstone.

Queen Elizabeth II of England, when she recently opened a meeting of Church of England dignitaries, said that in a world filled with information, much of it without lasting value, "there is a renewed hunger for what endures and gives meaning...At the heart of our faith stands the conviction that all people, irrespective of race, background or circumstance, can find lasting significance in the Gospel of Jesus Christ." She did not, however, tell us that the Gospel of Jesus Christ is the Gospel *about the Kingdom*.

I propose that Christianity is to be built firstly on Jesus, and Jesus without his teaching and preaching of the Gospel is not really Jesus at all. "Jesus" can be made the subject of all sorts of pious religious ideas and hopes. But the Jewish Jesus of history, the only Jesus, now at the right hand of God, claimed to be the Jewish-Christian Messiah (Christ) and to have the secret of immortality. He preached the saving Gospel-Message about the Kingdom. So did the Apostles after him. Jesus is by far the most challenging and gripping figure ever to have stepped the earth. As his contemporaries observed, "no one ever taught like this."

I echo the words of distinguished scholars of the Bible. I quote just one example among many. I think that their words should sound the alarm. Please read this quotation slowly:

> Neither Catholic nor Protestant theology is based on biblical theology. In each case we have a domination of Christian theology by Greek thought...Pagan ideas have largely dominated "Christian" thought...The immortality of the soul is not a biblical idea at all.[3]

If you do not understand the phrase "immortality of the soul," please read on. I am going to explain it later. It has to do with who we are as human beings, and what our destiny is — what happens when we die.

I wonder sometimes if Jesus would be welcome in our contemporary churches. The reader will have to decide. Jesus might well direct them back to his words and tell them to learn to "worship God in spirit and truth" (John 4:24) and not according to inaccurate church traditions. Many churchgoers have simply assumed that what they have learned about Jesus and the meaning of life in church is what Jesus would approve. My suggestion to

---

[3] Professor Norman Snaith, *The Distinctive Ideas of the Old Testament*, p. 188, 89.

the reader is that you do some serious investigation of the words of Jesus himself. It is always wise to go back to the original faith as Jesus believed and preached it.

Chapter 1
What Did Jesus Preach About?

My sole purpose in this book is to describe in uncomplicated language what I think the Bible tells us about God — about what the Creator of the universe had in mind when He created the heavens and the earth. About God's grand design. What is His great purpose for you and for the world? I want to explain to you what He expects of you and me, in whatever condition we find ourselves. What God's goal is for you, as you battle your way through life's difficulties. And I want to show you what God has in store for those who really love Him and His Son, Jesus.

Perhaps you are an important and influential financier, controlling large sums of money. Perhaps you are a teacher touching the minds of the young as they gather before you daily in school. Perhaps you are thankfully working as a housekeeper in a Malawi guest-house, mopping floors and washing dishes, or serving breakfast to the constantly changing population at your workplace. In Malawi, a country in Africa quite well-known to me, one is very thankful to have a job at all, and a salary, however meager. Most of the good Malawians we have been privileged to know have no job and no prospect of ever having one. Many live on a form of maize as a staple diet. They call it nsima. Many of our friends in Malawi, as in many other countries, do not have electricity or plumbing. Yet God is interested in them, not a bit less than anyone else. God is not impressed with social standing. But He is interested in His creation. He is interested in you — whoever you are, wherever you are. He is in search of people who will take His words and instructions through Jesus with utmost seriousness.

I repeat: God is not much interested in your "station" in life, your titles or your degrees or your accomplishments. But God is interested in your immortality, in your living forever. He created you with immortality in mind. Immortality means you cannot die. To be immortal means to be indestructible. It means that once you acquire immortality (which you do not yet have) you cannot ever cease to be alive! You will have life forever. When you are immortal, you cannot be diseased. You can never be killed. You will simply be indestructible (as is claimed for some of those "unbreakable" children's toys!).

I want to tell you about God's immortality plan for human beings. It is actually not a very complicated plan. If it were, one would have to have special intellectual skills and ability to understand it. You do not need any brilliance or special training to grasp God's immortality plan. But you do need an open mind — and a passionate, Truth-seeking attitude. You need a strong desire to know the Truth. Jesus called it "hungering and thirsting" after the right way to understand and act. And Jesus described the quest for the secret of immortality as a hunt for priceless treasure.

You need no special skills to read this book. I want to make things simple. But I want you to understand that you may not have learned much of what the Bible tells us about immortality in church. I will ask you to evaluate that last statement when you have finished reading this book.

If God had provided us with a Bible which only a learned scholar with years of training can understand, He cannot have intended ordinary people to understand Scripture, the Bible. But the records we have of Jesus when he was on earth show that he preached to the uneducated as well as the educated. He wanted his immortality Message, what he called, and we should call, the Gospel, to be accessible to everyone willing to listen with an open mind. All they had to do was to pay careful attention, give themselves wholeheartedly to what Jesus said, and then pursue the goal for their lives which Jesus laid before them. And they were to pursue that goal relentlessly for the rest of their lives. They were never to give up, whatever opposition or trial might come their way. Nothing could be more important than obtaining immortality — life forever and ever. "He who endures to the end will be saved," Jesus said.

People pursue goals in different fields with single-mindedness. They often give themselves wholeheartedly to the pursuit of goals which have no ultimate value. Is it too much to ask that we dedicate ourselves to gaining immortality, the only goal which really lasts, and lasts forever?

What goal did Jesus present to his audiences? What was the heart and core of all of his preaching and teaching? Quite simple.

Just open your Bible[1] to Luke, chapter 4 and verse 43 and you will find Jesus telling us there what he was "all about." You will find him in that verse giving his mission statement, the purpose for all his preaching and teaching, the reason for his whole activity in the service of God, his Father. You will find here Jesus' precious master-word, the genius of all he stood for and loved.

(Jesus as you know claimed to be the Son of God. If you had asked him who his father was, he would have looked you in the eye and said, "God is my Father." I trust that would have got your attention, your undivided attention. How many people do you know who can say "God is my Father," meaning that they have no human father? Yes, Jesus had no *human* father. The difference between Adam and Jesus is that the life of Jesus began in the womb of Mary his mother. Adam was made from the dust of the ground. Both Adam and Jesus are called son of God.)

More about who Jesus is and was in a later chapter. For the moment I want to be sure that you have grasped the stunning information given by Jesus in that verse in Luke 4:43 I just referred to. Luke 4:43. Write it down. Memorize it. It is a marvelous unpacking of the mind of Jesus. It tells you about his career, what his aims were, or rather what his single aim was. To know what *Jesus* thought the purpose of life was is indeed a great privilege and treasure. You can share his aims.

Christianity is about thinking and being like Jesus. Luke 4:43 provides a brilliant insight into the mind, the career and the purpose of Jesus, and therefore of Christianity.

And what drove the whole career and mission of Jesus? Let him answer. "I came to preach the Gospel (Good News) of the Kingdom of God. That is what I was commissioned to do." Yes, that is what Jesus was sent by God to do — to announce the Gospel of the Kingdom of God. Since that was Jesus' mission statement, that is the heart of the Christian faith. This is where your study of Jesus and his message must begin. Not to grasp what Jesus said here is to miss out on the whole point of his activity for some three years in Israel 2000 years ago. So please look again at Luke 4:43. Read it in any translation. The sense will be very clear.

---

[1] If you do not happen to have a Bible, please read on. At some point you will probably at least have access to a Bible, and I am going to tell the story of the Bible and often quote large sections of it in this book.

Jesus was an impassioned preacher of what he called the Gospel (Good News) about the Kingdom of God. God sent him, commissioned him, authorized him to do just that — preach the Gospel of the Kingdom.

The Gospel is about the Kingdom of God. That is fact number one about Jesus' version of Christianity. It is a fact which can be verified very easily by any reader. I have to repeat this: The Gospel of the Kingdom is the summary statement of the Christian faith. Jesus said it was, and if you are going to follow Jesus, it is wise to adopt his Gospel of the Kingdom as the center of your interest from now on. It was Jesus' "magnificent obsession" as someone has said, and if you want to think like Jesus and be like Jesus, the only sensible policy is to adopt his mission statement as yours. The Kingdom of God is Jesus' rallying cry and slogan.

I don't mean of course that you rush out today to preach the Kingdom of God because we need to find out first what he meant by Gospel or Good News and what he meant by Kingdom of God. (Don't let anyone tell you that it is impossible to know what Jesus meant by the Kingdom — or that the Kingdom is just something in your heart! And never let anyone tell you that Jesus' Gospel of the Kingdom is not for you!) But it is futile to proceed further in your search for the meaning of the universe, for the purpose of God in your life, until you have thoroughly taken in the basic fact that Jesus' purpose — and he was the spokesman for God, his Father — was to announce the Gospel about the Kingdom. That Gospel will open up the secret of living forever. It will also open up your understanding of the whole Bible.

I invite you, if possible with open Bible, to notice the verses which immediately follow Jesus' great and classic statement about the whole point of his mission and about Christianity, in Luke 4:43. You will find in Luke 5:1 that people listening to the Gospel of the Kingdom were listening to what Luke calls the "word of God." Now that phrase "word of God" is one which you really *must* understand, if you are going to make sense of the Bible and especially the New Testament books. Just as we in the West all recognize the term "the States" as shorthand for the United States of America, so Luke establishes for us here a "shorthand" for the Gospel of the Kingdom. Since the Gospel of the Kingdom is the heart and core of everything Jesus said and did, it is natural for those "in the know" to refer to that great saving Gospel message about the Kingdom simply as "the word of God," which means "the message," the Gospel message. Other New Testament writers refer to the Gospel of the Kingdom simply as "the word." This is no more difficult than understanding the fact that we often refer to the President of the United States of America as simply "the President." We all recognize this, but most people do not know what "the word" or "the word of God" means.

They lose out on a massive piece of vital information if they do not know that "word" or "word of God" in the New Testament almost invariably means "**the Gospel of the Kingdom as Jesus preached it.**"

I want to make this point crystal clear. Please do not confuse this important phrase "word of God." *It is not just another way of referring to the whole Bible.* Unfortunately in churches and on radio and TV, this vital phrase "word of God" is constantly used as just another way of referring to the Bible. Why is this point so important? Because within the whole Bible, which is called the *Scriptures* or holy writings, we have what is called "the word," or "the word of God." And both those phrases mean the saving Gospel message of the Kingdom of God which both Jesus and the Apostles always preached to the public. Is that point clear to you? Let me give you just one of many examples: In Acts we very often read that the preachers preached "the word." What does that mean? Is that just a general and vague statement about preaching anywhere from the Bible?

No. "The word" or "word of God" is the specific Gospel preaching about the Kingdom of God. This goes back to Jesus' own preaching. "Next Sabbath almost the entire city gathered to hear the word of God" (Acts 13:44). They "went everywhere preaching the word" (Acts 8:4). This was not a general lecture on the Bible. It was the Gospel as Jesus had preached it. Acts 8:12 defines the "word" for us beautifully. "The word" is the "core" of the Bible. The Bible is certainly "the words of God," but the heart of the Bible is called the Gospel or "word" or "word of God" many times in the New Testament.

To confuse "word of God," thinking that in the New Testament it simply describes the Bible, would be like not knowing the difference between London and England. If someone says they are going to London, they do not just mean a journey to somewhere in England.

To misunderstand that phrase "word of God" is to throw away a very great key to understanding the teaching of Jesus. It is to throw away a key to God's immortality plan for you.

Jesus was the first and authoritative preacher of the saving Gospel. And it is quite untrue (in fact a disastrous mistake) to say that Jesus' Gospel was meant for Jews only![2] It is meant for everyone! Hebrews 2:3 is a verse which everyone should memorize. "Salvation was first preached by the Lord (Jesus)." If you are interested in salvation, you must therefore determine to find out what *Jesus* preached. And the Gospel about the Kingdom is for everyone. It is the Christian Gospel. (The death and resurrection of Jesus are part of the Gospel but not the whole Gospel.)

We are going to see that it is this Gospel of the Kingdom (including of course the facts about Jesus' death and resurrection) which we all must grasp and understand and take into our lives as vital spiritual food. It is the Gospel about immortality, and we insist with Hebrews 2:3 and a mass of Bible verses that Jesus is the first, model preacher of immortality. Here is how Paul put this fascinating and important concept: Paul wrote to Timothy, his student in the faith, that Jesus had "brought life and immortality to light *through the Gospel*" (2 Tim. 1:10). There it is! Stop and ponder that wonderful statement. It was Jesus, preaching his Gospel of the Kingdom, who brought the secret of how to live forever to light. It was in Jesus' Message, and in no other, that we are invited to find the amazing secret of living eventually forever.

But in church this simple fact about "the word" being the Gospel is not clear. In fact the Gospel itself is not clearly defined. Often it is defined with no mention of the Kingdom! Many in churches have very vague ideas about what the Gospel is. In church circles you will almost never hear the phrase "Gospel of the Kingdom."

Has the voice of Jesus been lost or suppressed? *Jesus and Paul spoke about the Gospel of the Kingdom of God, but churches do not. They do not sound like Jesus and Paul.*

---

[2] It is true, of course, that Jesus preached the Gospel of the Kingdom to his own Jewish people first. But later he commanded his disciples to preach the very same Gospel of the Kingdom to everyone.

Now people today sometimes go to extraordinary lengths to preserve their lives for a few extra years (many die much too early due to smoking or other practices which take years off their lives). Some in California have their dead bodies frozen in the hope that science will find a way of bringing them back to life! What these people do not understand is that Jesus has already told us how we can have life forever, indestructible life. **He said that the secret is bound up with his Gospel Message about the Kingdom of God.** In another chapter we are going to look at, and hopefully listen very carefully to, that Gospel of the Kingdom which Jesus said was the very purpose of all his preaching and teaching. Remember that Paul said that Jesus had revealed the way to immortality in that Gospel or "word."

Presumably you are interested in living forever. Does the idea of having eternal youth — in fact finding the fountain of youth — and not being able to die grab your attention? It does mine! The secret of life forever and ever is sitting right there in the pages of the Bible, but I doubt that it has been clearly explained to you in church. If that sounds incredible please hear me out. Read on and see for yourself. (There are historical reasons why important Bible truths have been largely lost to huge church organizations.)

May I remind you to listen carefully and see if churches use the same language about the Gospel as Jesus did. Do they speak constantly about the *Gospel of the Kingdom*? Jesus always did. Paul always did. They both "welcomed the people and began talking about or preaching the Gospel of the Kingdom." Both Jesus and Paul were impassioned Kingdom preachers. Please look up Luke 9:11 and Acts 28:30, 31 for this vitally important fact. Ponder it deeply and compare it with what you have heard in church.

So what have we said so far? That God, alone the creator of all things (Isa. 44:24) and the one who gives us every breath we breathe and equips us with our amazing bodies and minds, has an ultimate plan and purpose for every human being born. That purpose can be discovered in the Christian Bible, though, due to a great muddle in churches, you may not have seen or heard that Plan clearly explained. It ought to be possible to remedy that situation.

In addition we have pointed you to Luke 4:43 which is the grand mission statement of Jesus himself. It reveals his whole purpose. It was to preach the Good News about the Kingdom of God and how to gain immortality in that Kingdom.

In the next chapter we begin to investigate what Jesus meant by the Gospel of the Kingdom. But before we do this, let me leave you with a question. Are you aware of having heard sermons on the Gospel of the Kingdom? If your answer is doubtful or "no," you might wonder why this is.[3]

Since churches are meant to be representing Jesus and his Gospel, are they in fact doing their job if they never or seldom talk about the very subject which Jesus said was the whole point of Christianity? Give that question some serious thought. You might even inquire among your friends if they define the Gospel as Jesus did. Ask them in a non-threatening way what the Christian Gospel is. If they do not immediately respond that it is the Gospel of the Kingdom, you might follow up by asking them why their answer was different from Luke 4:43 (and hundreds of other verses we have not yet had time to look at). You could make your point like this: You could invite them to look up Matthew 4:17, 23 and 9:35, and Luke 8:1 as well as Acts 8:12, 19:8 and 28:23, 31. You need no special skills to see what it was which kept Jesus fully occupied. And there are masses of verses like these.

These conversations about the Gospel and immortality can be fascinating. So much more interesting than talking about football or the weather.

The lady cutting my hair recently, who had attended church since childhood, was astonished when I pointed out that she had been praying for years, in the Lords' prayer, for the Kingdom to come. She confessed to not knowing what "Thy Kingdom come" meant. It apparently had not occurred to her that her prayer was for Jesus to come back and relieve the present world-system of its awful problems and injustices. And that the Kingdom is the central subject of the Christian, saving Gospel.

---

[3] In our book, *The Coming Kingdom of the Messiah: A Solution to the Riddle of the New Testament* (2002) we document numerous statements by leading preachers and writers admitting they do not preach the Gospel of the Kingdom and that the Church really has not for much of the past 2000 years!

Chapter 2
More About the Kingdom

We need to say lots about the Kingdom of God since "Kingdom of God" was really Jesus' way of speaking of the Christian faith which he taught everywhere and for which he also died. Jesus was driven by the commission which God, his Father had given him: to announce the greatest Good News (Gospel) ever: that the Kingdom of God is coming (Luke 4:43; Mark 1:14, 15).

You really know this, since almost everyone knows the Kingdom prayer: "May your Kingdom come!" You do not pray for something to come if it is already here. And Jesus did not say "Your Kingdom spread." He asked us to pray that the Kingdom will *come*. To imagine that it has *already* come would be a quick way to confuse the Bible story.[1] The Kingdom prayer is still the key Christian prayer, and we are still praying for a future event, the coming of the Kingdom in power and glory.

Jesus told us to pray "Thy Kingdom come" and we are to pray that prayer intelligently, knowing what we are saying! The last words of the Bible echo that passionate longing for Jesus to come back and bring peace on earth (Rev. 22:20).

Jesus knew the Old Testament well and he knew a passage in the prophet Micah (4:7, 8), which had just the same coming of the Kingdom in mind. It defines the Kingdom beautifully. "The Lord will rule over them in Mount Zion [Jerusalem]...To you [Jerusalem] it will *come* — the former dominion will come, the *Kingdom* of the daughter of Jerusalem." The Hebrew Bible is chock full of such promises of the future Kingdom of God to be established on earth.

---

[1] The notion held by some that after Jesus ascended to the Father we are no longer to pray the Lord's prayer with its petition "Thy Kingdom come" is fundamentally wrong. Such an idea would put us in direct disobedience to the Messiah, which is dangerous (John 3:36).

That wonderful passage in the prophet Micah is a prophecy of a restored government, operating with headquarters in Jerusalem. This has obviously not yet come to pass.

One of the simplest and most enlightening facts about the Kingdom of God can be learned from the first chapter of the book of Acts. The promised Kingdom of God did not arrive on the day of Pentecost. The nations have not abandoned international or local wars as they will in the Kingdom of God (Isaiah 2:1-4). The churches are hopelessly divided. There is no lasting peace on earth. The Bible expressly and clearly says that the coming of the Kingdom of God will be at a time unknown to us (Acts 1:7). The resurrected Jesus, however, stated that the coming *of the spirit of God* in a special outpouring of power on the young church would be "not many days from now" (Acts 1:5). When the disciples then asked if the Kingdom of God would come at the same time, Jesus replied that this was a separate event, whose date was reserved in God's plan, and not to be known by us (Acts 1:6, 7).

The coming of the Kingdom is obviously, then, *not the same event as the coming of the spirit* in spectacular power at Pentecost. The coming of the Kingdom of God is future, and it includes the restoration of the Kingdom to Israel, as Jesus' highly trained Apostles and Gospel preachers well knew.

I trust that our first chapter impressed on you the hopelessness of trying to understand Jesus or the New Testament (or in fact the Old Testament) if we do not get a firm grasp *firstly* on the fact that Jesus always preached the Gospel of the Kingdom, and secondly what Jesus meant by the Kingdom of God. So what did he mean by it?

I want to deal with that question by first tackling a related question: What happens when we die? You will see very soon how that question is closely related to the Kingdom of God. Let me direct your attention to the basic question about what happens to the dead. Where are they when they are dead? Are they really dead or in fact alive somewhere else? We need to understand the answer to this question as part of our search for understanding on the Kingdom of God, the center of all that Jesus preached.

Where did Jesus get his information about the Kingdom of God and the future of human beings? And about what happens when we die?

The answer to that question lies largely in the Old Testament Bible background which Jesus learned from the synagogue. He learned also from his parents, and of course from God his Father who constantly inspired his thinking and all his activity. You will perhaps remember that from the age of 12 Jesus was able to "run circles" around the official doctors of religion of his day. He was "streets ahead" of them in his understanding of the great theological questions. Jesus appeared as a kind of Mozart or Einstein of his day, a prodigy, an exceptionally brilliant and talented exponent of God (of theology) and of the meaning of the universe and life itself. The religious doctors of his time were amazed at his questions and answers as he discussed the great issues of life with them (see Luke 2:40-52).

We all need to soak ourselves in the wisdom and teaching of Jesus, that virtuoso of spiritual understanding. But have you been taught to think of Jesus as a tireless teacher and rabbi? The New Testament says that Jesus *taught* daily in the temple, no doubt for hours and hours (Luke 19:47).

I said that Jesus' understanding was largely due to his grasp of the Old Testament Bible which he had grown up with. The Old Testament we might reasonably call "the Hebrew Bible." It is written in the Hebrew language from Genesis to Malachi. Some parts of Daniel and a very few other passages are written in Aramaic, which is a language like Hebrew. Jesus had the same books in his Bible as you and I have in our Old Testament, 39 books. The *order* of the books was different in the Bible Jesus knew. The books were the same. Jesus actually referred to that order of the books in Luke 24:44 where he spoke of these precious sacred writings, the Hebrew Bible, as "the Law, the Prophets and the Writings."

Jesus loved those writings. (Christians who have the spirit and mind of Christ will love them too.) He believed in their inspiration. That means that he believed that God had used the writers of those books to record what God wanted revealed to us. God did not dictate His words to the Bible writers, using them as robots. But He taught them His will, and without bypassing their different capacities and backgrounds, God caused them to put on paper what He wanted communicated about His great Plan in world history, and of course His Plan to give immortality to those who choose to listen carefully to God and His agents the prophets, and to the final prophet and Messiah, Jesus. Yes, Jesus was the ultimate prophet. He was also the Son of God. (Luke 1:35 tells us the *basis* for his being the Son of God.) You probably have not heard Jesus called a "prophet" but according to a great prophecy in Deuteronomy 18:15-19 he is called a prophet like Moses, though of course greater than Moses. The New Testament links that prophecy with Jesus in Acts 3:22 and 7:37. Peter in Acts 3:22, 23 uttered some pretty strong words. He said that every human being who will not pay attention and respond to the words of "that prophet" Jesus has very little future. He is in terrible trouble with God. Jesus said the same thing powerfully in John 3:36.

When God inspired the writers of the Old Testament, the Hebrew Bible, as He did later the writers of the New Testament, God's very mind was expressed. God used the individual talents of the different writers. As we pointed out, He did not just impose on them a form of "guided writing," using them as passive instruments. Rather He gave them understanding of His will and purpose. He gave them wisdom. He taught them, sometimes through great trials, and He used them to write the Bible. That is why we refer to the Bible as Scripture, or holy writings. This means that the words of Scripture are reliable and true.[2] It means that the words of Scripture carry the very spirit, mind and heart of God. We can learn how God thinks from the Bible. David was one of the great Bible writers and he expressed how God had used him as a vehicle of inspiration: "The spirit of the Lord spoke by me; His word was in my mouth" (2 Sam. 23:2). David's words were expressions of the mind, spirit and will of God.

As Jesus put it "the Scripture cannot be broken" (John 10:35). Jesus over and over again claimed to be speaking on behalf of the One God, his Father. God has seen to it that the precious words of Jesus have been preserved for us. Paul put it this way: "All Scripture is given by inspiration of God" (2 Tim. 3:16). He said in fact that Scripture was "inspirited" by God. God breathed His

---

[2] There are a few passages which have been corrupted by copiers. But the evidence for this is usually clear, and scholars are able to help us get at the original version. God has not left us without a clear statement of His will and intention. Jesus promised to send "scribes," i.e. professional Bible scholars to help declare the Gospel (Matt. 23:34; cp. Dan. 12:3).

mind and will and spirit into the words of Scripture so that they tell us exactly what God wanted known. They reveal what God is thinking and what He wants us to know for our own good. The Bible, especially the teachings of Jesus as the foundation of Christianity, equips us with the information needed to make sense of life, with all of its difficulties. We can rely on the Bible as a sacred record of what God has communicated to the human race, to help us on the journey of life towards our goal, which is immortality in the Kingdom of God.

God spoke in ancient times through various prophets and only in New Testament times did he give His ultimate Message, the Gospel of the Kingdom, through His Son Jesus. For this fundamental fact please read Hebrews 1:1-2. You will find there too that God created the ages of the world with Jesus in mind. The whole Bible centers on God's immortality program as it was finally revealed to us by Jesus as God's agent.

The Bible tells us where the world is headed, and what we must do to fit into God's plan. The Scriptures are given us as a great comfort that God is in charge, whatever happens to us. It is our job to find out and follow God's plan.

You may notice that I did not say that God guides us "on our journey of life towards *heaven*."

One of the greatest of all confusions and muddles ever to hit churches is the use of the word "heaven" as the goal of the Christian. Neither Jesus, nor the Bible anywhere, ever spoke of "heaven" as the goal Christians are aiming at. There is no place called "heaven" in the Bible, meaning a place where your "soul" goes when you die. God and Jesus are in heaven, certainly, but the dead are not!

You may find this a bit shocking. But I ask you to think deeply about this question of human destiny and destination. I am hoping to convince you that speaking about "heaven" as your future destination is a quick way to get confused about the Bible. I repeat: the Bible never says that when we die, if we are believers in Jesus, we go "to heaven." It never says that anywhere. Jesus never preached a Gospel about "heaven." Jesus did not believe in going to heaven when you die. He himself did not go to heaven the day he died.[3] Jesus did not believe that any human being had gone to heaven when he or she died.[4] And Jesus plainly said that those who had died as the faithful in Old Testament times were still dead in their graves. He never said that they or anyone else had gone to a celestial heavenly mansion, or to a burning hell.

Pick up a New Testament for yourself and simply read, asking yourself, "What objective or goal did Jesus offer his followers?" Where did he ever say "If you want to go to heaven, follow me"? He never said, "you are going to rejoin your dead relatives in heaven." Much less did Jesus ever imagine that disembodied souls (souls without bodies) had left the earth for a heavenly existence with God.

So, you might ask, where did I learn all that language about "going to heaven"?

The answer is that you learned it by listening to other church members, by sitting in Sunday or Sabbath school, by singing hymns in church and listening to sermons. But you could not possibly have learned it from the Bible. There is a very important conclusion to be drawn from this amazing fact. It is that huge numbers of churchgoers, united in one great organization, do not often stop to ask themselves about where they learned what they believe and what they understand about their faith. They do not in fact generally ask many questions at all about what they believe. After all, their leader has been trained. He must know. And who are they as pew sitters to question what is taught from the pulpit?

The fact is that countless good Bible scholars have complained bitterly about the fact that "heaven in the Bible is nowhere the destination of the dying."[5] These men have been leaders in the

---

[3] Jesus promised the thief that he would be with him in the future paradise of the Kingdom of God. The thief had asked to be remembered in the future "when you come in your Kingdom" (Luke 23:42). Jesus replied emphatically that indeed the thief would be in the Kingdom, when Jesus returned (Luke 23:43). Jesus clearly said that he would be three days in the grave (Matt. 12:40) and after his resurrection he still had not yet gone to heaven to be with God (John 20:17).

[4] Enoch and Elijah had been taken up into the sky, it is true, but Hebrews 11 tells us that they later died. They are certainly not in heaven now and nor is any other human being except Jesus who is there with God his Father.

[5] Dr. J.A.T. Robinson of Cambridge, *In the End God*, p. 104.

field of Bible studies. But the public either does not bother to read what they have to say, or are simply not interested in a clear understanding of their future hope. (And hope is the second great Christian virtue, along with faith and love. The *content* of your hope is very important. The Bible has lots to say about what a Christian is to hope for.) For whatever reason, the churchgoing public is content to rely on "what everyone believes" — that is, that at death our "souls" leave our bodies in the grave and we continue to live on. We sing about "John Brown's body" rotting in the grave while "his soul goes marching on." We just change our address, from earth to heaven. We shed our physical clothing, our body, and our "immortal soul" soars off to heaven to be with Jesus. One popular hymn speaks of flying off to heaven.

All this may sound comforting, but is it in any way true?

We have all had the "heaven at death" idea enforced at funerals, repeatedly. How many of us have looked at an open casket and thought: "Isn't that a pleasant thought? The dead person is not really in the coffin"? He or she is really somewhere else, enjoying (?) watching us as we grieve over their "departure" to a better place. And we go on reinforcing our grand misunderstanding by speaking of the dead as having "passed away," which in some vague way seems to mean that they have gone to heaven to be fully conscious with God and Jesus.

We tell our children that dead relatives have just left their clothes, their body, in the grave, and have gone off to be with God and Jesus, alive and well. How a person can exist without a body we cannot imagine, but longstanding tradition has convinced us that the dead are really alive somewhere else.

Of course Christian bookstores confirm our false understanding with popular descriptions of people who have had "after death" experiences. These people claim to have died and gone to heaven. Some say that they have visited hell. Somehow these books, and not the Bible or Jesus, are taken as "gospel truth." The public is deluged with the idea that the dead are really alive somewhere else.

But none of this is true. Moreover it cleverly diverts your attention from the real Christian goal. And that goal is an essential part of the Gospel of the Kingdom which Jesus invites us to believe.

We must say frankly that anyone who speaks of the dead
going to heaven does not sound at all like Jesus. Jesus never ever
said such a thing[6] and so people who do use that "heaven when
you die" language appear to tell us that they have been listening to
the Church and not to Jesus and the Bible. I trust that you will
accept this as a challenge to further careful study. How is it that
the Church, your church perhaps, could be poles apart from Jesus
on such an elementary and basic question as "what happens when
I die"? If you are prepared to read on, I want to try to convince
you from simple Bible verses that the whole popular idea that a
man or woman consists of a physical body and a separable
conscious soul which never dies, is just a myth, or should we call
it what really it is, a lie.

It was the Devil who originally promoted the falsehood that
disobedience to God would *not* lead to death (Gen. 3:4). Adam,
however, failed to listen to God and lost his life. He died. The
New Testament speaks of Christians who die. But the great
difference is this: For them as believers that is not the end. They
will *come back to life*. They will be resurrected, brought back to
life from death. They will return to life at "the resurrection of the
just" (Luke 14:14). Jesus is going to resurrect them when he
comes back. Until then they remain dead and buried.

Once you understand this, you will be able to look forward to
the Kingdom of God as your goal, the grand purpose for which
you presently exist.

Is it reasonable that lies should be promoted in the name of
Jesus? Is that safe for us and our church, or is it time for us all to
raise a protest against falsehoods of any sort preached in the name
of Jesus, who did not believe what our church teaches? One might
even ask whether Jesus would be welcome in our church. He
might be asked politely or impolitely to leave and not come to our
church if he were to report on the dead as he did in the case of
Lazarus, his friend: "Lazarus is asleep. Lazarus is dead. I am going
to wake him up from the dead." (Please look this up in John 11:11,
14.) He did not say Lazarus has gone to heaven! Jesus said he

---

[6] Jesus spoke sometimes of rewards in heaven, but this is a typical
Jewish way of telling us that our *future* reward is now prepared in heaven
with God, and will be given to us on earth *in the future* at the return of
Jesus to this earth.

would bring Lazarus back to life by calling him back *from his tomb* (John 11:43). That is where the dead Lazarus was. He had not gone somewhere else. Nor have your dead relatives and friends. Mary, the mother of Jesus, is also dead and buried. Neither she nor any so-called special "saints" can possibly hear prayer. The notion that dead "saints" respond to prayer is a huge fairytale. But about a billion people in one large denomination believe it.

The grief counseling of Jesus, as reported by John, sounds radically different from the erroneous counsel offered by churchmen, when they comfort the bereaved with assurances that their relatives are alive and well, in "a better place," heaven.

One clergyman reacted this way when we put it to him that the Bible does not teach that the dead are in heaven: "You are quite right, of course." Then he added, "But I could not possibly say such a thing from the pulpit!"

Do those words of Jesus — that his dead friend Lazarus was asleep in his tomb — challenge you, even shock you? I believe they are meant to drive you and me to some earnest thinking. After all, believing falsehoods in the name of Jesus or supporting organizations which promote falsehoods in the name of Jesus is likely to be dangerous. A very risky business, I would think, since Jesus always insisted that we must believe the truth and never falsehoods, that we must always be willing to stand up for him and what he taught against all opposition. And remember that Jesus encountered most opposition not from the general public, but from the churches (synagogues) of his day. He also warned that "anyone who is ashamed of me *and my words*, I will be ashamed of him when I come back" (Mark 8:38).

Jesus was a tireless opponent of careless worship. Of worship not based on Scripture but based on tradition, carelessly and thoughtlessly inherited from our parents and perpetuated, unopposed, in our churches. Jesus complained bitterly against teaching tradition rather than truth in church. We are all meant to be intelligent truth-seekers, not passive receivers of unexamined tradition. We must worship God within a framework of "spirit and truth" (John 4:24). Tradition which contradicts the Bible is a deadly poison in the church and Jesus issued a forceful warning to this effect (Matt. 15:7-9). Religious tradition embedded in our lives because our parents taught it, and our church taught it, and our best friends believe it exercises a mighty power over our thinking. And the one question which apparently only a very few seem to ask is "What is the Gospel?"

Jesus had learned from the Hebrew Bible a number of very simple basic facts about death. In Ecclesiastes he had read and probably memorized Ecclesiastes 9:5, 10. We read there a clear statement about the state of the dead. "The dead know nothing at all and they have no more reward...There is no activity or thought or knowledge in Sheol ['gravedom,' the world of the dead] to which you are going." "The dead do not praise the LORD, all those gone down into silence" (Psalm 115:17). And scores of verses say the same thing.

That hardly sounds as if the dead are fully conscious in bliss watching their surviving relatives from a privileged position in heaven. Would that in fact be any sort of privilege? Happily God has arranged things quite differently. He places the dead in a state of unconsciousness, at rest in their graves until a great future moment. That grand and amazing moment is the event of the resurrection, which will happen when Jesus comes back to inaugurate worldwide his Kingdom of God, the subject of his Gospel. All this is concisely and plainly stated in that wonderful verse in Daniel 12:2. Here is how the dead will one day return from death to life: "Many of those who are sleeping in the dust of the ground will awake, some to the Life of the Age [to come]." You are familiar certainly with the idea of "everlasting life." Here is its first mention. It is literally "the life of the *age* to come," that is life in the future Kingdom of God. Life to be gained fully only via *resurrection*!

In this chapter we have been speaking more about the Kingdom of God. But in order to unfold the biblical story — the greatest story and drama ever — we have had to take up two related subjects: the question of what happens when we die and just briefly the grand future arrival of Jesus back on earth. Why must he come back? To raise the sleeping dead from their graves. And to make possible the great promise contained in his Gospel of the Kingdom. Jesus is coming back to reorganize the whole world so that it works properly and fairly as God intended. Jesus is going to supervise a new world administration with headquarters in Jerusalem. The Bible, especially the writings of the Hebrew prophets, is simply filled with this information, on page after page.

Isaiah 32:1 (from various versions) predicts: "There will be a king who reigns uprightly and princes who rule with fair judgment." "Behold, a king will reign in righteousness, and princes will rule with justice." "Look, a righteous king is coming! And honest princes will rule under him."

I wonder if you realize that Jesus' aim in preaching the Good News about that Kingdom was to invite you to be one of those "honest princes" or princesses, to administer that future world with Jesus. The Gospel of the Kingdom calls you to royal office in the first really successful government. Put away then the feeble idea that your destiny is to strum a harp in a far-off celestial place.

Your training as a Christian now and the talents God has given you are designed to equip you to bless the world on a grand scale when the Kingdom comes. God is not finished with you in this present life. He desires to "give the earth to those who are pleasing to Him" (Jer. 27:5). Can you imagine being given the earth?! God wants to appoint you as a servant-administrator in the Kingdom which God and Jesus are preparing. This is not a form of oppressive government, but the wise and loving supervision of the affairs of the nations by Jesus himself and those whom he is equipping for the same royal service. All talent comes from God, and it is our duty to develop those gifts not only now but in readiness for the time when Jesus puts in place and power his world government, the Kingdom of God. Here are the words of Jesus looking forward to the time when he comes back. He will say to those who have persisted: "Well done! You are a trustworthy servant. You have been faithful with the little I entrusted to you, so you will be governor of ten cities as your reward" (Luke 19:17).

Unfortunately, if you have been listening to a world-famous evangelist who represents millions of believers, you may have learned that "in heaven, we will polish rainbows, tend heavenly gardens and prepare heavenly dishes."[7] Jesus said nothing at all along those lines. "Polishing rainbows" is frankly just pious nonsense. Jesus offered the public to prepare now to join him in the brand new administration he will introduce when he returns to our planet. "Don't you realize," Paul the Apostle said, perhaps a bit frustrated with his audience's ignorance of the basics of the

---

[7] Billy Graham.

faith, "that the saints are going to manage the world? And if the world is going to come under your jurisdiction..." (1 Cor. 6:2). For Paul and the early Christians this was a most elementary and foundational fact about Christianity. "Polishing rainbows in heaven" would have seemed to them quite ludicrous.

I have friends who say that this popular fiction about "heaven," if that is what Jesus promised, puts them off Christianity entirely. They are totally bored at such a prospect. They find such a destiny repulsive.

I will add here a grand statement from a famous London preacher who hit the nail on the head on this matter of the Christian goal, the heart of the Gospel.

> We will dwell in glorified bodies *on the glorified earth.* This is one of the great Christian doctrines that has been *almost entirely forgotten and ignored.* Unfortunately the Christian Church — I speak generally — *does not believe this,* and therefore does not teach it. It has lost its hope, and this explains why it spends most of its time in trying to improve life in this world, in preaching politics...But something remarkable is going to be true of us according to the Apostle Paul in 1 Corinthians 6:1-3: "Dare any of you having a matter against another, go to law before the unjust and not before the saints? Do you not know that the saints will rule the world?"...*This is Christianity. This is the truth by which the New Testament Church lived.* It was because of this that they were not afraid of their persecutors...This was the secret of their endurance, their patience and their triumphing over everything that was set against them.[8]

What happens when we die, future resurrection and the future Kingdom. A lot of information in two chapters, you may say. Let us see if we can pull this together clearly in our next chapter. Remember that the whole biblical story is about the Kingdom of God, which was the Gospel as Jesus and Paul preached it. It is God's great plan to achieve peace on earth — and to involve you in that process, if you are willing to respond positively to Jesus and his Gospel of the Kingdom.

---

[8] Martin Lloyd-Jones, *Commentary on Romans,* pp. 72, 75, 76, emphasis mine.

Chapter 3
Jesus Is Coming Back to the Earth

If your church has been telling you that your objective as a Christian, your goal, is "heaven," I believe they have been making the Bible a confusing book for you! If at funerals they have been sending the dead to heaven, alive and glorified, they have been offering you a pagan, philosophical concept, not the teaching of Jesus. It was the pagan philosopher Plato, not Jesus, who taught that "souls" go to heaven. Plato is given lots of scope in churches.

What would you think of someone who is convinced that the objective in a game of soccer is to kick the ball as high as possible into the air, not to kick it through the goal posts? You would consider such an opinion to be totally misguided and uninstructed.

From childhood the Church has been telling you that "going to heaven when you die" is the objective of the Christian faith. I propose that this concept puts you seriously at loggerheads with Jesus and the Apostles, who believed no such thing. Jesus promised "heaven at death" to none of his followers. He told them that they should aspire to "inherit the earth" or land. And this is precisely the same as "inheriting the Kingdom of God." The Kingdom of God will be set up in the land of Israel and across the whole earth. That marvelous event is the subject of Christian prayer. We are taught to pray, "May Your Kingdom come!"

If you are prepared to believe Jesus' words in Matthew 5:5 that the "meek are going to have the earth as their inheritance," you have taken a major step towards understanding the Gospel of the Kingdom, towards following the biblical story intelligently and accurately.

Try dropping the "heaven" word from your vocabulary about the life to come and see if you experience a marked improvement in your comprehension of the Bible, indeed in your spiritual health. You do not need pagan philosophical ideas in your mind. You need truth as Jesus and the Bible teaches it. Greek philosophy and the Bible do not mix well at all, and if they are mixed they produce a spiritual poison. What possible sense is there in preaching or believing Plato in the name of Jesus?[1]

The fact is that the Bible says nothing about going to heaven as a "soul" when you die. Nothing at all. What Jesus and the Bible do teach is that everyone who dies as a successful Christian will be *brought back to life* at what is called the resurrection. And that resurrection is going to happen when Jesus comes back to begin his new government or Kingdom on earth. You can grasp this simple system and program once and for all by reading 1 Corinthians 15:22-28. Paul is here discussing the sequence of events in regard to the resurrection. Only one person has been already resurrected, brought back from death to *permanent* life. That is Jesus. The Christians of all the ages will be resurrected at Jesus' future coming. Here are Paul's words: "In Christ all will be made alive, but each one in proper order: Christ the first fruits; then, at his [second] coming, those who belong to Christ [the Christians]" (1 Cor. 15:22, 23).

The plan for resurrection is not complex. Those who are Christians will be raised to life, resurrected, at the coming of Jesus. They will have been dead, and then they will come to life again. They will then inherit the earth with Jesus. They will take part in a new worldwide government, which is going to work!

I think you will not find it hard to understand that it is fearfully confusing to point you in one direction, "heaven at death," when the Bible points you in a completely different direction. We all know how devastatingly frustrating it is to be told that a certain event is going to happen at a particular place and time, when that event is to be held at a different time and at a different place. While Jesus points you towards the Kingdom of God to be established on earth *when he comes back*, the Church has been promising you a place in "heaven" the moment you die. The place is wrong. You are not going to heaven. The timing is wrong. You are not going anywhere, alive, the moment you die. You are going to be "asleep" in the grave for however much time

---

[1] We have a set of three CDs entitled "Platonic Christianity" in which a missionary, Edward Acton, complains of the dangers of Platonic philosophy which has crept into the churches, and is firmly embedded in our mostly unquestioned traditional teachings.

elapses between your death and the future arrival of Jesus to bring in the Kingdom on earth.

This is the biblical program from start to finish. This is the framework of the whole Bible story, the outline of God's great Plan. You are alive now. If you are a true believer when you die, you will "go to sleep" in death and rest in the grave until Jesus comes back. R.I.P is correct. The dead are "resting in peace." When Jesus comes back he will bring all the faithful dead out of their graves, making them alive again and giving them immortality and a place in his royal government — the Kingdom of God, the subject of his Gospel.

This is essentially a simple and comprehensible story. It is confirmed throughout the Bible. Try reading the New Testament with this "model" in mind and see if it does not make perfect sense. I believe that all the New Testament writers shared this straightforward account of God's immortality program.

When Job asked the great question about "life after death," he said: "If a person dies, will he live again?" (Job 14:14). Notice he did not say: "If a man dies, will he go on living?" That is quite a different question. Job did not expect to go on living after he was dead. This would be a confusing contradiction. A person who is continuing to live does not have to be "made alive" at the resurrection (1 Cor. 15:22). But the Bible teaches that the dead are to remain dead until they are made alive at the resurrection which Jesus will bring about when he returns. This is a simple and coherent program of events. We all need to live in the certain knowledge that this is what God intends to do, using Jesus as His human agent.

"The dead know nothing at all," says Scripture (Ecc. 9:5). "The dead Lazarus is asleep and I am going to call him out of his tomb," says Jesus (see John 11:11, 14). But churches have demonstrated their impatience with Jesus and his viewpoint. They have wanted to "jump the gun" and promise their followers an immediate conscious presence in heaven the moment they die and not a moment later! Churches have ruined one of the greatest of all teachings — the future resurrection of dead persons.

The survival of an "immortal soul" is not a biblical teaching at all, but rather an import from pagan philosophy. Paul warned against philosophy in Colossians 2:8: "See to it that no one takes you captive by philosophy." If you have taken on board unbiblical philosophy you have been taken captive and you need to be made free by learning Truth. Jesus said that "the Truth will make you free" (John 8:32).

You can see what happens when the Bible's hope is replaced with a non-hope invented by Church tradition. If we are to go to conscious glory the moment we die, what possible sense is there in Jesus coming back to restore the dead to life? And what need is there for a Kingdom following that resurrection? Resurrection means "standing up again from the condition of death." Why would we need to come back to life if we are *already alive* before that time? It makes no sense at all. The Bible is against the idea of making the dead alive, *apart from* resurrection in the future. (Note: Various religious groups seem to be mesmerized by the idea of spirit beings. Jehovah's Witnesses say that Jesus was a spirit, angel-being and thus not really human. Mormons hold that Jesus was the spirit-brother of Satan, and that God chose Jesus to come down to the earth. Other churches tell their adherents to pray to invisible spirits of departed saints. The Anglican Church thinks of departed saints as somehow in communion with the living.)

The most spectacular event of the whole of human history will be the Second Coming of Jesus. Jesus was born the Son of God, by a miraculous generation and conception in Mary. He died in his thirties. He now sits with God in heaven (the only one who has gone to heaven). Jesus is now immortal, the pioneer and forerunner of the whole of God's immortality program. Jesus is waiting now at the right hand of God, a position of supreme authority next to God, until he is given the signal to leave heaven and return to the earth. Angels said, "Men of Galilee, why do you stand looking into the sky? This Jesus, who has been taken up from you into heaven, will come in just the same way as you have watched him go into heaven" (Acts 1:11).

And when he comes he is going to bring the faithful dead back to life, back to life from death. They are going to live again, and when they do, it will seem as if no time has passed since they closed their eyes in death.[2] Together with the Christians who survive until Jesus comes, the resurrected Christians will be together with Jesus forever and they will take part in restoring

---

[2] For confirmation of this idea see F.F. Bruce, *Paul, the Apostle of the Heart Set Free*, p. 312.

sanity to our shattered world. Both they and Jesus will be together here on this planet. Jesus promised his followers not that they "will go to heaven," but that they "will inherit the land/earth" (Matt. 5:5).

1 Thessalonians gives us one of Paul's clearest descriptions of the future return of Jesus to raise the Christians have died:

> And now, brothers and sisters, I want you to know what will happen to the Christians who have died so you will not be full of sorrow like people who have no hope. For since we believe that Jesus died and was raised to life again, we also believe that when Jesus comes, God will bring to life [see New English Bible] with Jesus all the Christians who have died. I can tell you this directly from the Lord: We who are still living when the Lord returns will not rise to meet him ahead of those who are in their graves. For the Lord himself will come down from heaven with a commanding shout, with the call of the archangel, and with the trumpet call of God. First, all the Christians who have died will rise from their graves. Then, together with them, we who are still alive and remain on the earth will be caught up in the clouds to meet the Lord in the air and *by this process* we will be with him forever. So comfort and encourage each other with these words (1 Thess. 4:13-18).

The picture here gives us the following facts. Jesus is going to reappear in the sky and the dead Christians will be resurrected back to life, leaving the graves where they have been asleep in death. Together with the Christians still living on earth at that time, they will be caught up ("raptured") to meet the Lord Jesus in the air and then escort him down to the earth, where he will take up his position as rightful ruler of the Kingdom of God.

The popular idea that Jesus will come back secretly *seven years before* he comes back in power and glory has no foundation in the Bible. It is an invented myth. When Jesus arrives the event will be spectacular and visible.[3] "Every eye will see him" (Rev. 1:7). Jesus is returning to the earth. He is certainly not going to

---

[3] The idea of Jehovah's Witnesses that Jesus will be invisible at his second coming or that he came back in 1914 or (as some others say) an earlier date has no basis at all in the Bible.

snatch the Christians away to heaven for seven years! This would not be a second coming at all, but a sort of "drive by." It would be a visit, rather than a permanent return. When someone says that they are going to the store and "will be back in a few moments," we have no difficulty understanding plain words. Nor should we have any problem with Jesus' promise that he is going to come *back to the earth and reside here.*[4] If he does not, then there will be no real second coming and no Kingdom on the earth with Jesus as King in Jerusalem. This would make the Gospel preached by Jesus a fraud!

I am sure you can see how important it is to know that the dead Christians are not now alive. If we know that the dead are presently unconscious, in their graves, peacefully "asleep," we immediately concentrate our attention on the future wonderful moment when Jesus reappears in the sky, brings the sleeping dead back to life, and comes down to the earth. And once we concentrate on that mighty event, we immediately center our entire interest on the Kingdom of God which is going to begin in power, on earth, worldwide when Jesus comes back. This is the Christian hope.

"Going to heaven when we die" is simply a clever diversion, which confuses and distracts us from the Biblical story and Jesus' Good News about the Kingdom. "Heaven at death" makes intelligent Bible reading almost impossible because our church story is not the story of the Bible. There are two incompatible stories, which cannot be harmonized. The whole great Kingdom plan becomes a huge muddle in the minds of churchgoers once the ultimate goal, the Kingdom at Jesus' return, is abandoned in favor of a "comforting" promise that our "souls" are with Jesus long before the Kingdom comes.

The "heaven at death" tradition places a filter between you and the words of Scripture.

Paul gave a strong warning against any who taught that one can be alive before the future resurrection. He even named two

---

[4] While we are talking about Jesus coming back, please note the wrong translation of the New International Version in John 16:28 and 20:17 where Jesus said nothing about going *back* to the Father. The Greek simply says that Jesus was going or ascending to the Father, not going *back.*

men: "Their teaching will spread like cancer. Hymenaeus and Philetus are an example of this. They have wandered away from the truth by saying that the resurrection has already taken place, and they have overthrown the faith of some" (2 Tim. 2:17, 18). Churches have proposed a similar mistake, by claiming that the dead are alive before the future resurrection.

But it is cold comfort to offer someone a hope which is not in the Bible. The hope of going to heaven at death is absent from Scripture. It is a later invention of man and of churches. The Church's story contains a dreadful dislocation of the Bible's story. Jesus had learned the Bible story very well. He looked forward to the Kingdom of God, of which he is to be the King, when he comes back. At that moment of future arrival in triumph, Jesus will call back to life all those who have died as his obedient followers. It will be one huge collective return to life, every one of the believers (from Old Testament and New Testament times) together in one mass. Not individual departures of "souls" to heaven, but a collective coming back to life of all the faithful of all the ages, at one wonderful moment.

Those who propose a different resurrection for the Old Testament saints, separating them from their fellow Christian believers of New Testament times, separate Abraham from the New Testament faithful. Abraham, however, is "the father of the faithful" (Rom. 4:11) and will be in the first resurrection with all the Christians.

Try reading the Bible and especially the New Testament with the sequence of events in mind which we have outlined above. See how beautifully it will fit and how it will make sense of the whole Bible story from Genesis to Revelation. In this way you will be grasping the Christian hope and believing the Gospel about the Kingdom which Jesus "promised to those who love him" (James 2:5).

You will also be grasping the Bible's teaching about resurrection, which is the return to life of whole people, not the joining back together of a surviving conscious soul and a body.

When Jesus comes back to raise the dead and reward them for their service in his Kingdom Gospel mission, the world will gradually experience a wonderful restoration (Acts 3:21; 1:6). A major factor in that new age coming is that Satan, who is currently deceiving the whole world (Rev. 12:9), will be put out of commission. At the arrival of Jesus to rule in his Kingdom an angel will arrest the Devil, bind him and imprison him for a thousand years (Rev. 20:1-3).

At that time the faithful will begin to reign with the Messiah on a renewed earth. Here is one of the clearest and most important Bible verses outlining God's great Plan for you and for the world:

> They sang a new hymn: "Worthy are you [Jesus] to receive the scroll and to break open its seals, for you were slain and with your blood you purchased for God those from every tribe and tongue, people and nation You have made them to be a Kingdom and priests to our God; and *they will reign upon the earth*" (Rev. 5:9, 10).

Jesus had earlier said, "Blessed are the meek: they are going to have the earth as their inheritance" (Matt. 5:5). Every time people talk of "going to heaven" they contradict Jesus' promise and obstruct an intelligent grasp of what God and Jesus promise the believers.

The event of the Second Coming means a severe judgment on those who have refused to take part in God's immortality program through Jesus' Gospel of the Kingdom. I advise you to consult the amazing words of the great prophet Isaiah. In his Kingdom vision he saw what God, through His servant Jesus, intends to do to present evil governments and people. Let me rehearse these words for you. You have here an advance picture of the state of affairs which accompanies the future intervention of Jesus at his second coming:

> Look! The Lord is about to destroy the earth and make it a vast wasteland. See how he is scattering the people over the face of the earth. Priests and laypeople, servants and masters, maids and mistresses, buyers and sellers, lenders and borrowers, bankers and debtors — none will be spared. The earth will be completely emptied and looted. The Lord has spoken! The earth dries up, the crops wither, the skies refuse to rain. The earth suffers for the sins of its people, for they have twisted the instructions of God, violated his laws, and broken his everlasting covenant. Therefore, a curse consumes the earth and its people.
>
> They are left desolate, destroyed by fire. Few will be left alive. All the joys of life will be gone. The grape

harvest will fail, and there will be no wine. The merrymakers will sigh and mourn. The clash of tambourines will be stilled; the happy cries of celebration will be heard no more. The melodious chords of the harp will be silent. Gone are the joys of wine and song; strong drink now turns bitter in the mouth. The city writhes in chaos; every home is locked to keep out looters. Mobs gather in the streets, crying out for wine. Joy has reached its lowest ebb. Gladness has been banished from the land. The city is left in ruins, with its gates battered down.

Throughout the earth the story is the same — like the stray olives left on the tree or the few grapes left on the vine after harvest, only a remnant is left. But all who are left will shout and sing for joy. Those in the west will praise the Lord's majesty. In eastern lands, give glory to the Lord. In the coastlands of the sea, praise the name of the Lord, the God of Israel. Listen to them as they sing to the Lord from the ends of the earth. Hear them singing praises to the Righteous One! But my heart is heavy with grief. I am discouraged, for evil still prevails, and treachery is everywhere. Terror and traps and snares will be your lot, you people of the earth.

Those who flee in terror will fall into a trap, and those who escape the trap will step into a snare. Destruction falls on you from the heavens. The world is shaken beneath you. The earth has broken down and has utterly collapsed. Everything is lost, abandoned, and confused. The earth staggers like a drunkard. It trembles like a tent in a storm. It falls and will not rise again, for its sins are very great. In that day the Lord will punish the fallen angels in the heavens and the proud rulers of the nations on earth. They will be rounded up and put in prison until they are tried and condemned.

Then the Lord Almighty will mount his throne on Mount Zion. He will rule gloriously in Jerusalem, in the sight of all the leaders of his people. There will be such glory that the brightness of the sun and moon will seem to fade away (Isa. 24:1-23).

This is a vivid picture straight from the pen of one of the great Bible prophets, Isaiah. You will see that he describes a calamity and catastrophe of which we have seen some very slight parallel in our days. We all know about the destructive tsunami and the terrifying hurricanes which destroyed so many people, so much property. Such events show that God's power, as He has ordained it in nature, can be devastating. In the future God will express His fury at the sinfulness of man deliberately. The Second Coming of Jesus is compared in the prophets to an earthquake and a powerful storm. We are meant to learn from what we are now seeing: that God's power should impress on us our infinite frailty. God will deal with human wickedness. He will deal with this deliberately on what is called "the Day of the Lord." A vast depopulation of the world will occur. This is the future and final intervention of God when He sends His beloved Son back to earth. That day is described in the long passage we just cited above. Many of the prophets wrote about this coming "day of the Lord," or "the day of His fierce anger." There will be international confusion, destruction and despair. It will affect all types of people. Jesus spoke of "people's hearts failing them for fear at the things coming upon the earth" (Luke 21:26).

But note the outcome of God's intervention: "A few persons will be left" when the Day of the Lord is over. Isaiah 24:6 says this expressly. Please take careful note of the fact that not every human person will be wiped out. That would leave the world vacant, and there is actually a large denomination which has misleadingly taught that not a single mortal person will be left alive on earth. That is plainly not true. There is an exact parallel here with the flood of Noah's time. A tiny fraction of the human population emerged unscathed from the protective ark. Noah and his wife and three children and their wives escaped death at that time. The rest of mankind was drowned in a colossal judgment event, which Jesus said is parallel and similar to his own coming. Listen to the words of Jesus: "Because as in a thunderstorm the bright light coming from the east is seen even in the west; so will be the coming of the Son of man" (Matt. 24:27). Jesus will arrive in power to save the world from a time of chaos and confusion.

The good news is that Jesus is coming back. But what about the bad news which precedes it? Jesus said:

> In those days before the Flood, the people were enjoying banquets and parties and weddings right up to the time Noah entered his boat. People didn't realize what was

going to happen until the Flood came and swept them all away. That is the way it will be when the Son of Man comes. Two men will be working together in the field; one will be taken, the other left. Two women will be grinding flour at the mill; one will be taken, the other left. So be prepared, because you don't know what day your Lord is coming. Know this: A homeowner who knew exactly when a burglar was coming would stay alert and not permit the house to be broken into. You also must be ready all the time. For the Son of Man will come when least expected (Matt. 24:37-44).

Paul's most vivid and powerful description of the Second Coming of Jesus is found in 2 Thessalonians 1:7, 8. Paul wrote to the Christians:

God will provide relief for you who are being persecuted and also for us when the Lord Jesus appears from heaven. He will come with his mighty angels in flaming fire, inflicting vengeance on those who do not know God and on those who do not obey the gospel of our Lord Jesus.

Jesus, the Bible says, is "the author of salvation for those who *obey* him" (Heb. 5:9). There is more to salvation than just believing that Jesus died to cover our sins, essential as this, of course, is.

I think you are getting the picture of the future clear. First the bad times, the destruction of the careless and unprepared, then the survival of a few, and then the Kingdom of God which will reconstruct humanity beginning with the surviving remnant. The Kingdom will restore peace and order to the whole world. Indescribable conditions will under Jesus' supervision extend across the globe. The Kingdom of God, consisting of Jesus as King and the faithful then immortalized, will reign from Jerusalem. All the prophets of Israel forecast this ideal future for our world. Begin to read the prophets of the Old Testament and see what a beautiful vision of the future of the world they present.

The prayer "May Your Kingdom come" is going to be answered!

Remember that your part in this grand prospect for the earth is to prepare in advance for the Kingdom, to escape the judgment (not by being taken to heaven!) and then to gain immortality and rule with Jesus in the Kingdom he is going to put in place when he comes.

Chapter 4
Filling in Some of the Blanks

If this Bible story is new to you (large numbers of professing Christians confess to having almost no knowledge of the Bible), or if you have had up till now only a very sketchy idea of it, let me now fill in some of the gaps and perhaps answer some of the questions which, as you read, may have formed in your mind.

Remember that the overall story of the Bible is not complicated. It is delivered in reasonably easy language. It is however an ancient Jewish story originating in a different culture from ours. It is a purely Messianic story. This is hardly surprising since Jesus claimed to be the Messiah!

We need to learn to relate to that ancient world. Nevertheless the Bible is meant for us all — not just for specialists. Certainly there *are* technical corners of the Bible which need specialist treatment, but the plot as a whole is very clear. There is a God, One God the Father, who created everything for a very good purpose. He had Jesus, His Son, and the Kingdom of God in mind from the beginning. That Messianic Kingdom purpose has been obscured and distorted, with God permitting it by allowing a measure of freedom for us to make our own (very often wrong) choices. Also He has allowed us to be fooled by the Devil who is called in the Bible "the deceiver of the whole world" (Rev. 12:9).

We human beings really ought to have been paying better attention to what God says and not to have allowed ourselves to be so easily and fully bamboozled by the Devil's false versions of religion. So massive is the present influence of the Devil (only as far as God allows) that he is called "the god of this present age" (2 Cor. 4:4). The Apostle John said that the "whole world lies in his power" (1 John 5:19). The present nations are nowhere in the Bible said to be Christian. They will belong to Christ only when Jesus comes back to inaugurate the Kingdom worldwide.

There is an invisible spiritual being called Satan or the Devil who is relentlessly opposed to God's immortality plan and he works hard, playing on the natural weakness of mankind, to make it incomprehensible. That Satan came up to Jesus in the wilderness, spoke to him and tested him, tempted him to take the easy or the spectacular way to "success" (Matt. 4:1-11). Jesus was wise enough and strong enough to resist the Devil's clever lies and half-truths (half-truths are usually the most pernicious and effective falsehoods). So well equipped was Jesus with the truth of Scripture, God's words to us humans, that the Devil was no match for the unique Son of God. But Satan continued to try to get Jesus off track at every opportunity. He works against God and God's design for human beings.

Jesus is the Son of God, and the explanation of what it means for Jesus to be the unique Son of God is provided for us in a simple statement from the angel Gabriel who announced to Mary, the virgin: "Holy spirit will come over you, and the power of the Most High God will overshadow you, and for that reason precisely the one to be begotten will be called the Son of God" (Luke 1:35).

Quite simple. The miraculously generated (begotten) son in Mary's womb is the Son of God. What does Son of God mean here? Gabriel explains that Jesus is entitled to be the Son of God precisely because he was miraculously created by God Himself using the power of His creative spirit, the holy spirit. It is tremendously important to follow the words Gabriel gives us here at the beginning of Luke's gospel. Luke has supplied us with an invaluable key to the proper understanding of the identity of Jesus. He explains what "Son of God" means. The basis and reason for Jesus being the Son of God is provided. Son of God means that Jesus had a supernatural beginning in Mary, due to a miracle performed by God. That miracle makes him Son of God. Jesus had no human father. God's power simply intervened to produce a pregnancy without the benefit of a human father. It is important to realize that this was a sheer miracle from God. So important was that miracle that Gabriel tells us that the miraculous begetting or fathering of Jesus is the exact reason for Jesus' identity as Son of God.

Luke 1:35 provides a precious definition of the meaning of "Son of God." But that definition has been discarded in traditional theology.

Here we must simply say that you almost certainly did not learn this stupendous fact about who Jesus is in church. I won't go into detail here, but a very different reason will be offered you by church tradition as to how Jesus is the Son of God. Churches have adopted a quite different account of why and how Jesus is the Son of God. They actually substituted the entirely unbiblical title "God the Son" for "Son of God."

I simply invite you to pay attention to God's messenger Gabriel and learn from him rather than from any contrary church creed or theory. "That is the reason why Jesus is the Son of God." What reason? The marvelous miracle worked by God in Mary. And for no other reason. Jesus is the second Adam. Adam is also called the Son of God in Luke 3:36.

You will, I am sure, immediately appreciate the direct parallel with the creation of the first man, Adam. Adam was formed from the dust of the ground. God then breathed His animating spirit of life into the man formed from the dust and Adam became a living creature.[1] A living creature is just that — a live being. In Genesis the great whales and other creatures are also called "living creatures." Neither Adam nor any of the animals was created with an "immortal soul," a part of them which could not die. Thus any church which teaches that men and women have an immortal soul which survives death is trading on a falsehood — and a serious one, since it was in fact the Devil and not God who told the first couple that they would not die, even when they disobeyed. God said that when and if they disobeyed Him they would surely be on the way to death. And indeed they died. The descendants of that first human pair also die. There is nothing more certain, it has been said, than death and taxes.

The only hope of living again for any of us is in the resurrection. The resurrection will happen, as we have seen, when Jesus arrives again on earth. That will also be the time when the nations of the present world are turned over to the control of the Kingdom of God which will then belong to God and to His chosen Son and Messiah, Jesus. You can read this in a beautiful and memorable statement in the book of Revelation 11:15-19. I am simply going to connect the two "seventh trumpet" passages to explain how the present world-systems are going to become the worldwide Kingdom of God. All good Bible study is done by

---

[1] The KJV translates the Hebrew word *nephesh* as "soul," but does not allow you to see that the same word is applied also to animals. Thus animals are also "living creatures" or "souls."

connecting related information from the various writers. Here first is the famous "seventh trumpet" statement in the book of Revelation, an important book given to Jesus by God and recorded by the Apostle John. It is a prediction and vision of the tremendous future event which will be Jesus' spectacular arrival back on earth:

> Then the seventh angel blew his trumpet, and there were loud voices shouting in heaven: "The whole world has now become the Kingdom of our Lord and of his Christ, and he will reign forever and ever." And the twenty-four elders sitting on their thrones before God fell on their faces and worshiped him. And they said, "We give thanks to you, Lord God Almighty, the one who is and who always was, for now you have assumed your great power and have begun to reign. The nations were angry with you, but now the time of your wrath has come. It is time to judge the dead and reward your servants. You will reward your prophets and your holy people, all who fear your name, from the least to the greatest. And you will destroy all who have caused destruction on the earth." Then, in heaven, the Temple of God was opened and the Ark of his covenant could be seen inside the Temple. Lightning flashed, thunder crashed and roared; there was a great hailstorm, and the world was shaken by a mighty earthquake (Rev. 11:15-19).

We could say that this brilliant passage of Scripture sums up the colossal revolution and restoration that is going to occur when God sends Jesus back to set up the Kingdom of God. No wonder the Kingdom of God is the heart of the Christian Gospel. It is the only ultimate and really Good News. The Kingdom is the only government which is going to survive permanently.

It is when the Kingdom comes at Jesus' return that the Christians who have died will come back from death (not from heaven!) to life.

Here is the related "seventh trumpet" passage which also links the coming of Jesus to establish the Kingdom with the resurrection of the faithful. Paul described the event like this: "In a moment, in the twinkling of an eye, *at the last trumpet*...the dead will be raised...Death will be swallowed up in life. We will put on immortality" (1 Cor. 15:52-54). This is the crowning moment of success for all who put their hope in Christ and his offer of indestructible life in the future Kingdom.

You see now how the Kingdom of God will be inaugurated by the return of Jesus to resurrect the faithful of all the ages.

Now back to the constitution of man for a moment. I trust this point is now clear to you: you and I were not born with immortality. This is a vitally important truth since it enables you to understand who you are as a human being. You are now mortal. You can and will die (unless you happen to survive alive until Jesus returns; and even then you will have to be transformed from mortal to immortal). Man does not have an internal part known as an "immortal soul." If he did, that soul would indeed have to go off to God in heaven while the body alone died. But if there is no immortal soul in man, then at death the whole man dies, and the only solution to that tragedy is that the *whole man* will be brought back to life in the resurrection when Jesus returns to earth. That is the biblical teaching about the destiny of man.

The other view, that man was made with an immortal part, is a piece of pagan philosophy which does not belong in true Christianity.

Several church groups, and many excellent scholars of various denominations, thankfully, understand this important fact about the make-up of man, who we really are. Martin Luther, the reformer (some sections of his writings have probably been "cooked" to weaken what he said), and William Tyndale, the heroic translator of the Bible into English, for which he was tragically martyred, understood what happens at death. But the vast majority of church members persist with the non-biblical idea that their "souls" cannot die and that the dead must still be alive now, in heaven or hell. The Roman Catholic Church at one point in its history even encouraged its members to pay for special "masses" conducted by the priests, to shorten the time that their dear, dead relatives would have to spend in "purgatory," which was said to be a temporary place of torment and suffering for those who were not yet fit for "heaven." Other mainstream churches never subscribed to this idea of a temporary hell, purgatory. They simplified the system by saying that all "outside Christ" go straight to hell, there to be tortured for endless ages of time. At the same time they want the public to believe that God is a God of infinite compassion.

We are trying to weave together the various strands of the Bible story so that it will make sense in all its brilliant simplicity. Again, some of this may be new to you. Take time to ponder it all. Wake up thinking about it. Go to sleep at night mulling it all over in your mind. Do not make hasty judgments about what you are reading. Study the Bible. Be a Berean. The Bereans were those noble-minded souls in Acts 17:11, 12 who painstakingly examined what Paul was telling them about the meaning of life and salvation. They "examined the Scriptures on a daily basis to see if what they were hearing was true. And many became believers," that is to say they were persuaded and compelled by Paul's revelation of God's immortality program in Christ.

They became members of the Church by being baptized in water, immersed in the presence of fellow believers, as a public statement of their intention to follow Jesus for the rest of their lives, through thick and thin. Jesus had made water baptism part of the instructions for ministry to his followers, for the whole period until he comes back (Matt. 28:19, 20). Jesus himself was baptized. He baptized his disciples (using his agents to perform this rite). (John 3:22, 26; 4:1, 2). Peter considered the act of baptism a response to a direct command of Jesus and "he commanded them to be baptized" in water (see Acts 10:47, 48). Peter took the matter of baptism in water very seriously. He recognized that he would be in direct disobedience to God if he prevented believers (in this case Gentiles) from undergoing water baptism. "'Surely no one can refuse the water for these to be baptized who have received the Holy Spirit just as we did, can he?' And he ordered them to be baptized in the name of Jesus Christ" (Acts 10:47, 48). The refusal of water baptism would be in direct opposition to God, Jesus and apostolic practice. Peter even rehearsed this story and noted that refusing water baptism would have been a direct confrontation of God's will (Acts 11:17). The refusal of baptism in water to new converts would have been a refusal to do what God and Jesus had commanded.[2] Some have been tragically led into direct disobedience to Jesus by being taught that water baptism is not part of Christian practice.

---

[2] Note the same word "refuse, forbid" in the Greek in Acts 10:47 and 11:17.

Note please that "believing" means being persuaded (Acts 28:23, 24). God gives us a mind and expects us to use it. God from the beginning has sent His agents in the form of prophets in the Old Testament and then the ultimate prophet, Jesus the Son of God. God's offers to mankind were very often refused by those who heard them. Even Jesus was largely rejected by hostile Jews in his own day and by many others of all the nations, when his Kingdom message was later brought to them. The human race has a terribly tragic history of not listening to what God says to us for our good. The records show that many of the prophets, God's spokesmen and agents, were simply murdered by the people who heard them speak. People are so confused that they easily become hostile to anyone who would kindly show them Truth. Some cult leaders confuse their followers so severely that it takes much time and study to de-program them, so that they can understand and follow the teachings of Jesus.

Jesus even promised to send "wise men" and professional theologians (scribes) to assist people to understand God's will and plan (Matt. 23:34).

If one has learned a piece of religious "truth" wrongly, it will require a sort of "spiritual surgery" to correct it. We all tend to cling tenaciously to what we have learned from beloved teachers, often without careful examination of other points of view. The technique of a cult is to isolate its members from the wider world of Bible study and commentary, and to instill a false sense of competence. If, for example, one proposes a doctrine or practice which is practically unheard of in the past history of biblical studies, it is almost certainly wrong! It is an illusion to suppose we do not need the advice of others and their input when arriving at proper understanding. Theology is done in community and not "on an island."

Jesus is the classic example of rejection for no good reason. Many of those who heard Jesus teach, including the religious authorities, believed that Jesus was an agent of the Devil and that he deserved to die. Religious leaders quite mistakenly, blinded by their own religious traditions, believed that the ordinary people needed to be protected against Jesus who (the authorities said) was working for the dark powers. Even Jesus' friends at one time suspected that he might have been an occult worker, a sort of magic man and a menace to public order and spirituality. Jesus responded by telling his followers that the time was going to come when they would be killed. And those killing the believers in Jesus would be people who "thought they were doing God a service" (John 16:2). Can you imagine that? Religious people were so totally confused that they thought they were helping God's cause by getting rid of Jesus! The question is, have things changed very much? Has the human race slowly become enlightened and wise? Do we now all instinctively know the difference between truth and error? Would we spot a false teacher or prophet if we saw or heard one? Or might we side with error against Truth?

Jesus took a very negative view of how his teaching would fare after he left. He even doubted that the faith would survive at all and wondered: "When the Son of Man comes, will he find faith on the earth?" (Luke 18:8).

In this connection, I want to finish this chapter by taking you to the most startling and alarming of all the recorded words of Jesus. Reading these words, we have all been duly warned. There is no possible way that we can be complacent or self-satisfied. These are terrifying words from Jesus. Listen to this:

"Not all people who sound religious are really godly. They may refer to me as 'Lord,' but they still won't enter the Kingdom of Heaven. The decisive issue is whether they obey my Father in heaven. On judgment day many will tell me, 'Lord, Lord, we prophesied in your name and cast out demons in your name and performed many miracles in your name.' But I will reply, 'I never knew you. Go away; the things you did were unauthorized.' Anyone who listens to my teaching and obeys me is wise, like a person who builds a house on solid rock. Though the rain comes in torrents and the floodwaters rise and the winds beat against that house, it won't collapse, because it is built on rock. But anyone who hears my teaching and ignores it is foolish, like a person who builds a house on sand. When the rains and floods come and the winds beat against that house, it will fall with a mighty crash." After Jesus finished speaking, the crowds were amazed at his teaching, for he taught as one who had real authority — quite unlike the teachers of religious law (Matt. 7:21-29).

This passage of Scripture has got to be the most unsettling section of the Bible. It is possible to be horribly deceived. One can be acting or *imagining* that one is active as a Christian preacher, even doing miracles and casting out demons, and be, as this translation has it, "unauthorized" — never recognized by Jesus as part of his team. These are awful verses.

I, for one, want to know how such a devastating and shattering state of affairs could come about. What, according to Jesus, is the decisive issue? It has to do with obeying Jesus which is the same as "doing the will of God." That is where the heart of the issue lies: Doing the will of God and of Jesus, God's final agent.

As we continue we want to look in more detail at this question of "doing the will of God and obeying Jesus." "He who hears and obeys" is on the right track. Others are not. Many will imagine, sincerely, that they are on the right track, but it will turn out that they are not and never have been. And others will start out on the right path to the Kingdom but will lose their way and go into darkness. It sounds as if being a Christian is going to involve some relentless effort, the effort to discern true from false, light from darkness. Our spiritual house must be built on a rock, but in this deceived world it is possible unknowingly to build it on sand. The collapse of the house on sand is inevitable. We want to avoid such a shattering collapse at all costs.

The outline of God's story is, as we have said, relatively easy. But it is going to take effort and dedication on our part to become fully versed in God's great immortality plan. Jesus did not just tell us to be "good" people. He began by issuing a command that we "believe the Gospel of the Kingdom" (Mark 1:14, 15). This means becoming involved in God and Jesus' Kingdom-immortality plan.

This is where that vital obedience Jesus talked about begins. Listening to Jesus' first command is the place to start: "Repent and believe the Gospel about the Kingdom" (Mark 1:14, 15). Peter said the same thing as he opened his first epistle. He spoke of "*obeying Jesus* and being sprinkled with his blood" (1 Pet. 1:2).

Why not start with Jesus' first comprehensive command in Mark 1:14, 15?

We are not going to learn everything in one day. But at least we can get started and "work out our salvation with fear and trembling," as Paul said (Phil. 2:12), that is, with a sober sense of the tremendous issues of life and death involved. What we need to do, obviously, is to pay the closest attention to the teachings of Jesus. Jesus is the ultimate, expert guide to success in the coming

Kingdom. He is "that final prophet" whom God from ancient times promised to send us (Deut. 18:15-18; Acts 3:22; 7:37).

He is the master teacher of the way that leads to immortality. He himself had to go through the course which leads to the Kingdom, and he was triumphant. He won the gold medal. He has gained immortality and he can never die. He has qualified to take his place on the throne of the Kingdom of God in Jerusalem. He is the pioneer in God's immortality plan. Meanwhile, at present, he is a compassionate and merciful High Priest to assist those on the way to salvation in the Kingdom of God.

We are to follow in his footsteps, in the adventure which leads to life forever in the Kingdom which the God of Heaven is going to establish on earth. Let us now add some more pieces of the puzzle in the great Plan unfolded in the Bible. As we do this, we must clearly keep our eye constantly on this business of "doing the will of God." It is the key to everything.

Chapter 5
More on the Gospel of the Kingdom, Including its Old Testament Background

Our survey of the Bible so far has revealed the supremely important fact that Jesus was a tireless and impassioned preacher of the Gospel of the Kingdom.[1] He preached that Kingdom message as the only message able to solve the human problem of mortality. Jesus claimed that he alone could teach the public the secret of immortality — how to get saved. And he claimed that the Kingdom would one day mean a solution to the problems of the whole world. Jesus made it quite clear that his whole activity centered on the preaching of the Kingdom Good News. That is what he was sent to do, as he declared in that memorable verse in Luke 4:43. That verse is one of those spectacular master texts which will let you in on the whole marvelous Bible story.

It must follow then from Luke 4:43 that the disciples of Jesus would imitate their rabbi and master and would themselves be energetic preachers of the Kingdom of God. The idea is simply this: when Jesus left the earth, after his resurrection from the dead, he ensured that his work of preaching the Kingdom would continue. He had carefully trained his first followers, an inner circle of executives sharing his work, for this Kingdom task. His final instructions to them in the famous Great Commission (Matt. 28:19, 20) were that they were to preach exactly the same Gospel as he had preached. That Gospel was, however, now to go to all the nations and not only to Israel. The Kingdom Gospel was now offered to everyone, as it is still is today. As the first followers of Jesus came to the end of their lives, they saw to it that their successors, thoroughly trained in the Gospel of the Kingdom,

---

[1]To confirm this simple fact please look up Matt. 4:17; 4:23; 9:35; Luke 4:43; 8:1; 9:11 to see that Jesus always spoke about the Kingdom before and after the cross (Acts 1:3). Paul was faithful to Jesus by preaching exactly the same Gospel of the Kingdom (Acts 19:8; 20:24, 25; 28:23, 31). There is only one Gospel message. It is for everyone. It is called the Gospel of the Kingdom.

would carry on the work. I should add that the Apostles (capital A)[2] were not replaced and we do not have them today. But we can learn from them and catch the spirit of their Gospel of the Kingdom, the Gospel for all nations.

But notice what learned commentators have observed. America's leading church planter: "I honestly cannot remember any pastor whose ministry I have been under actually preaching a sermon on the Kingdom of God...I now realize that I have never preached a sermon on it. Where has the Kingdom been?"[3]

An expert on Christian missions: "When is the last time you heard a sermon on the Kingdom of God? Frankly, I'd be hard put to recall ever having heard a solid exposition of the Kingdom. How do we square this silence with the widely accepted fact that the Kingdom of God dominated our Lord's thought and ministry?"[4]

A Roman Catholic Bible teacher: "To my amazement, the Kingdom of God played hardly any role in the systematic theology I had been taught in the seminary."[5]

An Archbishop of Canterbury: "To us it is quite extraordinary that the Kingdom of God appears so little in the theology and religious writings of almost the entire period of Christian history. Certainly in Matthew, Mark and Luke the Kingdom has a prominence that could hardly be increased."[6]

An evangelical writer on the Gospel: "How much have you heard about the Kingdom of God? It is not our language. But it was Jesus' prime concern."[7]

Historian H.G. Wells: "As remarkable is the enormous prominence given by Jesus to the teaching of what he called the

---

[2]The New Testament uses the word apostle in a secondary sense also as a missionary or supervisor of a number of churches. The Apostles (capital A), in the primary sense, were distinguished by having personally seen Jesus, and they were accredited by the amazing signs and wonders they performed (2 Cor. 12:12; 1 Cor. 9:1).

[3]Peter Wagner, *Church Growth and the Whole Gospel.*

[4]*Missiology*, April, 1980, p. 13.

[5]B.T. Viviano, *The Kingdom of God in History*, 1988, p. 9.

[6]William Temple, *Personal Religion and the Life of Fellowship*, 1926, p. 69.

[7]Michael Green at the Lausanne International Conference on World Evangelization, in 1974.

Kingdom of God, and its comparative insignificance in the procedure and teaching of most of the Christian churches. This doctrine of the Kingdom of Heaven, which was the main teaching of Jesus, and which plays so small a part in the Christian creeds, is certainly one of the most revolutionary doctrines that ever stirred and changed human thought. Is it any wonder that to this day this Galilean is too much for our small hearts?"[8]

I invite you to ponder these amazing — extraordinary — statements from top church authorities. Do you see that Jesus' Gospel is missing from what we call Christianity?

In a striking saying in Jesus' prophecy discourse in Matthew 24 Jesus said, "This Gospel of the Kingdom will be preached in the whole world to all the nations and then the end [of the present age] will come" (Matt. 24:14). The end of the age means, of course, the time of his return to take charge of the Kingdom of God worldwide. Before that amazing event, the world must be duly warned that God is about to step in, massively and decisively. The preaching of the Christian Gospel of the Kingdom is the divine statement of intention on the part of God and Jesus. It is a promise to those who heed and a threat to the unrepentant. A promise and a menace. The world is given advance knowledge of what God is going to do. He is going to have to intervene to save the world from its own perverse ways. We are destroying ourselves. The world is full of injustice and tragedy.

We are to heed the warning issued by Jesus in his Kingdom Gospel, and believe the message about the Kingdom and the death and resurrection of Jesus, who died to reconcile wayward human beings to God. And he died so that we might be forgiven for all our failures, not least our rejection of his Gospel about the Kingdom. Repentance, of course, implies that we begin to obey Jesus. Forgiveness is pointless if we *continue* in disobedience. Thus Jesus begins his ministry by commanding repentance and belief in the Gospel of the Kingdom (Mark 1:14, 15).

I want now to take you back into the Old Testament, which Jesus knew in detail and loved so much. Particularly let us look at the book of Daniel, who worked in the great city of Babylon (in modern Iraq, 50 miles south of Baghdad) in the 6th century BC. Daniel was one of several royal young men who had been

---

[8]*The Outline of History*, vol. 1, p. 426.

deported to Babylon when Nebuchadnezzar invaded and conquered his country, Judah. This event happened in about 605 BC.

Daniel was given a broad outline of the history of the Middle East as it would unfold. Or rather he was privileged to see in advance what would happen there at specific times in history. This information was provided for him when he interpreted a dream given to the king of Babylon. The king had seen a colossal statue. It consisted of a head of fine gold, chest and arms of silver, stomach and thighs of bronze, legs of iron and feet of a mixture of iron and baked clay (Dan. 2:31-45).

Daniel was able through inspiration from God to explain to the king the meaning of the dream-vision. The head of the statue represented the king of Babylon himself, Nebuchadnezzar. The trunk stood for the following empire in Babylon, namely the empire of the Medes and Persians.[9] The third section of the statue pictured the Greek kingdom which ruled over the same general area, and the fourth kingdom, most violent of them all, pictured a final Babylonian kingdom. (The final kingdom is identified as one of four divisions of the *Greek* kingdom in Daniel 8 and as a kingdom "of the north" in chapter 11. The Greek/Syrian kingdom of the second century BC, with Antiochus Epiphanes as its cruel leader, foreshadowed the final ruthless kingdom of the statue.)

That final form was pictured as having ten toes. And as we will see, there would also be a final eleventh power, a contemporary of ten final rulers, who would be a single destructive Antichrist. The book of Revelation adds further details to this vision, especially in chapters 13 and 17. In the book of Revelation the final wicked individual is called the Beast (Rev. 11:7; 13:4-7; 17:8, 11, 12, 16, 17, 19). Paul referred to him as the Man of Sin or Man of Lawlessness (2 Thess. 2:3-10). Jesus referred to the Abomination of Desolation standing where *he* ought not to (Mark 13:14).

The Bible is united in its testimony to a future wicked person who will embody all that opposes God and His plan. He will be a direct tool of the Devil.

---

[9]Some commentators have taken the Kingdom of the Medes to be a different Kingdom from that of the Persians. The interesting point about the statue is that it is centered in Babylon from top to bottom.

What is to happen when the final Beast power comes to an end — when the time of great trouble or "great tribulation" (Matt. 24:21; Dan. 12:1; see Dan. 7:21-27) is over? The answer is directly related to the Christian Gospel, since Jesus found in that revealed dream the vision of the Kingdom in which he expected to rule. That Kingdom is beautifully described in the vision (chapter 2 of Daniel) as a "stone cut out without hands," i.e. a stone supernaturally produced. That stone struck the image of Nebuchadnezzar's dream on its brittle feet, and the whole colossus collapsed at once. The "stone" was the Kingdom of God. The "stone" pictured the Kingdom of God arriving. Here is Daniel's inspired interpretation: "In the days of those [final] kings the God of heaven will set up a Kingdom which will never be destroyed. It will break in pieces all those former kingdoms and will itself endure forever" (Dan. 2:44). It is to be a Kingdom not *in* heaven but "under the whole heaven" (Dan. 7:27).

The goal of the Bible story is a Kingdom on a renewed earth and never a Kingdom off in a distant "heaven."

It is called the Kingdom of Heaven because the God of heaven will bring it into existence on earth. And Jesus, the Son of God — the Messiah — will be in charge of it. It is the Kingdom of God because God is going to bring it into being on earth when Jesus returns. Kingdom of God and Kingdom of Heaven have the same meaning exactly.

This is precisely the Kingdom of God which Jesus made the center of his Gospel. It is the Kingdom for which church members have been taught to pray "Your Kingdom come!" It is the time, as the next line of the "Lord's prayer" tells us, when the will of God will be done *on earth.* And when, as Jesus promised, the faithful will "inherit the earth" (Matt. 5:5). And rule with Christ *on earth* (Rev. 5:10).

The Christian Gospel is lost when *Jesus' point of reference to the Hebrew Bible's idea of the Kingdom is suppressed.* Once the roots of the saving Gospel are discarded, then it becomes possible for the uninstructed to imagine the Gospel of the Kingdom *as any form of vague spirituality.* Christianity is Messianism, as taught by Messiah Jesus. But the Jesus currently presented to the public is often almost entirely unmessianic!

I think it is fair to say that many church members do not know quite what they are praying for when they say "Thy Kingdom come." It is not a general wish that things may go better now. It certainly does not mean, "May your present kingdom *spread*." It is a prayer and cry that God would send Jesus to intervene in human affairs and provide us with a government which really works. It points to and longs for a time when "the earth will be filled with the knowledge of God as much as the waters cover the sea" (Isa. 11:9).

Even wild animals will live peacefully together. The nations will thankfully give up international warfare forever. Senseless violence which now kills and maims will be no more. No one will be allowed to build a tank or point a weapon threateningly at another human being. When the Kingdom comes, the nations are going to melt down their terrifying weapons of destruction into farm tools. It will be illegal to build lethal weapons (Isa. 2:4). Peace will be mandatory. People will soon learn that there is a better way of organizing themselves. Conflicts of all sorts will be resolved. The Messiah, who will then be present on earth, will arbitrate national disputes and formerly hostile nations like Assyria and Egypt will rejoice in a common faith and be at peace with each other and with Israel. You can catch a glimpse of that wonderful coming society in Isaiah 19:22-25. The Old Testament prophets repeatedly speak of this glorious time coming.

Even nature is going to reflect the dramatically different conditions across the globe. The lion is going to lie peacefully with the lamb and children will play unharmed with now poisonous snakes. A veritable paradise will return to the earth (Isa. 11; 65:17-25, etc.).

Daniel speaks of that Kingdom to come as a Kingdom "under the whole heaven" (7:27). This is a Kingdom quite different from any of the popular and mistaken notions of a Kingdom *in* heaven or in the sky. The Bible nowhere speaks of us floating as souls in the upper atmosphere. This idea is no more than a popular fairy tale. The whole point of the biblical story is that God is going to succeed in bringing about peace on earth. If He were to scrap the planet and take everyone off to heaven, there would be no resolution of His great immortality project on earth. Paradise was once here on earth, and it is going to be restored. But only those who prepare for this event and help to promote it so that others can enjoy it too, will be in that Kingdom on earth. The essence of true faith is to believe in Jesus as the executive of God's grand design for our planet.

At present the deeply ingrained idea that we are supposed to go to heaven has all but submerged Jesus' outstanding utterance that "the meek are going to inherit *the earth*" (Matt. 5:5, quoting Ps. 37:11). This revealing teaching of Jesus about the Kingdom needs to replace all the careless language we now hear about "going to heaven." If we read the Bible with an honest desire to understand its grand promise, we would do well to drop all reference to "heaven" as our future home and honor Jesus by imitating his language about the Kingdom.

Is it unreasonable to expect Christians to *sound* like Jesus when they speak of their aims and hopes?

The book of Daniel is a marvelous treasure of background information to Jesus' preaching of the Kingdom. In chapter 7 we learn that just before the Kingdom comes, a terrible and beast-like kingdom will dominate the politics of at least the Middle East. It will be led by an antichristian figure called in the book of Revelation the "Beast" and by Paul in 2 Thessalonians the "man of sin." Jesus spoke of this agent of evil who would destroy on a large scale just before the coming of the Kingdom. This tyrant of evil is known also as "the Antichrist" (1 John 2:18). The Apostles taught that the lying spirit and tendency of antichrist was and is already powerfully at work in society. The final individual Antichrist has not yet appeared. The only defense against falling for the lies of this evil person is "the love of the truth in order to be saved" (2 Thess. 2:10).

Daniel in vision saw both a government and its leader, as a final form of evil human rule. He saw "a little horn." A horn in the Bible pictures a ruler. Daniel was anxious to know about how the dreadful antichristian figure would be defeated:

> Then I wanted to know the true meaning of the fourth beast, the one so different from the others and so terrifying. It devoured and crushed its victims with iron teeth and bronze claws, and it trampled what was left beneath its feet. I also asked about the ten horns on the fourth beast's head and the little horn that came up afterward and destroyed three of the other horns. This was the horn that seemed greater than the others and had human eyes and a mouth that was boasting arrogantly. As

> I watched, this horn was waging war against the holy
> people and was defeating them, until the Ancient One
> came and judged in favor of the holy people of the Most
> High. Then the time arrived for the holy people to take
> over the kingdom (Dan. 7:19-22).

That critical moment of time will be at the end of the great
tribulation. It will be marked by the return of Jesus in power and
glory to establish the Kingdom on earth.

Let us summarize what we have seen in these verses: There
will be a brief time of domination by the Antichrist. Then his
power will be permanently removed. Note the spectacular solution
to the chaos brought about by the reign of Antichrist: "But in the
end, the holy people of the Most High will be given the kingdom,
and they will rule forever and ever" (Daniel 7:18).

Jesus echoed this promise when he said to his followers,
"Don't be afraid, little flock; it gives your Father great pleasure to
give you the Kingdom" (Luke 12:32).

The vision of Daniel 7 shows that the saints are going to
receive the authority to rule with Jesus. Daniel 7 makes this point
three times, concluding with this grand vision of the Kingdom.
First, a short burst of evil as the Antichrist is on a rampage. Then
the blessed relief to be brought by the Kingdom of God:

> He will defy the Most High and wear down the holy
> people of the Most High. He will try to change their
> sacred festivals and laws, and they will be placed under
> his control for a time, times, and half a time. But then the
> court will pass judgment, and all his power will be taken
> away and completely destroyed. Then the sovereignty,
> power, and greatness of all the kingdoms *under heaven*
> will be given to the holy people of the Most High. They
> will rule forever, and all rulers will serve and obey them
> (Dan. 7:25-27).

This is what Jesus meant by his promise that his followers
would inherit the land or earth (Matt. 5:5) and rule the world with
him (see Rev. 5:10).

Daniel's reaction to what he had seen was alarm. It should
likewise capture our imagination and interest. "That was the end
of the vision. I, Daniel, was terrified by my thoughts and my face
was pale with fear, but I kept these things to myself" (Dan. 7:28).

Today the revelations Daniel received are public information and should be passed on to others.

Later chapters of Daniel give more detail about that final evil ruler who will be replaced by Jesus and his Kingdom. He is called the King of the North in Daniel 11 and after a dramatic military career will "come to his end" in Israel. Here are the words of Daniel:

> He [the final King of the North] will enter the glorious land of Israel, and many nations will fall, but Moab, Edom, and the best part of Ammon will escape. He will conquer many countries, and Egypt will not escape. He will gain control over the gold, silver, and treasures of Egypt, and the Libyans and Ethiopians will be his servants. But then news from the east and the north will alarm him, and he will set out in great anger to destroy many as he goes. He will halt between the glorious holy mountain and the sea and will pitch his royal tents there, but while he is there, his time will suddenly run out, and there will be no one to help him (Dan. 11:41-45).

The final days of the evil King of the North will involve the world in a time of great, unparalleled tribulation, but the blessed relief of the Kingdom of God will put an end to that terrible period of suffering. Daniel described those future times like this:

> At that time Michael, the archangel who stands guard over your nation, will arise. Then there will be a time of anguish greater than any since nations first came into existence. But at that time every one of your people whose name is written in the book will be rescued. Many of those who are sleeping in the dust will rise up, some to everlasting life and some to shame and everlasting contempt. Those who are wise will shine as bright as the sky, and those who turn many to righteousness will shine like stars forever. But you, Daniel, keep this prophecy a secret; seal up the book until the time of the end. Many will rush here and there, and knowledge will increase (Dan. 12:1-4).

Jesus in his famous prophecy discourse likewise spoke of this final time of unprecedented "great tribulation," quoting and elaborating on the verses he found in Daniel. Jesus said, "Then there will be a great tribulation such as has never occurred before and never will again, and unless that tribulation was cut short, no one would be left alive" (Matt. 24:21, 22). "Immediately after the tribulation of those days," Jesus went on to say, "the sun will be darkened and the moon will not give its light...and then they will see the Son of Man coming in power...and he will gather his elect" (Matt. 24:29-31).

The picture of the future is not complicated. Before the arrival of Jesus to take up his position as world ruler in the Kingdom, the world will experience a unique burst of agony, just as a woman goes through birth pangs (as Jesus said). This time of anguish is a necessary prelude to the rebirth of the world which will follow the time of great tribulation.

When the world is finally reborn, under its new government directed by Jesus himself, the Apostles will occupy positions of servant-rulership. Jesus told them, "Truly, I say to you, in the new world, when the Son of Man will sit on his glorious throne, you who have followed me will also sit on twelve thrones, judging [administering] the twelve tribes of Israel" (Matt. 19:28).

Later he confirmed this event: "But when the Son of Man comes in his glory, and all the angels with him, then he will sit upon his glorious throne" (Matt. 25:31).

I am hoping that these details about how present world history will end will recall the basic outline we described earlier from other Bible verses. You see in Daniel 12:2, 3 the resurrection of the faithful dead and their glorious transformation as shining beings. Immortality is conferred on them by that resurrection. Jesus loved this passage of Daniel and quoted it in his own description of the same events. Jesus spoke of "the resurrection of the just" (Luke 14:14). Jesus was deeply interested in prophecies of the future. As Matthew reports it, Jesus spoke of the faithful Christians "shining forth like the sun in its strength in the Kingdom of their Father" (Matt. 13:43, quoting Dan. 12:3). He also described the appalling fate of the non-believers:

> The enemy who planted the weeds among the wheat is the Devil. The harvest is the end of the age, and the harvesters are the angels. Just as the weeds are separated out and burned, so it will be at the end of the age. I, the Son of Man, will send my angels, and they will remove from my Kingdom everything that causes sin and all who do evil, and they will throw them into the furnace and burn them.

There will be weeping and gnashing of teeth. Then the godly will shine like the sun in their Father's Kingdom. Anyone who is willing to hear should listen and understand! (Matt. 13:39-43).

All this material about the future of the world and of humanity was of the greatest interest and concern to Jesus as he preached the Gospel of the Kingdom. We should etch into our memories these indelible images of the future of the world. The Bible is a vivid and exciting book designed to capture our full interest. The Kingdom of God is coming, and we are to be prepared by believing and living out those marvelous promises of a sound and permanently stable government under the supervision of Jesus and his chosen associates. Social justice is notably absent in so much of our world. All that injustice is going to come to an end. A revolutionary new government is coming to the earth. Jesus will be its first and supreme president and king. That is what it means to be the Messiah. He is God's chosen world ruler. As "prince of peace" he is going to achieve what no one so far has been able to produce, peace across the globe for all peoples.

At his first coming Jesus announced God's future, and then he died at the hands of evil religious opponents and other fanatics. His death was reckoned by God as a fitting substitute for the death we all deserve. He "covered" for us, relieving us of the death penalty we deserved. We are spared and forgiven. Forgiveness is obtained by embracing that substitutionary death of Jesus for every human being *and by believing also in his Kingdom Gospel* (Mark 4:11, 12; I Pet. 1:2).

Daniel provides us not only with a great vision of the resurrection. He impresses on us also the condition of the dead before the resurrection. Like Jesus and the New Testament Daniel had never heard a word about "souls going to heaven to be with God." He and Jesus were firmly of the opinion that the dead are now dead, unconscious in their graves. This makes the promise of future resurrection and a return to life all the more riveting. "Many of those who are sleeping in the dust of the ground will awake, some to the life of the age to come" (Dan. 12:2). This simple verse tells us what the dead are doing and where they are doing it. They are "asleep" in the ground. But when Jesus comes back they are going to awake from the sleep of death and from then on live forever. They will be given what the Hebrew Bible and the New Testament tell us is "the life of the age to come."

Daniel was comforted by the prospect of rising from the sleep of death. The angel told him: "As for you, go your way until the end. You will rest, and then at the end of the days, you will rise again to receive the inheritance set aside for you" (Dan. 12:13).

This is the biblical hope so absent from preaching in church.

In Daniel 12:2 Daniel meant by this famous phrase "life of the age" "the life of the age *to come*." Since it is to be life following the future resurrection, it is naturally the life of the age *to come*. The age to come of course is the Kingdom of God, the subject of Jesus' Gospel. In the New Testament the age to come has the same meaning as the Kingdom of God.

In our Bibles you will find this expression "the life of the age to come" translated as "everlasting life" or "eternal life." This is an inaccurate translation, and hides from you the fact that the future Kingdom is going to replace the present evil age dominated by Satan. Satan is said to be "the god of this age" (2 Cor. 4:4) and in that capacity he "is deceiving the whole world" (Rev. 12:9). His control over this dark present evil age is so widespread that John the Apostle said that "the whole world lies in the power of the evil one" (1 John 5:19). That is a sort of blanket coverage and suggests that we must work hard to free ourselves from the Devil's deception and darkness. We must rid ourselves of his clever lies and embrace the truth. This is the only way to be safe and to live within the grace of God. Above all we should not be complacent. We should earnestly pursue truth.

The power and promise and spirit of that future Kingdom can be tasted now in advance. Christians at conversion are transferred into the Kingdom, in the sense that they are candidates for immortality when the Kingdom comes (Col. 1:13). At conversion and belief in the Gospel of the Kingdom they cease to be part of this world or age and take on a new loyalty to Jesus as King of the Kingdom. Christians are now heirs to the Kingdom, joint heirs with Christ (Rom. 8:17). They will inherit the Kingdom when Jesus comes back. Christians, as we will see, are now to undergo a "rebirth." Jesus said it plainly: "you must be born again" (John 3:3). Without rebirth now in this present life, we cannot enter the Kingdom when it comes. Rebirth is absolutely essential if we are to be prepared for life in the future Kingdom. Jesus instructed a rabbi, Nicodemus, who came to see him: "Unless a person is born again, he cannot see or enter the Kingdom of heaven" (John 3:3, 5). Jesus made intelligent reception of his Kingdom Gospel a necessary condition for being saved. "I tell you the truth, anyone who will not receive the Kingdom of God like a little child will never enter it" (Luke 18:17).

How this rebirth happens — by receiving the Gospel as Jesus preached it — we will explain in greater detail in a later chapter. Please read on.

From this present chapter I hope you will see that the prophet Daniel was deeply important to Jesus, as he should be to us. It is impossible to grasp the saving Message of Jesus if we do not know about the background to his teaching in the Hebrew Bible, the Old Testament. All the prophets of the Old Testament looked forward to the time coming when peace is going to prevail all over the world. The Kingdom of God is going to put an end to all the problems we now face as individuals and as society. Daniel in his seventh chapter was given a grand revelation of the future activity of the Son of Man and his associates.

The Son of Man means *the* human being. The title refers to Jesus and secondarily to the followers of Jesus who will, as a group, administer the affairs of the Kingdom when it comes. "Son of Man" was Jesus' favorite title for himself. He knew about his own destiny in the future of the world, and he found that destiny described in Daniel's visions. Jesus is the supreme human being, supernaturally begotten by the One God of the Bible, the Father of Jesus. Jesus is the perfect model of a human being in relation to God. He faithfully carried out the will of God, despite terrible opposition and trial. Jesus was also the model preacher of the Gospel, the Gospel about the Kingdom of God. He successfully carried out his commission to preach the Gospel of the Kingdom. As he said, preaching the Kingdom Gospel was the purpose for which God had commissioned him.

In our next chapter we need to trace the Bible drama further back to the time of Abraham, some 2000 years before Jesus was born, and in the chapter after that to David who lived approximately 1000 years after his ancestor Abraham, and 1000 years before Jesus' birth.

As we will see, Abraham and David are key figures in God's great Kingdom-immortality program. That is why the New

Testament's very first verse introduces Jesus as the descendant of Abraham and David (Matt. 1:1). They are prominent members of the great Kingdom drama. Both David and Abraham were specially anointed by the spirit of God. Everyone who wants to understand the Gospel will need to know how these great men fit into God's plan. They too are models for us, and they underwent some of the same trials and tests which Christians should expect. God and Jesus need to know what we are really "made of." God will not appoint rulers in His Kingdom who have not been thoroughly groomed for royal office — and found to be irreproachable and reliable.

Chapter 6
God Picks Abraham, the Father of the Faithful

The world, after its creation by the One God of heaven and earth, soon fell into terrible trouble. Adam and Eve were taken in by the subtle lies of the Devil and they lost their place in the paradise garden of Eden. They listened to the Devil and not to God. This was the beginning of a downward spiral of evil. Cain, son of Adam and Eve, murdered his brother. Subsequent generations were not able to reverse the trend of violence and sin which overwhelmed the young human race.[1] Eventually in Genesis 6 an extraordinary account of supernatural evil in collaboration with human evil is given us. We read that certain angelic beings[2] cohabited with human females and produced a hybrid offspring of giants who terrorized the world. They are remembered also in Greek literature as renowned "heroes" of old. This disaster allowed evil of all sorts to prevail in even greater measure. God, who allowed mankind freedom to make his own good or bad choices, actually regretted that He had made man at all (Gen. 6:6). He therefore purposed to exert His almighty strength in the form of a totally devastating judgment, the flood.

For some 120 years Noah, who understood God's immortality plan, warned his fellow human beings that catastrophe was facing the human race unless they repented of their evil. There are, of course, direct parallels between the situation on earth which led to the great judgment of the flood and the conditions which Jesus predicted will prevail on earth just prior to his return to destroy the wicked and bring in the Kingdom. Jesus said that conditions just before his return will be like the careless and godless times of Noah.

---

[1] The account can be read in Genesis, chapters 1-6.

[2] The expression "sons of God" in Hebrew (Job 1:6, 2:1; 38:7; cp. Dan. 3:25) always means angelic beings and not humans. One Greek version of the Old Testament translates the term in Gen. 6:2 correctly as "angels." The New Testament refers to this disastrous evil in 2 Peter 2:4 and Jude 6.

Eventually, after the vast majority mocked Noah's warnings and dismissed him as some sort of religious fanatic, God sent a flood which drowned everyone except for Noah and his immediate family, eight persons in all. Peter in the New Testament reminds his readers of the awful dangers of complacency (2 Pet. 2:5-9). God will continue to judge evil societies. He has done this before and He will do it again. We cannot afford to lose our grip on the need to pursue what Jesus called the will of God. Doing the will of God, for Jesus, was closely connected with believing and helping to propagate the Good News (Gospel) of the Kingdom of God. To "do the will of God" is the same according to Jesus as "hearing the word [Gospel of the Kingdom] and doing it." We will examine that connection between the Kingdom and the will of God in a later chapter. God does not impose on us a burdensome religion, but His standards for us are very high. God is relentlessly opposed to violence and sexual impurity of all sorts. The Bible is strongly against all forms of sexual perversion and present attempts to redefine the word "marriage" represent the lengths to which humanity will go to defy the Creator.

Jesus warned against false prophets and advised us that they are to be recognized by their "fruits." Where sexual perversion of any sort is practiced or taught by religious leaders and their followers, one can be sure that they are not representing Jesus. Some leaders not only practiced adultery but advocated it as beneficial to their disciples. One group set themselves not only in this regard against the will of God, but they counseled opposition to the Messiah by denying the need for water baptism.

Despite the terrible judgment caused by the flood, it was not long after that the human race began once again to fill the earth with evil. Noah's children had not learned the lesson of the flood. In Babylon, the land of Nimrod, who was an anti-God figure, people combined their resources to build a monumental tower, the tower of Babylon (Gen. 11). It was a symbol of man's attempt to reach up to heaven. God's response was to prevent a further disaster by dispersing the people in all directions and confusing their languages. This move on the part of God diffused the enormous danger to humanity caused by a united world movement in opposition to God.

Then God began, so to speak, all over again. He decided to call out of the pagan city of Ur in Babylon a single couple whose names have been known throughout history as heroes of true faith. God invited Abram (later called Abraham) to give up everything for His cause. He was told to leave his country and his relatives and to depart, relying simply on God and His promises, for an unknown land. Abraham and his wife Sarah obeyed, and they are the model for us all of the right response to the Gospel. [3] We are meant to have what Paul called "the faith of Abraham" (Rom. 4:16). Christians are defined in the New Testament as the spiritual children of Abraham (Gal. 3:29).

Staying for a time in a place called Haran, Abraham eventually left that city and journeyed on to the land we now know as Israel. It was known also as the land of Palestine. God had determined to make this country the center of His great plan. Abraham was promised a permanent inheritance in that land (Gen. 13:15; 17:8, etc.). This he has never yet received, though he died fully assured that he would receive it at the future resurrection when Jesus returns.

Here is the plain statement from the Bible which supports this point: "All these died in faith without receiving the promises" (Heb. 11:13, 39). The writer was referring to all the biblical heroes of faith who believed in God's Kingdom plan.

Christians are those who follow in the steps of Abraham to whom God promised the world (Rom. 4:12).

Abraham is celebrated in the Bible as "the father of the faithful" (Rom. 4:11, 16). "The faith of Abraham" (Rom. 4:16), we repeat, is a phrase used by Paul to describe what true believing is — true Christianity, in fact. The reason for this Abraham connection is simply this: God promised to give to Abraham a descendant who would be the Messiah, the Christ, Jesus. At the same time the promise to Abraham included a guarantee that if Abraham obeyed God, he and his descendant (Christ) and descendants (plural, the Christians) would inherit the whole land of Israel, and since Israel would be the center of a world Kingdom, the whole world. Paul spoke of this great promise as "the promise to Abraham that he would be heir of the world" (Rom. 4:13). This is a key biblical phrase which opens up important vistas of understanding of God's immortality program. Inheritance of the

---

[3]The story of Abraham begins in Gen. 12 and chapters 13, 15 and 17 deal especially with the covenant God made with him.

world promised to Abraham, "the father of the faithful," is *exactly the same as the inheritance of the Kingdom promised to Jesus and by Jesus to his followers.* The story is essentially simple. The Christian Gospel of the Kingdom preached by Jesus cannot be properly grasped without the vital Old Testament information about the land and seed promise made by God to Abraham.

Yes, we may describe the divine promises to Abraham as simply the promise of seed (descendant) and of soil, land. The seed and the soil. The concept is not complicated. If you have a land you need a king to be in charge of it. The land needs a manager. Thus God's whole plan to establish the Kingdom of God on earth involves both land and landowner. The promise to Abraham was that the Messiah would one day be born, as a blood descendant of Abraham, and that the Messiah, after teaching and dying and rising from death, would take over the politics of the world by ruling in his Kingdom. It is to be a Kingdom over the land and the whole earth. It will be God's Kingdom ruled by His supreme agent, Jesus the Messiah. God has decided to give the land and the world to those who please Him (Jer. 27:5).

There is a key here to the whole biblical story. The basic fact to get hold of is this: The land promise to Abraham is exactly the same as the Kingdom of God Gospel-promise in the New Testament. The background to the Gospel preaching of Jesus, in other words, was the announcement to Abraham that he would possess the land forever. The land would belong to Abraham and his special descendant, the Messiah Jesus. Jesus knew that he was a lineal descendant of Abraham and that he, Jesus, was that distinguished "seed" who would arise in Israel to rule in the coming Kingdom. Jesus knew that he was the ultimate heir to the land and thus the king of the Kingdom of God. He invites others, through the Gospel, to be part of that Kingdom in the land. "Blessed are the meek: they will have the land as their inheritance" (Matt. 5:5). How strikingly different this is from the hopelessly vague promise of "heaven" for disembodied souls promoted in churches! No wonder many are completely "turned off" from church. The point of the Christian venture as presented by church makes no impact on them. They find the prospect of disembodiment in heaven almost repulsive, and certainly very boring and uninviting.

The Bible is all about who gets "the land," the very issue now causing so much trouble in the Middle East. Jesus will get the land. And he will share it with his followers when he returns. To try to take it over now, or engineer policies to make Jews or Arabs own it now, lies completely outside the range of the teaching of Jesus.

It is surprising that this wonderful connection between what God promised to Abraham and what He promises to Christians is not common knowledge in church. It is written in Scripture for all to see:

Genesis 28:4: Isaac's son Jacob was told: "May God pass on to you and your descendants the blessings he *promised to Abraham*. May you own this land where we now are foreigners, for God gave it to Abraham."

And what exactly is that promised blessing? Let the New Testament answer:

Galatians 3:14: "Through the work of Christ Jesus, God has blessed the Gentiles with the same blessing he *promised to Abraham*, and we Christians receive the promised Holy Spirit through faith."

The blessing promised to Abraham is exactly the same blessing that is promised to Christians. It is the future inheritance of the land, in other words the Kingdom of God.

This promise of the land to Abraham is so utterly crucial to understanding the Bible and Christianity that I want you to hear the whole passage in which God established His firm agreement, a covenant, with Abraham. These are indeed fascinating words:

When Abram was ninety-nine years old, the LORD appeared to him and said, "I am God Almighty; serve me faithfully and live a blameless life. I will make a covenant with you, by which I will guarantee to make you into a mighty nation." At this, Abram fell face down in the dust. Then God said to him, "This is my covenant with you: I will make you the father of not just one nation, but a multitude of nations! What's more, I am changing your name. It will no longer be Abram; now you will be known as Abraham, for you will be the father of many nations. I will give you millions of descendants who will represent many nations. Kings will be among them! I will continue this everlasting covenant between us, generation after generation. It will continue between me and your offspring forever. And I will always be your God and the God of your descendants after you. Yes, I will give all this land of Canaan to you and to your offspring forever. And I will be their God. Your part of the agreement," God told Abraham, "is to obey the terms of the covenant. You and all your descendants have this continual responsibility" (Gen. 17:1-9).

You too can be a part of this astonishing program promised to Abraham and finally to Jesus himself.

Although most Jews rejected the claims of Jesus, some did not. The claim of Jesus was that he was indeed the long-promised Christ, the King, the Son of God. On a most important occasion during the Kingdom ministry of Jesus, Jesus put the most fundamental of all questions to his disciple and Apostle, Peter. Jesus wanted to be assured that Peter understood who Jesus was. Jesus noted that some people thought various things about who he was. Some thought he was John the Baptist resurrected or perhaps one of the prophets. But these views were quite mistaken. Hence Jesus' pointed question to Peter: "Who do *you* say that I am?" Peter gave the only correct answer to this decisive question. "You are the Christ [= the Messiah], the Son of the living God." Jesus recognized that it was by supernatural revelation that Peter understood that Jesus was the Messiah — the chosen descendant promised to Abraham, the heir to the Kingdom, the savior of all who turn to him. It was on this rock confession of Peter that Jesus proposed to build his true Church (Matt. 16:16-18).

The whole Bible story is about the land or Kingdom and its King, Jesus the Christ (Messiah).

It is essential not to miss the extreme importance of this episode when Peter correctly identified who Jesus is. The key is to know and understand that Jesus is the Christ, the Son of God. These titles are complementary. They have the same meaning. As we saw, Jesus is the Son of God because of the marvelous miracle performed in Mary, the mother of Jesus. Please review this vitally significant fact in chapter 4.

Later church traditions changed and obscured the identity of Jesus drastically. The idea arose, after Bible times, that Son of God meant "God the Son," the second member of what was called the Triune God or Trinity. Unfortunately Jesus would not have recognized such a far-reaching switch of his identity. Jesus claimed always to be the Messiah. Certainly he never claimed to be God Himself. He never ever raised his own status to that of the uncreated God. Not once did he ever say "I am God." Jesus was always subordinate to his Father and Jesus recited and affirmed as the only acceptable creed, the creed of Israel: "Hear O Israel, the Lord our God is one Lord." One Lord, not two or three Lords! If both the Father and the Son are God, that would of course make two Gods! Jesus would have dismissed such a belief as dangerous paganism. Jesus agreed with a Jewish scribe that the creed given to Israel was the all-important key for worshiping God "in spirit and truth" (John 4:24). Jesus obviously believed in the central creed of Israel and of the Bible. So should his followers, of course. Jesus' creed as recorded in Mark 12:28-34 is the Christian creed, and he would have been puzzled and disturbed by later theories about God which no Jew will accept today. And of course the billion Muslims on earth likewise reject belief in the Triune God developed after the Bible was written.

This issue about who God is, is no minor question. Some three billion religious people on earth, claiming to be monotheists,[4] are unable to agree on their definition of God. It would be immensely valuable to proclaim once again the creed of Jesus that God the Father is "the only one who is truly God" (John 17:3). That was indeed the creed of Jesus himself, and ought to command our utmost respect.

This enormously significant fact — about the later invention of a new status for Jesus which he would not have recognized — has not been told you in church. In fact if any church member raises questions about the much later claim that the important thing is to know that Jesus *IS God*, he is likely to be viewed as a traitor to Jesus! Far from that being true, a questioner as to who Jesus is simply calls attention to Jesus' own description of who he really is. He should know. He never ever claimed to be anyone other than the Messiah, *the* Son of God. All sons are subordinate to their fathers who produced them. A son cannot possibly be the same age as his father. And since the Bible tells us that Jesus was the *begotten* Son of God, this merely confirms what is anyway quite obvious, that Jesus was brought into existence by his Father.

---

[4]Believers that God is one.

That is what the word beget means, as any dictionary of English, Greek or Hebrew will tell you. Yes, "to beget" means to become the father of someone, to bring that person *into existence*. Jesus was brought into existence as the Son of God in Mary's womb. That is what Luke 1:35 says. When that precious text enjoys a comeback it will undo a mass of traditional teaching about Jesus which has been accepted blindly and uncritically as "tradition."

To say then, as churches customarily do, that the Son had no beginning of existence, is to contradict the Bible badly. The word "beget" in that case has been emptied of all meaning. The texts which speak of Jesus as the begotten — i.e., brought into existence — Son of God have been cleverly ruled out of court by churches. Their obvious meaning has been obliterated. And a false tradition that Jesus was *always* the Son and had no beginning has been put in their place. This is destructive to God's plan to save humanity by a sinless *man*, the appointed mediator between the One God and ourselves. Paul said this very clearly: "There is one God and one mediator between that One God and man, Messiah Jesus, who is himself man" (1 Tim. 2:5). Is this a difficult teaching to understand?

Equally important in this question of the identity of Jesus is the promise made to Abraham of a coming "seed" or descendant who would appear on the scene of history and eventually rule the land and the world. It is obviously important that we identify that seed and recognize him as the legal and biological descendant of Abraham. All other claimants would be frauds. Abraham was not promised that "God" would be his seed and heir. God is not a created being. God has always existed.

The Son of God, the Messiah, is strictly a member of the human race. One contemporary leader of a big church said that "Mary changed God's diapers." Another said that "God came to Mary and asked, 'Will you please be My mother?'" The Bible writers would have rejected such ideas as nonsense. God was never a baby! God is not a man. He is God and alone has immortality (1 Tim. 6:16). God cannot die, therefore, and the Bible says that the Son of God, Jesus, died. The whole point about the Messiah is that he originates as a member of the human race. And it is essential that the Son of God *died*. Otherwise there is no sacrifice for sin.

If Jesus is God, and God is immortal (1 Tim. 6:16), then Jesus cannot have died. Then there is no sacrifice for the sins of humanity. If the Father is God, which is stated thousands of times in the Bible, then the Son cannot also be God. That would make two Gods. The Bible warns against any deviation from the truth that there is only One God.

While the Father was in heaven, the Son of God came into existence on earth and taught on earth. If both are God, that adds up to two Gods. Just look at some of the terribly confusing statements about who God is, offered at websites: "God is a Person...three Persons, and yet but one God." It is logical nonsense to propose that God is one Person and three Persons! Three 'x's cannot equal one 'x.'

At present church members are taught that they *must*, for salvation, believe that God is three-in-one. However, sermons are not preached on what this means. It is just to be believed, on the basis of a heavy-handed official teaching of "the Church."

John Calvin, the reformer, actually authorized the judicial burning at the stake of a young theologian who dared to question the Trinity.

The centuries-long disputes which racked the Church over who Jesus was in relation to his Father are the sad monument to the awful results of abandoning the Hebrew creed of Jesus. Meanwhile millions of Jews and Muslims knew better. They knew that God is One and only One. Certainly not three. And as many theologians know the average churchgoer does not know what to make of the mysterious idea that God is one and three. Yet, woe betide anyone who questions that dogma! He is likely to be given the "left foot of fellowship"! Kicked out.

Thankfully, in our time, there is enough literature around from first-class scholars to call attention to the fact that the Church has been promoting for nearly 2000 years a creed which contradicted the belief of Jesus.

To say that the seed of Eve and of Abraham would actually *be* God would make nonsense of the whole promise to Abraham. Abraham looked forward to the birth of the Messiah, a descendant of his. Mary conceived that royal descendant at a given moment of history. That seed was indeed the Son of God (certainly not "God the Son"!) because God was responsible for his existence which began in the womb of his mother (just as all human beings originate in their mothers). Mary did not act as a sort of "conduit" or channel through which an *already existing* "Son of God" passed, moving from a spiritual life to a human existence. That sort of idea belongs in pagan religions. It reminds us of pagan concepts of "reincarnation." It would be a sort of metamorphosis and not a begetting at all.

You cannot be human if you are pre-human. We are what we are according to our origin. And the origin of Jesus, Son of God, was in the womb of Mary. He was brought into existence in the womb of his mother. He is the beginning of God's new and final creation. Adam failed but Jesus succeeded and we are all summoned to follow him and gain life forever.

Matthew wrote a whole section at the beginning of his gospel about the "*origin* of Jesus" (Matt. 1:1, 18; the Greek word is "genesis"),[5] and churches have substituted a completely different story by saying that the Son of God had no beginning!

It was to the arrival of this promised royal descendant that Abraham looked forward with such excitement. Abraham died without having received the promise of permanent ownership of the land, which God had guaranteed to him. He died looking forward with great joy and excitement to the future coming of his promised descendant, Jesus. Abraham died believing firmly that what God had promised He would accomplish in due time. Believing that what God has said is true and will one day become reality is the essence of faith. There is a great key verse in Genesis 15:6 which announces that "Abraham believed God and this was counted to Abraham as making Abraham right with God." Paul quoted that verse three times in the New Testament (Rom. 4:3, 9; Gal. 3:6). James also quoted it (James 2:23). Faith is simply believing what God has said — believing that it is true, and living on the basis of those promises. In the New Testament faith is concentrated on believing what Jesus said and living in accordance with those promises. What Jesus promised was itself a confirmation of God's promises to Abraham (Rom. 15:8).

The key here is coming to know what it is that God has promised. It is highly problematic to make up one's *own* ideas about God's will and promises. To believe our own theories about

---

[5]Some Greek manuscripts were corrupted by substituting the word "gennesis" (with two n's) to avoid the clearer term "genesis" (one n).

what God should or might do is perilous. To imagine our own method of achieving everlasting life is risky. True faith is based on the words of Scripture. And now that the Son of God has come, faith is based on the covenant, Kingdom words of Jesus and those whom Jesus appointed as his messengers who also wrote Scripture for us all.

Man's failure from the dawn of human history has been his willingness to believe the falsehoods of the Devil rather than the truth told him by God. Reversing that tragedy, which is the cause of all of our problems, means beginning to listen carefully to and heed the words of the new Adam, Jesus, and his agents.

All true faith rests on the recorded words of the Jesus of history, summarized as his Gospel about the Kingdom. That phrase sums up the entire Bible story. It is all about the Kingdom, about who "gets the land." This is the very issue over which people in the Middle East and elsewhere struggle apparently endlessly today. The solution to the problem is given us in the Bible. Jesus gets the land. He is the Messiah and he promised his followers, of all nations, that if they are meek, they "will inherit the land" (Matt. 5:5). That too is what Abraham looked forward to.

That land/Kingdom promise is of course simply the great promise of God to Abraham confirmed by the one who is the object of all the promises, Jesus, the Messiah. Another key figure in the unfolding drama of the Kingdom is the celebrated King David. He understood very well the vastly important role he had been chosen to fulfill in the Messianic, Kingdom, immortality program. The whole activity of God in history took on an even greater clarity when Nathan the prophet explained God's intentions for David's royal household and dynasty.

That part of our story belongs to the next chapter.

Chapter 7
King David: Another Great Figure in the Kingdom Story

About 1000 years after Abraham, there occurred another major framework event in God's unfolding immortality-Kingdom program. It was God's selection of a king from among eight sons of a Jew, Jesse. God selected his youngest son, David, the one with a ruddy complexion and beautiful eyes. He was, his brothers thought, the least suitable candidate for royal office as king of Israel. But God looks on the heart, the Bible reminds us, and not on outward appearance. God was in search of someone whose loyalty to the great Kingdom program would be fixed and firm. This does not mean that David did not make some serious mistakes in the course of his journey of faith. But genuine repentance brought him back on track. He was deeply broken over his sin, and he died after a long life, as did Abraham, believing in God's Kingdom plan, without having seen the fulfillment of the great promise of the Kingdom to come.

First, the selection of King David. We have here a picture not only of David, but in principle all Christians who align themselves with the Messianic program to be realized in Christ, who is the blood descendant or "seed" of David (Matt. 1:1). Christians are said to be anointed, in the New Testament, because they have received the holy spirit of God as an anointing. That spirit is in our hearts (2 Cor. 1:22). The holy spirit in the Bible is the operational presence and power of God. It is God and Jesus (since New Testament times) in personal outreach to us. The spirit is also the mind of Christ (1 Cor. 2:16). The spirit is a foretaste of the immortality to be granted to believers when Jesus comes back. For the present, the Christians, those who obey Jesus (Acts 5:32; Heb. 5:9), receive the spirit as an anointing in advance of the future Kingdom. The spirit is received by believing the Gospel (Gal.

3:2).[1] Christians are said to be "born of the spirit" (John 3:5) or born of the word, the Gospel (1 Pet. 1:23; James 1:18; Gal. 4:28, 29). I love this story of the selection of David to royal office. We watch the work of God in the choice of this celebrated ancestor of Jesus, David the famous psalmist and king. Let the Bible itself tell the story:[2]

> Finally, the Lord said to Samuel, "You have mourned long enough for Saul. I have rejected him as king of Israel. Now fill your horn with olive oil and go to Bethlehem. Find a man named Jesse who lives there, for I have selected one of his sons to be my new king." But Samuel asked, "How can I do that? If Saul hears about it, he will kill me." "Take a heifer with you," the Lord replied, "and say that you have come to make a sacrifice to the Lord. Invite Jesse to the sacrifice, and I will show you which of his sons to anoint for me." So Samuel did as the Lord instructed him. When he arrived at Bethlehem, the leaders of the town became afraid. "What's wrong?" they asked. "Do you come in peace?" "Yes," Samuel replied. "I have come to sacrifice to the Lord. Purify yourselves and come with me to the sacrifice." Then Samuel performed the purification rite for Jesse and his sons and invited them, too. When they arrived, Samuel took one look at Eliab and thought, "Surely this is the Lord's anointed!" But the Lord said to Samuel, "Don't judge by his appearance or height, for I have rejected him. The Lord doesn't make decisions the way you do! People judge by outward appearance, but the Lord looks at a person's thoughts and intentions." Then Jesse told his son Abinadab to step forward and walk in front of Samuel. But Samuel said, "This is not the one the Lord has chosen." Next Jesse summoned Shammah, but Samuel said, "Neither is this the one the Lord has chosen." In the same way all seven of Jesse's sons were

---

[1]The evidence of the spirit is shown by an understanding of the Gospel and Truth. To teach that the real evidence of the spirit is "speaking in tongues" is a catastrophic departure from the Bible.

[2]From the *New Living Translation*.

presented to Samuel. But Samuel said to Jesse, "The Lord has not chosen any of these."

Then Samuel asked, "Are these all the sons you have?" "There is still the youngest," Jesse replied. "But he's out in the fields watching the sheep." "Send for him at once," Samuel said. "We will not sit down to eat until he arrives." So Jesse sent for him. He was ruddy and handsome, with pleasant eyes. And the Lord said, "This is the one; anoint him." So as David stood there among his brothers, Samuel took the olive oil he had brought and poured it on David's head. And the Spirit of the Lord came mightily upon him from that day on. Then Samuel returned to Ramah (1 Sam. 16:1-13).

The background to this royal appointment of David is of the greatest importance. Abraham, you will remember, had been promised the seed and the soil, a descendant and a land or Kingdom which he would inherit permanently. The promises to Abraham consisted of a geographical place and a prince to go with it. Abraham was guaranteed, subject to his proper response of obedience and faith, progeny, prosperity and property. With the land promise now firmly established, under the terms of the Abrahamic covenant, God decided to provide a king, a royal household, beginning with David. You cannot have a land without a prince or king to supervise it. David was anointed as king, and was thus a messiah (an anointed one), but God promised him a descendant who would be the *ultimate* promised seed, Jesus *the* Messiah, God's unique Son.

It is surprising that in countries calling themselves Christian the true Christian history is not faithfully taught in schools. Our real history and roots are not to be found in the country in which we happen to have been born, but in our spiritual, biblical heritage. Americans often speak of their so-called Judeo-Christian heritage, but they say nothing about the Abrahamic and Davidic covenants which form the backbone of God's dealings with believers.

Christians are firstly members of the royal household of Judah. The members of the New Testament church are titled "God's Israel" (Gal. 6:16). We are also called the "true circumcision" which means the true spiritual "Jews" (Phil. 3:3). We are spiritually brothers and sisters of the Jew Jesus. Our passports really read "Kingdom of God." Our "birth certificates" speak of "rebirth," being born again into the royal family of King Jesus. Our relationships are not firstly with our physical relatives or the country of our birth, but with the international relatives of Jesus. Jesus made this marvelous observation: "Who are my mother and father and brothers and sisters? Those who hear the word of God — the Gospel of the Kingdom — and do it" (see Luke 8:21). Hearing the word of God is defined as "doing the will of God." "For whoever does the will of God, he is my brother and sister and mother" (Mark 3:35; cp. Matt. 12:50).

Don't miss this important point: hearing the Gospel as Jesus preached it and doing the will of God are intimately related. This is a key to understanding the Christian faith.

Jesus redefines the family as an international brotherhood of believers in and disciples of the Messiah. He intended his international Church to be a mini picture of the future Kingdom of God. The church would be noted for its love and compassion, one for another (John 13:35). At present, however, the ideal of love amongst believers has not been lived up to. The identifying "badge" of Christians has been lost. International wars have occurred in which believers have killed each other in support of their countries of origin. Would Jesus have taken the lives of others in international wars? Or was he an ambassador for a foreign Kingdom, modeling that status for his followers also? David was disqualified from building the temple because he had shed blood (1 Chron. 28:3).

Paul was very distressed about the large-scale rejection of Jesus by his natural kith and kin, Jews. He made it very clear that God had not given them all up permanently, but while they rejected Jesus as their Messiah, they were "enemies of the Gospel" and needed to be grafted back into their own olive tree (see Rom. 11). Paul of course acknowledged that Jews of his day "had a zeal for God, but without knowledge" (Rom. 10:2). (This is a peril for us all.) They were "doing religion" on their own terms but were not willing to submit to the terms of the New Covenant inaugurated by the blood of Jesus, the great Kingdom covenant (Luke 22:28-30).[4] Paul's Jewish compatriots were not without

---

[4]Luke 22:28-30 reports Jesus as "covenanting" the Kingdom to his followers. The Kingdom is the heart of the Gospel and thus of the New Covenant.

enthusiasm for God and religion, but they had not accepted the only religion which ultimately counts — faith in Jesus as the Messiah who has already come and is coming again — who came with the saving Gospel message about the Kingdom.

This truth about Christian identity is found in the model believer Abraham as much as it is found in the life and example of David. Abraham was an advance believer in Jesus and the Gospel of the Kingdom of God. He is thus rightly entitled to be called the father of the New Testament faithful (Rom. 4:16). In the same verse Christian faith is called "the faith of Abraham." Paul noted that the Gospel had been preached in advance to Abraham (Gal. 3:8). Abraham knew about the Kingdom and about Jesus, and looked forward excitedly to the birth of Jesus and the later coming of the Kingdom at the return of Jesus.

As we go on to see how God made a royal covenant with David, we must remind ourselves of the model and example of David's ancestor, Abraham. Abraham, like all followers of Jesus, was asked to break ties with all that was closest and dearest. He was asked to obey God by leaving his native country and his father and mother and relatives. He was then to proceed to the land of the promise, the promised land. He lived there in that promised land as a resident alien, a sort of "green card" person. He was a foreigner, in fact, in the land which actually belonged to him by promise. But he did not yet own it because Jesus the Messiah, the seed of Abraham, had not yet been born. Please consult the important information in Hebrews:

> By faith Abraham, when he was called, obeyed by going out to a place which he was to receive for an inheritance; and he went out, not knowing where he was going. By faith he lived as an alien *in the land of promise*, as in a foreign *land*, dwelling in tents with Isaac and Jacob, fellow heirs of the same promise (Heb. 11:8-9).

The royal element in the promise to Abraham was given a richer meaning by the appearance of King David. God's wonderful binding agreement with David, His covenant with David, is described so delightfully in the words of the Bible that I want you to hear it straight from Scripture. Here is the famous encounter of the prophet Nathan with King David. You will easily understand how the great immortality program is advanced by this next stage in the unfolding activity of God in history. This is not only

David's story. It is yours if you are beginning to take seriously the aims and claims of Jesus, if you want to be part of the great immortality program.

We take up the story in 2 Samuel 7:

> When the Lord had brought peace to the land and King David was settled in his palace, David summoned Nathan the prophet. "Look!" David said. "Here I am living in this beautiful cedar palace, but the Ark of God is out in a tent!" Nathan replied, "Go ahead and do what you have in mind, for the Lord is with you." But that same night the Lord said to Nathan, "Go and tell my servant David, 'This is what the Lord says: Are you the one to build me a temple to live in? I have never lived in a temple, from the day I brought the Israelites out of Egypt until now. My home has always been a tent, moving from one place to another. And I have never once complained to Israel's leaders, the shepherds of my people Israel. I have never asked them, "Why haven't you built me a beautiful cedar temple?"' Now go and say to my servant David, 'This is what the Lord Almighty says: I chose you to lead my people Israel when you were just a shepherd boy, tending your sheep out in the pasture. I have been with you wherever you have gone, and I have destroyed all your enemies. Now I will make your name famous throughout the earth! And I have provided a permanent homeland for my people Israel, a secure place where they will never be disturbed. It will be their own land where wicked nations won't oppress them as they did in the past, from the time I appointed judges to rule my people. And I will keep you safe from all your enemies. And now the Lord declares that he will build a house for you — a dynasty of kings! For when you die, I will raise up one of your descendants, and I will make his kingdom strong. He is the one who will build a house — a temple — for my name. And I will establish the throne of his kingdom forever. I will be his father, and he will be my son. If he sins, I will use other nations to punish him. But my unfailing love will not be taken from him as I took it from Saul, whom I removed before you. Your dynasty and your kingdom will continue for all time before me, and your throne will be secure

forever.'" So Nathan went back to David and told him everything the Lord had said (2 Sam. 7:1-17).

David's reaction to these wonderful promises about his own future and that of his descendants and of the world follows. David knew that the arrival of Jesus would be the ultimate fulfillment of the covenant God was making with him. (There was only a partial fulfillment in the life of Solomon, David's son.) The covenant with David would be the center of God's great charter for mankind, resulting in peace and prosperity for all nations obedient to Jesus.

David understood the vast importance of God's gracious dealings with him and his family:

> Then King David went in and sat before the Lord and prayed, "Who am I, O Sovereign Lord, and what is my family, that you have brought me this far? And now, Sovereign Lord, in addition to everything else, you speak of giving me a lasting dynasty! Do you deal with everyone this way, O Sovereign Lord?[5] What more can I say? You know what I am really like, Sovereign Lord. For the sake of your promise and according to your will, you have done all these great things and have shown them to me. How great you are, O Sovereign Lord! There is no one like you — there is no other God. We have never even heard of another god like you! [Note that David's creed was just like Jesus' — belief in one Person as God, certainly not two or three!]
>
> "What other nation on earth is like Israel? What other nation, O God, have you redeemed from slavery to be your own people? You made a great name for yourself when you rescued your people from Egypt. You performed awesome miracles and drove out the nations and gods that stood in their way. You made Israel your people forever, and you, O Lord, became their God. And now, O Lord God, do as you have promised concerning me and my family. Confirm it as a promise that will last

---

[5]This phrase probably means rather, "And this is the charter for human history." For a fuller account of the Davidic covenant, please see my *Our Fathers Who Aren't in Heaven: The Forgotten Christianity of Jesus the Jew*, especially chapter 6.

forever. And may your name be honored forever so that all the world will say, 'The Lord Almighty is God over Israel!' And may the dynasty of your servant David be established in your presence.

"O Lord Almighty, God of Israel, I have been bold enough to pray this prayer because you have revealed that you will build a house for me — an eternal dynasty! For you are God, O Sovereign Lord. Your words are truth, and you have promised these good things to me, your servant. And now, may it please you to bless me and my family so that our dynasty may continue forever before you. For when you grant a blessing to your servant, O Sovereign Lord, it is an eternal blessing!" (2 Sam. 7:18-29).

With this marvelous revelation of God to David the Kingdom drama of the Bible became even clearer. All the pieces of the unfolding plan came together. There remained only the arrival of Jesus the Messiah, coming into existence as the Son of God in Mary by supernatural generation (Luke 1:35).

David fell asleep in death, not having received the promises (Acts 13:36), but writing in many of his psalms[6] about them and the future of the world. David, as he wrote, eventually "slept the sleep of death" (Ps. 13:3). He knew that in the grave "no one thanks God or praises him" (Ps. 6:5; 115:17). But he died full of hope and faith in the future Messiah and the Kingdom. Your hope can be that of David, expressed so beautifully:

These are the last words of David: "David, the son of Jesse, speaks — David, the man to whom God gave such wonderful success, David, the man anointed by the God of Jacob, David, the sweet psalmist of Israel. The Spirit of the LORD speaks through me; his words are upon my tongue. The God of Israel spoke. The Rock of Israel said to me: 'The person who rules righteously, who rules in the fear of God, he is like the light of the morning, like the sunrise bursting forth in a cloudless sky, like the refreshing rains that bring tender grass from the earth.' It is my family God has chosen! Yes, he has made an

---

[6]See Particularly Psalms 2, 21, 96-100, where "the Lord reigns" is a prophecy of the future Kingdom, when the Lord will begin to reign. Also Psalms 72, 89.

everlasting covenant with me. His agreement is eternal, final, sealed. He will constantly look after my safety and success" (2 Sam. 23:1-5).

The New Testament makes it clear that the prophecy of Nathan about David's future son did not reach its climax in Solomon, who failed dismally as king. The prophecy had its true, final fulfillment in Jesus Christ. The New Testament applies the prophecy of 2 Samuel 7:14 about David's descendant to Jesus as the Messiah. "I will be his father and he will by My son," God had promised to David. Hebrews 1:5 tells us that Jesus was the object of this prophecy. It quotes the words of the Davidic Covenant and applies them to Jesus. It also proves the same point by quoting Psalm 2:7 about the coming into existence, the begetting, of the Son.

And so, some 2000 years ago, the Messiah Jesus was begotten by God in the womb of Mary (Luke 1:35). And note especially Matthew 1:20, where the Greek reads "that which is *begotten* in you is from holy spirit." Matthew has described in detail *the genesis* (Matt. 1:18) of the Messiah Jesus, son of Abraham and David (Matt. 1:1). That important word, "genesis," reminds us that the Son of God had a definite beginning of existence. It would be quite false to say that he has always existed. Someone older than David could not be David's descendant.

Truly the coming into existence of the Son of God was a stupendous miracle. No other person was born from a woman without the cooperation of a human father. Had you asked Jesus about his father, he would have replied, "God is my father."

This makes Jesus absolutely unique, in a class of his own. He was not "just a good man"! Nor was he selected to be God's Son sometime during his career. He was created in Mary as Son of God. No human being is his equal and there is no Savior except him. He is the perfect model of what it means for a human being to be in intimate relation with the Father, the Creator. God desires to be intimately related to His creatures and He was supremely active in the life of the perfect creature, Jesus.

Satan tries to make nonsense out of Jesus' status as Son of God by saying that a human being could not claim what Jesus claimed or do what Jesus did! But this is to deny God His perfect right to produce a human person of infinite dignity and value, and worthy of the homage paid to him as Messiah, not God. The New

Testament word for the worship *of God* alone is never applied to Jesus — not once.[7] Homage was paid to Jesus as Messiah. Jesus was intensely and passionately interested in God's great covenants with Abraham and David, his ancestors. No wonder that Jesus worked tirelessly at the task of announcing the Gospel of the Kingdom (Luke 4:43) which was nothing less than the Good News about God's great plan in fulfillment of His covenants with Abraham, David and of course with Jesus himself, as the centerpiece of the whole marvelous biblical drama.

---

[7]"There is no instance of *latreuein* [to worship as God] which has Christ as object" (Arthur Wainwright, *The Trinity in the New Testament*, p. 103).

Chapter 8
The True God, the True Messiah and the
Precious Seed of Immortality

Christianity is firstly about understanding God's great Kingdom-immortality program for the human race, and understanding that Jesus is the human Messiah, the Son of God. God is carrying out this Plan through Jesus the Messiah. Christian faith is about acting on that knowledge. It is about "getting with the Kingdom program." About treating the knowledge of the Kingdom Gospel as priceless treasure (Matt. 13:44). About understanding what the great God of Abraham, Isaac and Jacob and of Jesus is working out in history. About cooperating with that divine program. About working, as we can, for God's Kingdom cause. All this amounts to knowing the destiny of man and the purpose of human life. Living forever, rather than dying forever. The choice is ours.

It is about realizing that we have not done what we should have been doing, that we have been careless with the Bible and that we should "repent" of our ungodly behavior and beliefs and seek to have the mind of Christ which is the same as the spirit or mind of God. Repentance means "thinking again," and gaining a new orientation on life and its meaning in the light of truth found in the Scriptures. It means learning to think like Jesus and sound and act like Jesus. Jesus counsels us to "live by every word which proceeds from God's mouth" (Matt. 4:4). God's final message, the Gospel of the Kingdom, was the focus of Jesus' entire ministry, and of the ministry of Paul.

Attention to the words of Jesus is the key to the Christian faith. Yet the public has been presented with a Jesus who did not really preach the Gospel! This disastrous mistake has been achieved in various ways.

There is a catastrophic theory taught by some churches that the Gospel which Jesus preached is not for us, but was only for Jews! This extraordinary notion would cancel the teachings of Jesus and divorce him from the saving Gospel. It flatly contradicts the Great Commission, by which Jesus ordered his own Kingdom Gospel to be announced to all nations, without distinction. Any departure from Jesus' clear marching orders regarding the Gospel should be firmly rejected and the warnings of 2 John 7-9, 1 Timothy 6:3, and Hebrews 2:1-3 noted carefully.

Paul could not have made the Gospel clearer. His whole career was dedicated to preaching the one Gospel about the Kingdom, which is of course *identical* with the Gospel of grace (Acts 20:24, 25). Paul was obediently following Jesus.[1]

We are told to think and be like Jesus, and Jesus was the perfect model of someone who thinks and acts like God. He was not of course himself God. That would make two Gods. You cannot say: The Father is God. Jesus is God. That makes one God! It does not. Everyone, I think, really knows this, but church tradition is very threatening and sometimes believers have been frightened into believing impossible things — for example that the Father and Jesus are both God, but that makes one God! This makes no sense. It communicates nonsense. And here are some other things to think about: God cannot die. Jesus died. God cannot be tempted. Jesus was tempted. God never sleeps. Jesus fell asleep. God is not a man. Jesus is a man.

And most significantly of all, Jesus quoted the Jewish creed of Israel, which certainly restricted God to a single divine Person (biblical unitarianism) and never permitted anyone to believe that God was mysteriously three, and yet one. Or two in one, which would also be a violation of the command to believe that God is one Person, the Father of Jesus. Listen to the very clear statement of Paul: "For us there is no God but the one God, the Father" (see 1 Cor. 8:4-6). That is the Christian creed. Paul has been discussing the fact that in pagan religions there are many so-called gods and lords. But for us Christians belief in more than one God is impossible. Christians should be committed to the creed which Jesus loved (Mark 12:28-34).

That creed Paul also referred to in 1 Corinthians 8:4-6, where he contrasted the Christian belief in One God, the Father with the

---

[1]"It is evident that the preaching of the Gospel of grace is identical with the preaching of the Kingdom. Proclaiming the Kingdom is the same as testifying to the Gospel of God's grace" (F.F. Bruce, *Commentary on the Greek Text of Acts*, pp. 379, 380).

belief in more than one, or many gods in other systems of religion: "We know that there is one God and no one else besides him...For us there is one God, the Father." Paul went on to speak of our belief in "one Lord Messiah, Jesus." But note that Paul believed that Jesus was the Lord *Messiah* — certainly not the Lord God! Luke had used that same phrase, "the Lord Messiah," in Luke 2:11.

Jesus is said to be the Messiah repeatedly in the New Testament. Jesus is not the Lord God. He is the Lord Messiah, the Lord Jesus Christ/Messiah. Psalm 110:1 mentions those two contrasted Lords. One is Yahweh, the Father of Jesus, and the other is the human lord Messiah. David referred to the lord Messiah as "my lord" (in Psalm 110:1 which should be memorized by every believer) a thousand years before Jesus was born. He called him in Hebrew *adoni* (pronounced "adonee"). That form of the word "lord," *adoni*, occurs 195 times in the Old Testament Hebrew Bible and it never once refers to God.[2] It is the word used to tell us that the person addressed is *not* God, but a superior human or occasionally an angel.

Peter, on whose confession Jesus founded the Church (Matt. 16:16-18), declared that Jesus was lord in the sense revealed by Psalm 110:1. "God has made Jesus Lord and Christ" (Acts 2:36). He had just quoted Psalm 110:1. Everyone should know that the second "lord" of that verse is not God!

If people paid attention to that verse in Psalm 110:1, very frequently quoted by the New Testament writers, there would be no confusion about who God and Jesus are. One is Yahweh, the One God of Israel and the Father of Jesus. The other is the Lord Messiah, addressed not by a title of Deity, but a title of superiority as a human person.

Jesus used this verse in Psalm 110:1 to make his audience think about who the Messiah is. He invited them to think about how the Messiah could be both the lord of David and the son of David (Matt. 22:41-46). But Jesus was not asking them to think of the Messiah as the *God* of David! By being the supernaturally

---

[2]Strong's concordance will not show you this distinction. But it is obvious to anyone reading the Hebrew, and supported by major lexicons. The RSV, NRSV correctly do not put a misleading capital L on the second lord in Ps. 110:1.

begotten son of Mary and of God (Luke 1:35), Jesus was both son and lord of David from birth and ultimately by being raised to the right hand of the Father at the ascension. Peter understood this perfectly. He quoted that precious verse to prove that God had made Jesus Lord and Messiah (Acts 2:36). No one imagined that Jesus was *God*. He was the Messiah!

This issue of the right creed is no small matter. Billions of believers in God across the world are divided and potentially hostile to each other on the basis of differing concepts about God. We need to unite around the Bible's view, which incidentally will help to open conversation with members of the Muslim and Jewish faiths, who are presently offended (and rightly) by the traditional Christian idea that God is three-in-one. The so-called triune God of Christians puts up a barrier between Christians and much of the rest of the religious world. That barrier is quite unjustified. Jesus did not believe in the "Trinity." Nor did Paul or any New Testament writer.

Who is Jesus? Jesus is a perfect and unique human person. He began miraculously in the womb of his mother. That is what it means to be a human being. Human beings are not angels, and angels do not become humans (except in the grotesque and evil case of fallen angels mating with human females, see Genesis 6). You cannot be pre-human and human. Jesus did not transition from one life into another. The womb of Mary was not a place of transit for Jesus. He is the second Adam. He is called *the man* Messiah. Thus he had a definite beginning in time. Jesus was six months younger than John the Baptist. He was not and logically could not be *also* millions of years older. A single line cannot begin at two different points. A single person cannot have two origins at two different times. The origin of the Son of God is traced to the miracle performed in Mary (see again Luke 1:35). The Son of God was supernaturally generated by God.

The Jesus presented in church creeds is supposed to be the Son of God who had *no beginning in time*. This would make him non-human. It would mean that he passed through the womb of Mary, entering it from his "pre-life," and then dressed up in human clothes and looked like a man, but really was not. If the ego of Jesus were God he automatically could not sin, or be tempted or die. In this case his whole temptation and resistance of temptation would be a sort of game, a charade, an act. It would not in any way be an inspiring model for us. *We* are certainly not God and having an immortal God as a model for mortal man would not even be fair! It would be like a concert pianist in a piano competition with children who had had two piano lessons. The whole idea of what the churches call "the preexistence" of Jesus is really incomprehensible. It makes no logical sense. Think of a verb which goes like this: "I pre-am, you pre-are, he pre-is." How can a single person "pre-exist"? Can you exist before you exist? Who preexists who in that case? The whole theory is baffling and incomprehensible. And alien to the plain descriptions of how the Son of God began in Matthew and Luke.

I want to let you in on an amazing fact of church history. When you read Luke 1:35 you probably had no difficulty understanding that you were reading about the beginning of the Son of God. But by 150 AD the Church, which was rapidly losing touch with the biblical portrait of Jesus, was beginning to teach that Jesus was alive before he was born and that he actually brought about his own conception in Mary! Yes, that Jesus performed the miracle of his own birth!

Think carefully about what happened here. A tradition was being formed, later written into the creeds of most churches, by which the Son of God could no longer be a descendant of Eve, Abraham and David, supernaturally given existence, begotten, in Mary. Justin Martyr was an important "church father" of the second century. He was beginning to turn the teaching of Gabriel in Luke 1:35 into a completely different account of the origin of Jesus. Justin said that the power which overshadowed Mary (Luke 1:35) was none other than the Son of God! On that theory the Son produced his own conception! This is really nonsense. But the idea is written into the creeds of churches. They teach that the Son of God did *not* originate in the womb of his mother. This concept is more akin to the pagan idea of reincarnation.

Leading scholars today know quite well that Justin made nonsense out of the biblical account here, though they do not seem too worried. A leading expert commentator on Luke wrote, "Later tradition made something quite other out of Luke 1:35."[3] "Quite other"? Yes, the text was made to say something that Luke never imagined. Justin invented a brand new origin for Jesus, which later

---

[3]Joseph Fitzmeyer, *The Gospel According to St. Luke*, 1981, p. 350.

tradition has embraced to this day. It was that the Son of God did *not* begin in Mary's womb, but was alive before his birth and actually "engineered" his own conception.

Happily scholars admit that Luke and Matthew knew nothing about the doctrine which is now said to be the heart of Christianity — the Incarnation of a second member of the Trinity as a man: "Incarnation is a notion foreign to Luke (as to Matthew)."[4]

Luke is more explicit than Matthew in his assertion of Jesus' divine sonship from birth (1:32, 35). But here too it is sufficiently clear that it is a begetting, a becoming, which is in view, the coming into existence of one who will be called, and will in fact be the Son of God, not the transition of a preexistent being to become the soul of a human baby, or the metamorphosis of a divine being into a human fetus...Luke's intention is clearly to describe the creative process of begetting...Similarly in Acts there is no sign of any Christology of preexistence.[5]

The Bible warns us that only the historical Messiah, the man Christ, is the real Savior. Other saviors are only imitations and should not be taken as real. Jesus obviously believed that the majority would think that they had understood his teaching and that they had acted as his representatives. But they did not really sound like Jesus. Their teachings were unsound. Churches have a way of building into their systems of belief ideas which are not really based on the Bible but only on tradition.

How can we ensure against "getting our faith wrong"? The key to success is to be well-versed in what Jesus meant by the word Gospel. "Gospel of the Kingdom" is really an overarching title for Christianity. It is a sort of label for the Christian faith. Christianity is all about the Kingdom of God. Jesus demonstrated this by being a tireless and fearless announcer of the Kingdom of God and teaching his followers to "seek first the Kingdom of God" (Matt. 6:33) and to pray to God to send the Kingdom: "Your Kingdom come, your will be done on earth" (Matt. 6:10). Jesus said that the Christians would be granted the land or the earth as their reward (Matt. 5:5). He said nothing about going to heaven. In the Old Testament, God, the Father of Jesus, had earlier promised

---

[4] *Ibid.*, pp. 340, 350.
[5] James Dunn, *Christology in the Making*, p. 51.

the land not only to Abraham and David, but also to the faithful of all nations. He guaranteed them possession of that promised land forever, which of course implies immortality. That immortality and how to pursue it now is the center of Jesus' Kingdom Gospel.

If Jesus talked about the Kingdom always and preached it as Gospel, it would make sense that the followers of Jesus would be doing the same. That seems to me to be a fair test. If our language does not sound like Jesus, are we following him? Is Christianity just a matter of being kind and good, as we define it? Do "good people" get crucified, or was there much more involved in the teaching of Jesus than just being "good"?

Christianity as Jesus taught it is a matter of living out every word of God. Jesus did give us this piece of sage advice: "Man is not to live by bread alone, but by every word which proceeds out of the mouth of God" (Matt. 4:4). Presumably that implies a thorough search of Scripture to see what it teaches us. (Note carefully that Jesus was not requiring us to live by the Old Covenant laws given as a temporary guide to Israel through Moses. Jesus introduced the New Covenant which unites all nations in one faith. The book of Galatians deals with this important subject.)

If the Kingdom of God is the central theme of the Bible, in connection with the Christ who always preached the Gospel of the Kingdom, then must it not be the center of all Christian activity and preaching? If not, how can we be sure that we are thinking like Jesus and doing what he commanded? "This Gospel of the Kingdom will be preached in the whole world to all the nations and then the end will come" (Matt. 24:14). "Preach the Gospel to all the nations" (Mark 16:15; Matt. 28:19, 20).

That would appear to be the simplest job description of the Church. The Great Commission is very clear. Jesus gave a standing order when he told his successors to "go to all the nations, making disciples, baptizing them and teaching them everything I have taught you" (Matt. 28:19, 20). Clearly the same Gospel of the Kingdom was to go unchanged to the whole world. Men and women were to be baptized in water, just as Jesus himself had been. Yes, the Jews were the first to get the saving Gospel of the Kingdom. But when the witness to them was complete and many of them rejected it and their Messiah, then the same saving Gospel of the Kingdom was to go international.

People of all races and languages would in this way have the opportunity to believe in Jesus and his Kingdom Gospel and be saved. Only when "this Gospel of the Kingdom" (Matt. 24:14) has crossed the globe with sufficient intensity can the end of the age come. Then it will be time for Jesus to return. The throne of David will be restored in Jerusalem and the Messiah will take up his office as king of the world.

This information about the Kingdom, the Christian hope, was given full and fascinating detail in Jesus' famous parable of the sower. According to Mark's reporting,[6] that parable is also a parable about parables. "If you do not grasp the point of this parable of the sower," Jesus said, "you will not understand any of the parables" (see Mark 4:13). The sower/seed parable is the key to all of Jesus' teaching and it is the "unpacking" of the Kingdom Gospel which is vitally important for our salvation.

Jesus used a perfect example to illustrate how spiritual rebirth takes place: a seed. We all know about seeds. We ourselves are all "seeds." Everything starts with a seed. We are surrounded by evidence of the power of the seed. "Seed" is the key to life in the natural world. It is also the key to the life which lasts forever, immortality.

"The sower went out to sow his seed." The sower is the preacher of the Gospel of the Kingdom. The seed is "the word of the Kingdom" (Matt. 13:19). Luke calls it the "word of God" (Luke 8:11). Mark abbreviates it to "the word" (Mark 4:14). And he and Luke did not just mean the Bible as a whole. They meant the Gospel of the Kingdom.

We have in these three parallel accounts the simplest of equations: "word/Gospel of the Kingdom" = "word of God" = "word." Carry these definitions given by Jesus with you as you read the rest of the New Testament. Above all, never ever drop the word "Kingdom." If you do, you will cease to think and sound like Jesus.

---

[6]Mark's version of the parable of the sower is in chapter 4, Matthew's in chapter 13 and Luke's in chapter 8. All three accounts should be read over and over to glean their important meaning for God's immortality program and the way to salvation.

Jesus was thus the model "seed-sower," creating the possibility of life forever and ever. Greeks knew that the "word"[7] described the principle of coherence in the universe. Jesus showed what the real meaning of life and the universe is by telling us what "the word" really is. "The seed is the word" (Luke 8:11). The seed is the vital spark of the new life which ends in immortality. It is the only "*logos*" of ultimate value, the pearl of great price. Jesus thus superseded all the wisdom of contemporary philosophy and science. No philosopher or scientist knows the secret to life forever. But we can all learn it from Jesus.

Some of the seed fell on rocky soil. This means that it really never penetrated the hearts and minds of those in the first category who heard. They heard it but they did not understand it. They were quickly distracted by a multitude of competing attractions, and the seed came to nothing. "In one ear and out of the other," "over their heads," as we say.

Others accepted the seed Gospel of the Kingdom with excitement. They did not last long however as Christians. They were shallow and put down no roots. They were not "rooted and grounded" in the Gospel. *They believed for a while* (Luke 8:13). Yes, they were real believers, but very short-lived. Temporary Christians. When trials and temptations arose, they dropped the message. They fell away from the faith and bore no fruit.

Only the fourth category really succeeded with the seed. The seed was deeply planted in their understanding and eventually with perseverance, amidst trials, it brought forth fruit. This is the fruit of the spirit. This of course implies that the seed carried in itself the very spirit of God. That spirit began to dwell in the hearts of the converts and fruit was borne in due time. The produce of fruit was sometimes astonishing — a hundred times more.

The seed message of the Kingdom contained the spark of new life, the secret of immortality. We might say that it transmits the very DNA of God Himself.

No wonder Jesus raised his voice as he preached this parable (Luke 8:8: "He used to raise his voice"). He preached it over and over again. He knew that human destiny was at stake. It was the immortality message, which the public needed to hear. Jesus, we

---

[7]The Greek word is *logos*. Some philosophers spoke of the "*logos spermatikos*," recognizing the energy which produces life and growth.

remember, "brought life and immortality to light in the Gospel" (2 Tim. 1:10). The seed was the germ of new life. It was the very life of God Himself transmitted through Jesus who was the perfect human agent of the One God, his Father.

Seed is about the most perfect illustration of new life, vitality and energy. We all know something about how seeds work. We ourselves are the product of a male seed uniting with a female ovum. Our life is generated by this miracle and the life of all animals follows this pattern. Seeds are planted everywhere and we are constantly exposed to the fruit of the seed.

Exactly the same seed process is true of the matter of being reborn, born *again*. We were once born of physical seed. That is not sufficient to bring us immortality. We have to be born over again. We must undergo a *spiritual* birth, a rebirth. We cannot reenter the womb of our physical mother. Instead we enter the womb of our mother the Church as the community of faith based on the promises. Paul spoke of the "Jerusalem above" (Gal. 4:26). This is the Jerusalem of the future, the Kingdom of God. It is being prepared by God and Jesus now. It will be manifested on earth when Jesus comes back. We are sons and daughters of that Kingdom Gospel, children of the promise (Gal. 4:28) and thus sons and daughters of God and brothers and sisters of Jesus. When we are born again, we become "newborn babies," and we must then seek "the pure milk of the word," so that we can grow into spiritual adulthood (1 Pet. 2:2). That milk for the reborn Christian is in fact the "Gospel milk." Peter used a word related to the "word" (*logos* in Greek). He refers to the milk of the Gospel, the "*logikos*" milk.

The seed is the Gospel preached by Jesus (Luke 8:11; Matt. 13:19). That seed must be intelligently received in our hearts, our understanding. Satan is determined to wreck this process wherever he can. He watches the progress of the seed and snatches it away wherever he is permitted to do so. We must make the choice to follow the Gospel message. If we do not pay attention to the seed Gospel of the Kingdom, the Devil "takes away the seed sown in our heart so that we cannot believe it and be saved." That is Luke 8:12, a spectacularly interesting verse. Jesus made that brilliant observation. It clearly describes what is going on in the realm of spiritual warfare. The Devil is relentlessly opposed to the Gospel *of the Kingdom*. Jesus understood God's will and purpose. He knew how the Devil was determined to obstruct God's will. He also knew that human beings are given a choice. "...so that they cannot believe it and be saved" (Luke 8:12). Note those words carefully. The Kingdom Message is directly linked here to salvation. Receiving the Kingdom Gospel is a matter of life and death. Of course, as we know today, the death and resurrection of Jesus are also a vital part of the message which we must grasp. These events were added to or included in the Gospel when they took place at the end of Jesus' ministry. Jesus shed his blood as a sacrifice for sin, as a substitutionary sacrifice on our behalf. He died in our place so that we could be forgiven. Our sins have been covered. But we are not forgiven if we do not change our minds radically and begin to live earnestly as Christians. "Jesus is the author of salvation for those who obey him" (Heb. 5:9). Paul speaks of the "obedience of faith." And repentance and forgiveness *depend directly on our reception of the Kingdom Gospel* (Mark 4:11, 12). Our obedience to the Gospel command of Jesus to *believe* God's Gospel of the Kingdom (Mark 1:14, 15).

The basis of this necessary change of mind is our acceptance of the Kingdom Gospel of Jesus. Mark 4:11, 12 gives us a fair warning. Jesus there declared that we can be forgiven only on condition that we change our minds, repent. But how does Jesus define repentance? Jesus makes an intelligent reception of the Kingdom Gospel *the condition* for us being accepted with God and Jesus. This is a most important teaching of Jesus. It should be read with utmost concentration, since it provides a key to the New Testament system of salvation. Jesus said in effect: "If they understood and accepted the Gospel word, then they would be able to change their minds and be forgiven." The choice is made very clear here. As one commentator as said, Jesus divides society into two opposing camps: "those who have heard, understood and received the Kingdom of God Gospel and those who have not."[8]

Is this not the plain meaning of Mark 4:11, 12? Luke reports the same truth in this way: "Satan comes and removes the word from their heart, so that they cannot *believe it and be saved*" (Luke 8:12). No belief in the Gospel as Jesus preached it, no salvation. Does not Jesus plainly make salvation depend on a willing

---

[8]George Ladd, *Theology of the New Testament*, p. 51.

acceptance and understanding of the Gospel of the Kingdom as he preached it? What about Luke 18:17? "Unless you receive the Kingdom of God as a little child you will not enter it." These are extraordinarily impressive and important words. To enter the Kingdom means to be saved. Believing the Gospel of the Kingdom is the key, the key of knowledge (Luke 11:52).

No wonder that throughout his ministry "Jesus welcomed the people and began talking to them about the Kingdom" (Luke 9:11). Paul's missionary style was exactly the same. Paul welcomed the people and preached the Kingdom of God (Acts 28:30, 31). Paul was obeying the Great Commission. He was preaching the Gospel. Jesus had commanded as the salvation message for all nations: "Go into the whole world and teach them everything I taught you" (Matt. 28:19, 20).

If Paul had preached a different Gospel, as some erroneously say, he would have put himself under his own curse! In Galatians 1 Paul became passionately concerned about anyone who would distort the Gospel by adding to it or taking away from it. Paul threatened Gospel-twisters with a kind of curse. Changing the Gospel in any way would be like adding foreign additives to good food and ruining it. In no way could the Gospel be altered or modified. It would lose its saving effects. To deprive it of its rock-firm foundation in the Kingdom preaching of Jesus would be to take a terrible risk. All the Apostles preached the same Kingdom-immortality Gospel. They were followers of the Kingdom Gospel preacher Jesus, but can the same be said of modern evangelists?

According to John's account of a famous interview between Jesus and a Jewish Bible teacher named Nicodemus, Jesus challenged this leader, "Unless you are born again you cannot see or enter the Kingdom of God" (John 3:3, 5). Nicodemus was apparently a prominent religious leader, and he visited Jesus by night. Jesus got right to the point. Without a rebirth there is no salvation, no immortality, no entrance into the coming Kingdom. Jesus wanted Nicodemus to understand that we must now be born again, and then as spiritual babies grow up to maturity. By this process we can enter the Kingdom when Jesus comes back. The Kingdom will have been prepared and we will then be invited "to enter the Kingdom prepared for you from the foundation of the world" (Matt. 25:34).

Luke reports Jesus as saying publicly exactly what he said to Nicodemus: "Unless you accept the Kingdom of God as a little child, you won't enter it" (Luke 18:17).

Some have made the interview with Nicodemus very confusing. They have thought that Jesus was saying that you cannot be born again until the future resurrection. Jesus did not say that. He simply pointed out that "flesh," human beings in their natural, unspiritual condition, cannot produce spirit. Only spirit produces what is spiritual. We are to be spiritual now, by repentance and conversion and by receiving the Gospel of the Kingdom, which carries the spiritual seed of immortality. The action of God's spirit on us now is the like the invisible power of the wind. After all the Hebrew word for spirit means also breath or wind. The words of God in the Bible are spirit-filled words (John 6:63). They transmit holy spirit to us. They convey the spirit and mind of God to us. This is how we learn truth — by tapping into the mind of God via His inspirited words. Paul's classic statement confirms this: "How did you receive the spirit? By works of the law or by hearing the Gospel and believing it?" (Gal. 3:2). "Having heard the word of truth, the Gospel of your salvation, you were sealed with the holy spirit of the promise" (Eph 1:13). The answer to the crucial question as to how the spirit is received was given by Paul. It was that the words of the true Gospel transmitted the spirit to them, put the spirit in their hearts (2 Cor. 1:21, 22). Remember that the Gospel of the Kingdom is actually called "the word" in the New Testament.

Back to Jesus' encounter with Nicodemus. It is very interesting that here in John's account of Jesus' teaching, being born again is made an absolutely essential condition for being saved in the future Kingdom. In the reports of Jesus' teaching written by Matthew, Mark and Luke, we do not find the exact words "born again" anywhere. Does this mean that Matthew, Mark and Luke were unaware of Jesus' primary and basic teaching about being saved? Had they forgotten to mention such a vitally important teaching? Had they failed to report the key to salvation? Of course not. The fact is that Matthew, Mark and Luke recorded the same teaching about being "born again" under a different picture. They used the concept of "seed." This was a picture drawn from farming, from agriculture. John's record of Jesus' talk with the scholar Nicodemus shows that Jesus spoke of the new life in the spirit as parallel to a rebirth, being born again. Jesus used a comparison with human birth in the report of John. In Matthew, Mark and Luke, talking to the public and the disciples, he used the agricultural comparison; that is, he spoke of seed sown in our minds as the vitalizing agent of the new birth.

The rest of the writers of the New Testament were united in their presentation of the secret of living forever. They were following Jesus and had learned the immortality "trade" from their Master. They knew that immortality came through the seed message of the Gospel. They heard Jesus teach this day after day in different settings. They had heard him raise his voice, expressive of his passion to rescue dying human beings (Luke 8:8; John 12:44).

James, the half-brother of Jesus, reminded his readers that God "of His own will has *given us birth* through the word of truth" (James 1:18). (This verse alone will convince the open-minded that we are not now in the fetal stage only!) Peter had heard Jesus speak about the seed and rebirth many times. Peter recorded this centrally important teaching when he said that Christians have been "born again [note the past tense] not from corruptible seed but from incorruptible seed through the abiding word of the living God...That word was the Gospel preached to you" (1 Pet. 1:23-25).

Listen carefully to Peter:

> Now you can have sincere love for each other as brothers and sisters because you were cleansed from your sins when you accepted the truth of the Good News. So see to it that you really do love each other intensely with all your hearts. For you have been born again, not from seed which is perishable, but from imperishable seed. This new life will last forever because it comes from the eternal, living word of God. As the prophet says, "People are like grass that dies away; their beauty fades as quickly as the beauty of wildflowers. The grass withers, and the flowers fall away. But the word of the Lord will last forever." And that word is the Good News [Gospel] that was preached to you (1 Pet. 1:22-25).

"As newborn babies, desire the Gospel milk, so that by it you may grow up to salvation" (1 Pet. 2:2). The Christian is likened to a new baby, not a fetus.

Do you see how Peter beautifully combines the ideas of truth, rebirth, seed, word and Gospel? Peter's teacher Jesus had spoken of rebirth, seed, word and Gospel. Paul shares the same understanding. He speaks of Christians as those who are "born of the spirit" (Gal. 4:29). By this he means "those born of the promise" (Gal. 4:28). They are the product of the great promise of immortality in the Kingdom of God. That promise has brought them the new life in Christ. Paul also observed that the ones "born of the spirit" are likely to be persecuted and opposed by those who are still in the flesh (Gal. 4:29). All this reminds us of Jesus' words about flesh producing flesh and spirit producing spirit (John 3:6).

Paul in this chapter 4 of Galatians likens the Old Covenant based on the Ten Commandments and the whole system of Law given at Sinai to "bondage" or "slavery" in comparison with the freedom in Christ under the New Covenant. This is a great truth overlooked by many who seek to understand the Bible. There is a new Law or "Torah of Christ" (1 Cor. 9:21; Gal. 6:2), which is not just a repeat of the Law of Moses! The Torah of Christ is in the spirit and not in the letter. Physical circumcision commanded for everyone seeking to be in God's Old Covenant (Gen. 17) was replaced by circumcision of the heart alone in the New Covenant. That sets the pattern of a huge difference between the two covenants.

The Apostle John was intensely interested in the seed which must dwell in the hearts of the Christians. In 1 John 3:9 he noted that Christians are preserved from habitual sin by *the seed* which lives in them. It is the seed which brings about rebirth. That seed is nothing less than the character and nature of God Himself transmitted to us by the Gospel and the words of Scripture. The seed, Jesus had said, "is the word of God" (Luke 8:11). The seed is the seed of life forever, of immortality in the coming Kingdom.

Let us never forget the equation "Gospel/word of the Kingdom" = "word of God" = "word." Nor the sequence laid out by Jesus for becoming saved: "seeing, hearing, understanding, repenting and being forgiven" (encapsulated by one of my students as "SHURF").

Christians are supposed to be "channels" or vehicles of the spirit and words of God. Receiving the seed, they become seeds and are supposed to propagate further seed. David claimed this for himself when he uttered those beautiful and memorable words in 2 Samuel 23:2. David described his own experience with God. "The spirit of the Lord spoke by me; His word was on my tongue." Here we see that David's mind was in tune with the spirit and mind of God. God was able to put His thoughts and spirit into the mind of David, and David expressed this spirit in words.

I like this definition of spirit very much:

The Spirit is not merely God's breath, but his self-awareness, his *mind*, his inner being. This may be the source or seat of God's vitality, but it is more. It is his self-consciousness, his very being, the center of his Person, as we might say. Just as a man's spirit is his ultimate reality, when he is stripped of all that is accidental to his being, so God's Spirit is his inner self. Spirit therefore contrasts with Christ, insofar as the latter is God's image, while the former is his inner being.[9]

The phrase "the spirit speaks" shows that the spirit makes itself clear in words. Words are verbalized spirit. Water is invisible in a tank, but when the tap is turned on the water becomes visible. Spirit exists first in the mind and when words are uttered they manifest that spirit and make it intelligible. So the effect of spirit and word is the same. Both spirit and word are the creative activity of God who is at work in us. No wonder Paul could speak of the Gospel-word as "energizing" in us (1 Thess. 2:13). All true spirit and word have their source in God Himself who communicates by spirit. Jesus said that his own words were "spirit and life" (John 6:63), and Peter knew that Jesus possessed "the words of the life of the age to come" (John 6:68) and Peter spoke "all the *words* of this life" (Acts 5:20). The New Testament leaders are in complete harmony on this subject as they go about offering the public the words of eternal life, which means the words of the life of the age to come, or the Kingdom.

No wonder then that the New Testament issues the strongest possible warning against neglecting the preaching/teaching of Jesus. To do so would be to jeopardize the gracious offer of immortality. It would be to throw away the pearl of great price and squander the secret of living forever. Did not Jesus say:

---

[9]W.R. Bowie.

> The Kingdom of Heaven is like a treasure that a man discovered hidden in a field. In his excitement, he hid it again and sold everything he owned to get enough money to buy the field — and to get the treasure, too! Again, the Kingdom of Heaven is like a pearl merchant on the lookout for choice pearls. When he discovered a pearl of great value, he sold everything he owned and bought it! (Matt. 13:44-46).

No wonder the Apostles did their utmost always to prevent their congregations from abandoning the words/teaching of Jesus. Paul's words have permanent value:

> Anyone who teaches anything different and does not keep to the sound teaching which is that of our Lord Jesus Christ, the doctrine which is in accordance with true religion, is both conceited and ignorant. Such a person has an unhealthy desire to quibble over the meaning of words. This stirs up arguments ending in jealousy, fighting, slander, and evil suspicions (see 1 Tim. 6:3, 4).

And John said this about the loss of the precious seed of the Gospel as Jesus taught it: "For if you wander beyond the teaching of Christ, you will not have fellowship with God. But if you continue in the teaching of Christ, you will have fellowship with both the Father and the Son" (2 John 9).

After all the whole purpose of Jesus was to impart a proper understanding to us. John wrote: "And we know that the Son of God has come, and he has given us *understanding* so that we can know the true God. And now we are in God because we are in his Son, Jesus Christ" (1 John 5:20).

An Old Testament passage, often neglected, prophesied that the suffering servant (Jesus) would "make many righteous *through his knowledge*" (Isa. 53:11).

The key to a good understanding is therefore to heed the words of God who said of Jesus: "This is my beloved Son...*hear him*" (Matt. 17:5). The death of Jesus is, of course, also essential, but God did not say, "This is My beloved Son; watch him die."

Chapter 9
Making Public your Confession of Jesus as the Messiah and of the God of Israel, the Father of Jesus

Jesus gave his marching orders to the Church when he addressed his chosen Apostles. He gathered them together and commanded them to relay to all the nations everything he had taught them. He instructed them to baptize in water the converts they made. This was a very clear order. They were to take exactly the same Gospel which Jesus had offered to Jews to all the nations (Matt. 28:19, 20).

There is a widespread theory that a different Gospel would be offered to Gentiles, but this is a huge mistake. There is only one Gospel, one Christianity, and it is founded on the Gospel as Jesus preached it.

Jesus was by then immortal. He had come back from death to life. The tomb was empty and Jesus had appeared to his close followers and had meals with them. "We were the ones who ate and drank with him after he rose from the dead" (Acts 10:41). Jesus had made it quite clear that it was he, Jesus, who had reappeared. He was not some invisible "spirit being,"[1] but a tangible human person who had been resurrected from the dead. He appeared alive in the presence of completely reliable witnesses. Because they had eaten with him, conversed with him, they knew that he had returned from death. His resurrection from death is the greatest fact of world history, backed by irrefutable proofs. There is no room for doubt.

You have to have a lot more "faith" not to believe that Jesus was resurrected. What would be the point of the Apostles testifying to a falsehood, when it cost them much suffering? They even claimed that women had seen him alive first. In those days, women were (quite unfairly) not thought to be dependable sources of information!

---

[1]Certainly not Michael the archangel as proposed by one large denomination.

Jesus' disciples knew perfectly well that Jesus was no longer dead. He is the pioneer of God's great immortality program. We know that this program is true, because Jesus has proved this by appearing alive after his death. God raised him from death to life. He now lives forever. You can too.

To be successful candidates for life in the Kingdom we have to be willing to obey what Jesus says. "He who loves me keeps my orders," Jesus said (John 14:15). It is pointless to go around claiming to be following Jesus if we reject his plain teachings. Jesus commanded belief in his Gospel of the Kingdom. He also commanded men and women to be baptized in water. This was a public ceremony of initiation into the Church he promised to build. The Apostles, throughout the book of Acts, obeyed Jesus by teaching and baptizing the men and women they converted to the faith.

Paul made it quite clear that no adulterer or fornicator, homosexual who goes on practicing homosexuality, no drunkard, no thief can hope to be in the future Kingdom (1 Cor. 6:9, 10). Our lives have to change drastically. Repentance and a completely new lifestyle are required of Christians. God will not make the immoral or drunks or the other categories listed in 1 Corinthians 6:9, 10 rulers in His Kingdom.

One of the very easy and clear teachings of Jesus is that when we have learned about the Gospel of the Kingdom and are ready to make a decision to believe it, and thus follow Jesus, then we should be baptized in water. A baptized friend who shares your beliefs can perform this baptism. If there are other members of the church available they can be witnesses to this solemn occasion. With a simple prayer one is just dipped in water. This is a public statement of one's intention to be a Christian. Baptism is an apostolic practice because Jesus commanded it. Peter followed the command and commanded it also. He was simply following the orders of his Master.

Jesus commanded water baptism in the Great Commission. He told the Apostles and their successors (we do not have Apostles like the original 12 today, but we must all be disciples of the Apostles) to baptize believers into the joint name of the Father, Son and holy spirit. This has nothing to do with a much later doctrine called the Trinity, that God is three and one. God is just One in the Bible and Jesus is the Son of God, God's agent who reflected his Father's will perfectly and always obeyed his Father. The spirit is the operational power and presence of God and of Jesus. The Apostles obeyed Jesus by baptizing converts "in the name of Jesus," which means representing Jesus. They baptized in his place as his agents. To baptize in the name of Jesus means to baptize as acting on behalf of, representing Jesus and the Kingdom.

Baptism is a symbolic washing away of our former life of rebellion against God and our ignorance of His great Plan. Paul also compares baptism with the death and burial of Jesus and his coming back to life. We start a brand new life when we are baptized to seal our response to Jesus' command to believe his Kingdom Gospel and live the Christian life. We do not need to have years of training before baptism. In the New Testament people committed themselves to Jesus after just some basic teaching, a basic exposure to the Gospel and the aims and claims of Jesus. The eunuch in Acts 8 was instructed by Philip in the fundamentals, and then he asked Philip to baptize him in water and they went down into the water together (Acts 8:36-39).

In Acts 8:12 Philip baptized some Samaritans "when they believed Philip as he preached the Gospel of the Kingdom and the name of Jesus Christ." Men and women got baptized to declare their allegiance to Jesus publicly. Just as Jesus had preached the Kingdom and sown the seed of immortality, so Philip carried on the same Kingdom evangelism. He was planting the seed of immortality in the heart of his converts. In the case of those Samaritans they were the first in the whole nation to become Christians, and they needed a special visit from the Apostles in Jerusalem to complete their introduction into the Church. Peter and John came down from Jerusalem and laid hands on these unique believers and the spirit of God provided a special sign of their position as Christians when they spoke in foreign languages which they had never learned. This was a complete and demonstrable miracle. It certainly does not mean that every convert ever after has to speak in foreign languages unlearned! Today's efforts in some groups to speak in other languages really do not clearly match the public miracle of miraculously spoken languages in the Bible.

Once our commitment to Jesus is sealed in baptism, we must continue to hold fast to the Kingdom Gospel and to Jesus as the Messiah, Son of God for the rest of our days.

We must live within the terms of the Sermon on the Mount which shows how candidates for the Kingdom should conduct their lives. Paul developed those teachings in the letters he wrote to churches and to his young ministers, Titus and Timothy.

The New Covenant introduced by Jesus is not just a repeat of the Old Covenant. Paul spoke of the Law of Christ, as distinct from the Law of Moses. There are two covenants (Gal. 4:24). The Ten Commandments were given to the nation of Israel as a summary of the whole legal system imposed on them. Jesus spiritualized the Law of Moses, getting at the real issue which is that our hearts must be in tune with the will of God and Jesus. "The Law was given by Moses, but grace and truth came through Jesus Christ" (John 1:17). There is a distinct contrast here. We must avoid mixing the two covenants.

For example Israel celebrated the Passover once a year, offering a lamb as a sacrifice in memory of the exodus from Egypt and as a "shadow" of the Messiah promised to come. The New Testament church, now that Jesus has come, replaced the annual Passover with the regular celebration of the Lord's supper, remembering the sacrificial death of Jesus and looking forward to his future coming and their reunion with him in the Kingdom (Luke 22:14-30).

We should celebrate daily the great fact that the Father "is the only one who is truly God" (John 17:3), as Jesus said. Paul rehearsed the same great fundamental truth when he wrote to Timothy: "There is one God and one mediator between the one God and man, the Messiah Jesus, himself man" (1 Tim. 2:5). Paul also urged Timothy to preach the Kingdom of God Gospel in season and out of season: "I solemnly declare to you as Gospel, before God and Jesus who is going to judge both the living and the dead, both his coming and his Kingdom. Preach the word" (2 Tim 4:1, 2).[2] Paul warned that the time was going to come when audiences would not put up with Truth but heap up teachers who

---

[2]I take the appearing and Kingdom as the direct objects of the verb "solemnly declare as Gospel" (*diamarturomai*).

would "tickle their ears" and tell them what they wanted to hear (2 Tim. 4:3).

The solemn fact about the Kingdom and God's plan remains at the heart of Christianity. God has appointed a day when He is going to judge and administer the world by a man whom He has chosen. "God has set a day for judging the world with justice by the man He has appointed, and He proved to everyone who this is by raising him from the dead" (Acts 17:31). That coming day is the Kingdom of God for which we are to prepare diligently. Jesus has risen from the dead and in company with him and believing him and his teachings, we can be assured of resurrection when he comes back.

God has demonstrated His intention to confer immortality on human beings. "He has proved His intention by raising the man Jesus from the dead" (Acts 17:31). With that wonderful account of the ongoing, unfolding immortality-Kingdom Plan of God firmly in mind, let us rejoice in the hope set before us and strive to enter the Kingdom of God.

Let Jesus' words of warning go with us as we proceed on the journey of faith:

> Do your best to go in by the narrow door, for I say to you, a number will make the attempt to go in, but will not be able to do so. When the master of the house has got up and shut the door, and you, still outside, knock on the door, saying, "Lord, let us in"; he will answer, "I have no knowledge of where you come from." Then you will say, "We have taken food and drink with you, and you were teaching in our streets." But he will say, "Truly, I have no knowledge of you or where you come from; go away from me, you workers of evil." There will be weeping and cries of sorrow when you see Abraham, Isaac, and Jacob, and all the prophets, in the Kingdom of God, but you yourselves are shut outside. And they will come from the east and from the west, from the north and from the south, and take their places in the kingdom of God. And the last will be first, and the first will be last (Luke 13:24-30).

The promise of the Gospel of the Kingdom, the teachings of Jesus, including his sacrificial death for our sins, provide the rock foundation on which our Christianity must be based.

The death of Jesus was substitutionary, as theologians say. The sacrifice of Jesus, foreshadowed by the whole sacrificial system involving animals under the Old Covenant, covers our sins. We are thus "covered" and protected from the death penalty, because Jesus bore it in our place. One life, Jesus' life, covers another when the one life is surrendered in love so that the other can be spared. "Behold and see if there has been any sorrow comparable to my sorrow," says Lamentations 1:12, speaking of God's punishment of Jerusalem. The Messiah was innocently "a man of sorrows" (Isa. 53:3), facing the appalling blindness and stubbornness of religionists, and he was "acquainted with grief." God "laid on him the iniquity of us all" (Isa. 53:6).

Nothing is more important than to understand that the Gospel is the Gospel of the Kingdom and nothing is more valuable than our full commitment to that Gospel, which is equated by Jesus as commitment to himself. Jesus spoke of the Gospel of the Kingdom as simply "the Gospel" or even his "name," that is, everything he stood for, his agenda.

In Mark 10:29, 30 Jesus said, "Amen, I say to you, there is no one who has given up house or brothers or sisters or mother or father or children or lands for my sake and for the sake of *the Gospel,* who will not get a hundred times as much now in this time, houses, and brothers, and sisters, and mothers, and children, and land — though with great troubles; and, in the age to come, eternal life."

Now notice how Matthew reported that saying: "And everyone who has given up houses or brothers or sisters or father or mother or children or property, *for my sake*, will receive a hundred times as much in return and will have eternal life" (Matt. 19:29).

Luke thinks of commitment to the Kingdom of God, which is the same idea in different words: "And he said to them, 'Truly I say to you, there is no man who has given up house or wife or brothers or father or mother or children, *because of the Kingdom of God*, who will not get much more in this time, and in the age to come, eternal life" (Luke 18:29, 30).

Only one Kingdom is going to survive. Only one Kingdom has permanent value. It is the Kingdom announced by Jesus as the Christian Gospel — the Kingdom he commands us to "seek first" and pray with urgency for its coming, so that the world may enjoy peace, at last.

This is our destiny, yours and mine, and the answer to the puzzle of the meaning of life.

A GUIDE TO THE FAITH OF THE BIBLE

Lesson 1
Becoming a Christian — Where to Begin

The discussion presented in these lessons on the Kingdom of God, the Christian Gospel, assumes an understanding of the sacrificial, atoning death of Jesus and of his resurrection and ascension. These are essential elements in the Christian Gospel (1 Cor. 15:1-3). But they are not the whole Gospel.

The need for an investigation of the Christian Gospel lies in the fact that the Kingdom of God is also an absolutely indispensable component of the evangelism of Jesus and the Apostles. The term "Kingdom of God" is never simply a synonym for the facts about the death and resurrection of Jesus. Moreover the Kingdom of God is often the first article of faith in New Testament descriptions of the saving Message (Matt. 4:17; Mark 1:14, 15; Luke 4:43; 5:1; Acts 8:12; 19:8; 20:25; 28:23, 31: 2 Tim 4:1, 2, etc.) both before and after the resurrection of Jesus. Jesus preached the Gospel of the Kingdom for some 30 chapters (as recorded by Matthew, Mark and Luke), without at that stage, mentioning his death and resurrection. He began to speak of this much later in Matthew 16:21. This must prove to the open-minded that the Gospel is not just that "Jesus died for me."

Master Texts:
"Jesus came into Galilee proclaiming God's Gospel [Good News] and saying, 'The time has come and **the Kingdom of God** is approaching: Repent and **believe the Gospel**'" (Mark 1:14, 15).

"When they believed Philip as he proclaimed **the Gospel about the Kingdom of God** and **the Name of Jesus Christ**, they were being **baptized**, both men and women" (Acts 8:12).

"Paul put his case to them, testifying to **the Kingdom of God** and trying to persuade them about **Jesus**, arguing from the Law of Moses and the prophets. This went on from early morning until evening, and some were convinced by what he said, while the rest were skeptical" (Acts 28:23).

"Paul lived there two whole years at his own expense, and welcomed all [Jews and Gentiles] who came to him, proclaiming **the Kingdom of God** and teaching about the Lord Jesus Christ with all boldness and without hindrance" (Acts 28:30, 31).

In every system of knowledge there is a fundamental idea to be grasped, a core concept around which all other data must be organized. This central, dominating idea will determine the character of the subject as a whole and give meaning to every part of it. The core concept, the basic thesis, becomes the criterion by which all subsidiary ideas are evaluated. What then is the axis around which all of the Christian faith revolves?

The Christian faith comes to us in the Bible as a body of information challenging us to response and action. The source of that information is ultimately God Himself transmitting His message through prophets and teachers and supremely in His principal representative, Jesus the Messiah, the Son of God.

What, then, is **the central core concept of the teaching of Jesus?** What forms the heart of **his Message?** What **one single idea** underlies all his preaching and teaching? What primary idea must be **grasped and believed** by any who want to follow Jesus? What did Jesus consider to be the essential Gospel/Saving Message?

The answer to this question can be discovered by anyone with an ordinary ability to read, any version of the Bible, and an earnest desire to find out what Jesus taught. The importance of Christianity's key idea so impressed the writers of the New Testament that they emphasized it over and over again.

It is a testimony to the extraordinary way in which fundamental concepts can be lost that **Jesus' master idea is very seldom, if ever, presented with clarity to the public in 21st-century Gospel preaching.** Equally amazing is the fact that leaders of organized Christianity admit that they are *not* proclaiming as Gospel what Jesus proclaimed as the Gospel. The Gospel as Jesus preached it is very often conspicuous by its absence from contemporary presentations of what is called the "Gospel."

Christianity's Central Idea

Without any possible fear of contradiction we can assert with complete confidence that the axis around which all Jesus' teaching revolves is the **GOSPEL OF THE KINGDOM OF GOD**. The genius of Christianity is concentrated in that one term. It is Jesus' and the Apostles' master-idea. It is the heart of their rallying cry to the public. It has been preserved for us meticulously in the pages of the Bible, especially in the records of the ministry of Jesus. It is the Gospel which comes from the One God of the Bible — "God's Gospel" (Mark 1:14).

There is *one* Gospel in the Bible, the Good News of God's plan to grant you immortality (indestructible life, life forever) and to prepare you to administer the world, on a renewed earth, with Jesus in the coming Kingdom (Matt. 5:5; Rev. 5:10; 2 Tim. 2:12; Rev. 2:26; 3:21; 5:10; 20:1-6; 22:5; Isa. 32:1; 1 Cor. 6:2; Matt. 19:28; Luke 22:28-30). It is called **God's Gospel** or the Gospel about the Kingdom of God (see Mark 1:14, 15). Notice next how Paul spoke always, as did Jesus, of "God's Gospel" (Rom. 1:1; Rom. 15:16; 2 Cor. 11:7; 1 Thess. 2:2, 8, 9). All the Apostles preached the same saving Gospel as Jesus had (see 1 Peter 4:17).

Those 8 references to God's Gospel, from Jesus, Paul and Peter, prove the New Testament's testimony to a single, saving Gospel.

Open a Bible to Mark 1:14, 15. Here the career of Jesus is launched with his preaching of **the Gospel about the Kingdom of God**. He came into Galilee and summoned his compatriots to a complete change of mind and lifestyle — repentance — and to **belief in the Good News, or Gospel about the KINGDOM OF GOD**. This is where all true faith and all true repentance must begin. The command to "repent and believe in the Gospel about the Kingdom" is Jesus' first command and a summary of the faith which he presented. It is only reasonable that we begin at the beginning of Jesus' ministry and teach the faith as he taught it. We should remember at once that "he who obeys the Son has life and he who disobeys the Son of God remains under the wrath of God" (John 3:36). Jesus thus urges us to believe what he taught as the saving Gospel. Our response to Jesus' Gospel is the criterion of judgment. We are going to be judged by his words (John 5:24; 12:44-50; Mark 8:35-38). We are urged to comply with his opening command to mankind: "Believe the Gospel about the Kingdom of God" (Mark 1:14, 15). The Gospel of the Kingdom is the gracious Message of God telling us what He expects of us. We are to obey that Gospel (2 Thess. 1:8; 1 Pet. 4:17). To disregard the Gospel of the Kingdom puts us in opposition to God and to Jesus.

Jesus was particularly indignant at those who claimed to follow him but disregarded his teachings. "Why do you call me Lord, and yet you will not do what I say?" (Luke 6:46).

All the gospel writers emphasize the fundamental importance of **the Gospel about the Kingdom.** (John uses different terminology for the same idea. He calls the Kingdom "everlasting life" or "the life of the age to come.") The first piece of information about Jesus, given us by Luke when the birth of the Messiah is announced, concerns **the Kingdom of God: "The Lord God will give him the throne of his father David and he will reign over the house of Jacob forever"** (Luke 1:32). The very last question posed by Jesus' trained disciples to their master was, "Has the time now come for you to restore the Kingdom to Israel?" (Acts 1:6).

As any religious Jew knew well, the promise of Gabriel concerning the role of Jesus in God's plan was a statement about **the Messiah's kingship** in the coming Kingdom of God to be established on the earth, with its headquarters in Jerusalem — a Jerusalem purged of evildoers and reconciled to God and His Messiah Jesus (see Isa. 1:26 and many passages in the Old Testament prophets, for example Isa. 2:1-5).

Jesus himself gives us a clear definition of the underlying purpose of his ministry. He informs us about the basis of his entire career with these words: "I must proclaim the Good News of **the Kingdom of God** to other cities also. That is the reason I was sent" (Luke 4:43). "That is what God commissioned me to do." "That is the driving force behind my Christian mission to the world." This text opens up the mind of Jesus for us and provides the key to the whole Christian faith, which must be based on his teaching. Jesus tells us the whole reason for his ministry in this verse. Have you heard this verse quoted often? Did you know that Luke 4:43 provides one of the most fundamental truths of the Christian faith?

Luke immediately goes on to tell us that Jesus was preaching "**the Message**" or "**the Word**" (Luke 5:1; Mark 2:2; Acts 8:4, 5, 12). This is the Bible shorthand for **the Christian Message of salvation**. It appears throughout the New Testament as "the Message about the Kingdom" (Matt. 13:19), "**the Word of God**" (Luke 8:11), or simply "**the Word**" (Mark 4:14) and other phrases with the same meaning. It may just be called "**the Gospel**," or "**this Gospel about the Kingdom**" (Matt. 24:14; Matt. 4:23; 9:35; Mark 13:10). We must grasp and believe *this* message and no other in order to embark on the process of becoming a Christian believer. Nothing could be more crucial for our spiritual welfare than to gain an understanding of this Message. It is one message and one message only — **the Good News (Gospel) about the Kingdom of God**. Luke 4:43, 5:1 equate the Message about the Kingdom with "**the Message (Word) of God**."[2]

The spreading of this Gospel Message was of paramount importance to Jesus and the disciples he chose to assist him. Without any doubt it was the Message of Good News about the Kingdom of God which they preached everywhere: "He went round the whole of Galilee teaching in their synagogues, proclaiming the Good News [Gospel] of the **Kingdom of God**" (Matt. 4:23; 9:35). Matthew repeats this summary account of what Jesus was doing. Later Jesus "sent them [the twelve] to proclaim **the Kingdom of God**" (Luke 9:2).

Jesus defined the ultimate purpose of life for his followers. It is the quest for the Kingdom of God. He instructs his followers: "Seek *first* **the Kingdom of God**..." (Matt. 6:33).

The same subject dominated the conversation between Jesus and the disciples after his death and resurrection. For almost six weeks he spoke to them about **the Kingdom of God** (Acts 1:3). Christianity as Jesus taught it is about the Kingdom of God and Jesus as the King of that coming Kingdom. The challenge to you is to prepare to enter that Kingdom when it comes in the future. No wonder that Jesus urged believers to pray "May Your Kingdom come" (Matt. 6:10).

---

[2]For further details of the different New Testament names for the one Gospel of the Kingdom, see Appendix 1. My book *The Coming Kingdom of the Messiah: A Solution to the Riddle of the New Testament* is available at 800-347-4261.

Information Vital to the Potential Believer

Luke tells us about the information required by potential converts before they could be baptized into the Christian faith. His statement reads like an early creed: **"When they believed Philip as he proclaimed the Gospel about the Kingdom of God and the name of Jesus Christ, they were being baptized, both men and women"** (Acts 8:12). Jesus promised a supreme reward to his disciples. They were to assist in the rulership of the New World or New Age of **the coming Kingdom:** "I assign to you [literally, **covenant** with you] **a Kingdom** as my Father has assigned [covenanted] **a Kingdom** to me, and you will sit on thrones to govern[3] the twelve tribes of Israel" (see Matt. 19:28; Luke 22:28-30).

No wonder, then, that Paul, faithfully following Jesus, could sum up his whole ministry by calling it a preaching of **the Gospel of the Kingdom** (Acts 20:25), which one verse earlier he called "the Gospel of the grace of God." Luke wishes us never to forget what the Apostles always proclaimed as the Gospel. He informs us that Paul preached **the Kingdom of God** for three months in Corinth (Acts 19:8). In order to leave no room for doubt or misunderstanding he ends his second treatise, the book of Acts, by describing Paul's activity in Rome: For two years he preached **the Good News about the Kingdom of God and the things concerning the Name of Jesus** (Acts 28:23, 31). This was the Gospel Message of salvation he addressed both to Jews and Gentiles alike (Acts 28:23, 31). Jesus had commanded one Gospel for all the nations until his return (Matt. 28:19, 20).

It is the Gospel of the Kingdom which must constantly be preached in all the world until Jesus returns at the end of the age: **"This Gospel of the Kingdom will be preached in the whole world...and then the end will come"** (Matt. 24:14).

With this evidence before us — and there is much more — we may say that no one honestly in search of Biblical Truth can miss

---

[3]The word "judge" which appears in many versions is properly translated "govern," "administer" or "rule." Cp. the OT "judge" in the book of Judges. Judges were rulers. Note also the fact that kings "judge" (Ps. 2:10, I Macc. 9:73, etc.). Many modern commentaries recognize the fact that "judging" in Matt. 19:28, Luke 22:30 means administering.

recognizing the principal idea behind the Christian Message of salvation. **The Kingdom of God** is undoubtedly the heart and core of Jesus' and the Apostles' preaching of salvation, the basic idea around which true Christianity revolves.

A Comparison with Traditional Preaching

Biblical Christianity is founded, as we have seen, on the Message **about the Kingdom of God and about the Messiah Jesus, the King of that Kingdom.** If, however, we inquire of the various contemporary church denominations, we soon discover that the Kingdom of God is one of the least well-known topics in their preaching. The phrase "Gospel of the Kingdom" is almost entirely absent from contemporary presentations of the Gospel.

Instead you hear much talk about a vague "heaven when we die." One popular preacher says that Christians are going to "polish rainbows in heaven," "prepare heavenly dishes" or "tend heavenly gardens." But such language has no basis at all in the Bible. Jesus nowhere promised "heaven" as the future reward of the faithful. He invariably invited his disciples to prepare to "enter or inherit the Kingdom of God." He wants his followers to inherit the earth (Matt. 5:5) and to rule the world with him *on earth* when he comes back (Rev. 5:10).

The following words of a former head of the Church of England point to a longstanding and extraordinary absence of Jesus' central message! Apparently the churches have not been proclaiming the same Message as Jesus and the Apostles did. Consider these words of a distinguished church leader:

> Every generation finds something in the Gospel which is of special importance to itself and seems to have been overlooked in the previous age or sometimes in all previous ages of the Church. The great discovery of the age in which we live is the immense prominence given to the Gospel of the **Kingdom of God**. To us it is quite extraordinary that **it figures so little in the theology and religious writings of almost the entire period of Christian history**. Certainly in the synoptic gospels

[Matthew, Mark and Luke] it has a prominence which could hardly be increased.[4] This leading scholar of the Church of England agrees with us that the Gospel of the Kingdom has "a prominence which could hardly be increased" in the New Testament accounts of Jesus' ministry. At the same time he recognizes that the Gospel of the Kingdom is barely evident in "the theology and religious writings of almost the entire period of Christian history." This he finds "quite extraordinary," as we do. It should be a cause for urgent concern among believers.

We trust that the impact of these astonishing facts will not be missed. While churches have continued to function for the past nearly 2000 years since the time of Jesus, there is a glaring difference between what Jesus taught and what they have been teaching. This does not have to do with matters of secondary importance. The factor which has been lacking in preaching and teaching is nothing less than the heart and center of all that Jesus taught — **the Gospel Message about the Kingdom of God.**

The Witness of Contemporary Scholars

There is no room for disagreement that the Kingdom of God was the subject of Jesus' entire message and mission. "On one central point there is a strong consensus of opinion...The consensus can be summarized thus: The central theme in the preaching and life of Jesus was the Kingdom of God."[5] This author points out, however, that in the message preached by the Church since those apostolic times "the Kingdom of God **has not occupied a central place.**"[6]

Further distinguished names will confirm the absolute centrality of the Message about the Kingdom in the teaching of Jesus: "This term [Kingdom of God] is at the center of his proclamation."[7]

The most certain historical datum about Jesus' life is that the concept which dominated his preaching, the reality

---

[4] William Temple, former Archbishop of Canterbury, in *Personal Religion and the Life of Fellowship*, 1929, p. 69, emphasis added.
[5] Thomas H. Groome, *Christian Religious Education*, 1980, p. 39.
[6] *Ibid.*, p. 42.
[7] Hans Küng, *On Being a Christian*, p. 214.

which gave meaningfulness to all his activity, was "the Kingdom of God." This fact and its implications are of fundamental importance. It provides us with two essential keys to understanding Jesus. First, Jesus is not the central focus of his own teaching; this fact is commonly admitted. As Karl Rahner put it, "Jesus preached the Kingdom of God, not himself."[8] [However, Jesus also made exclusive claims for himself.]

Other prominent witnesses corroborate our thesis: "The whole message of Jesus focuses upon the Kingdom of God."[9] "It is generally admitted that the focal point of Jesus' message was the inbreaking of the Kingdom of God."[10]

At the turn of the last century, A. Robinson, D.D., giving the Bampton Lectures on the Kingdom of God, asserted: "There can be no question that in our Lord's teaching the Kingdom of God is the representative and all-embracing summary of his distinctive mission...Throughout, his message is the good news of the Kingdom."[11]

What Has Happened to Jesus' Gospel Message?

It is highly instructive to note that a leading writer on evangelism in our time frankly admits that the Kingdom of God is conspicuously absent from modern preaching: "How much have you heard here about the Kingdom of God? Not much. It is not our language. But it was Jesus' prime concern."[12] The statement comes from a prominent evangelist after he had attended the Lausanne International Conference on World Evangelization in 1974.

Equally remarkable is this admission by a prominent spokesman for the church growth movement:

> Modern scholarship is quite unanimous in the opinion that the Kingdom of God was the central message of Jesus. If this is true, and I know of no reason to dispute it, I cannot help wondering out loud why I haven't heard more about it in the 30 years I have been a Christian. I certainly have

---

[8] Jon Sobrino, S.J., *Christology at the Crossroads*, 1976, p. 41.
[9] Norman Perrin, *The Language of the Kingdom*, p. 1.
[10] Reginald Fuller, *Essays on the Love Commandment*, p. 51.
[11] *Regnum Dei*, 1901, pp. 8, 9.
[12] Cited by Tom Sine, *The Mustard Seed Conspiracy*, pp. 102, 103.

read about it enough in the Bible. Matthew mentions the Kingdom 52 times, Mark 19 times, Luke 44 times and John 4 times. But I honestly cannot remember any pastor whose ministry I have been under actually preaching a sermon on the Kingdom of God. As I rummage through my own sermon barrel, I now realize that I myself have never preached a sermon on it. Where has the Kingdom been?[13]

Once again, we hope that the devastating implications of these statements will not be overlooked. Michael Green notes the absence of Kingdom of God language amongst leading evangelists. Peter Wagner has not preached on the Kingdom of God. **Jesus, however, always preached about the Kingdom of God** (Matt. 4:17; 4:23; 9:35; 24:14; Luke 4:43; Luke 16:16). The ministry of Jesus was continued, after his resurrection, through the Apostles who always proclaimed the same Gospel of the Kingdom (Acts 8:12; 14:22; 19:8; 20:25; 28:23, 31; 2 Tim. 4:1, 2).

Another well-known theologian observes:

During the past sixteen years I can recollect only two occasions on which I have heard sermons specifically devoted to the theme of the Kingdom of God...I find this silence rather surprising because it is universally agreed by New Testament scholars that the central theme of the gospels and of the teaching of Jesus was the Kingdom of God...This phrase was used by Jesus more than any other...One would expect that the modern preacher who is trying to bring the message of Jesus to his congregation would have much to say about this subject. In fact my experience has been the opposite and I have rarely heard about it.[14]

But how can Christ be preached at all, if his Gospel is not communicated to the potential converts? Does not "faith come from hearing and **hearing from Messiah's message**" (Rom. 10:17)? It is agreed on all sides that Jesus' supreme purpose concerned the Kingdom of God. At the same time those who claim

---

[13] Peter Wagner, *Church Growth and the Whole Gospel*, p. 2.

[14] Dr. I. Howard Marwill, "Preaching the Kingdom of God," *Expository Times*, Oct., 1977, p. 13.

to be propagating the Gospel as Jesus preached it say almost nothing about the Kingdom!

Elizabeth Achtemeier writes:

> One of the central messages of the New Testament, which is now rarely heard by the average churchgoer, is the proclamation of the coming of the Kingdom of God in the person of Jesus Christ. That coming was promised in every major theological complex in the Old Testament...The prophets promised the new age of the Kingdom, on the other side of the judgment of the exile, with a new exodus (Isa. 52:11-12) and wilderness wanderings (Isa. 48:20-21) to a renewed promised land (Ezek. 34:25-31), where Israel would dwell in faithfulness and security, in a new covenant relation with her God (Jer. 31:31-34), and would by her light attract all nations into her fellowship (Isa. 60:1-3; 56:6-8). Israel anticipated that coming kingdom and knew a foretaste of it in her worship (Ps. 47, 96-99). Throughout most of the pages of the Old Testament she strains forward toward its arrival.[15]

A final example will help to reinforce our contention that for modern preachers the Gospel of the Kingdom of God does not have anything like the comprehensive significance it had for Jesus. In an editorial in the journal *Missiology* Arthur F. Glasser says:

> Let me ask: When is the last time you heard a sermon on the Kingdom of God? Frankly, I'd be hard put to recall ever having heard a solid exposition of this theme. How do we square this silence with the widely accepted fact that the Kingdom of God dominated our Lord's thought and ministry? My experience is not uncommon. I've checked this out with my colleagues. Of course, they readily agree they've often heard sermons on bits and pieces of Jesus' parables. But as for a solid sermon on the nature of the Kingdom of God as Jesus taught it — upon reflection, they too began to express surprise that it is the rare pastor who tackles the subject.[16]

---

[15] *Preaching as Theology and Art*, pp. 41, 42.

[16] *Missiology*, April, 1980, p. 134.

The Loss of the Gospel as Jesus Preached It

The above facts lead to a simple conclusion. Jesus and the Apostles made the Kingdom of God the principal theme of all their teaching. They proclaimed the Gospel of the Kingdom of God everywhere. The Good News Message of salvation consisted of information concerning the Kingdom of God. Generally speaking the churches calling themselves Christian admit that they have never said much about the Kingdom. Modern preachers do not preach it. Contemporary evangelists confess that the Kingdom is not part of their evangelistic agenda. This may be easily demonstrated, too, by pointing to the absence of the word "Kingdom" in tracts promoting what is called the Gospel. We conclude, therefore, that there is a glaring loss of Gospel content if we compare the Christianity of Jesus and the Apostles with what has been called Christianity for some 1900 years.

Throughout the biblical accounts of the preaching of Jesus and the Apostles we find a plain record that the Kingdom of God, to be inaugurated by Jesus as King of that Kingdom, is Christianity's principal concept. It is not, and never has been, the principal concept in traditional Christianity.

It must follow, we contend, that the Christianity of Jesus and the Apostles and traditional Christianity are substantially different in this important matter of defining the content of the Gospel.

A Summary of the Biblical Facts

We may gain a sense of the massive importance of the Kingdom of God in Biblical Christianity by quoting some of the many verses in which Jesus spoke of it. (The term **"Kingdom of Heaven," used only by Matthew, is the exact equivalent of "Kingdom of God." They are interchangeable terms.**):

Matt. 4:23: "Then Jesus traveled through all Galilee, teaching in their synagogues and proclaiming the Gospel of the Kingdom."

Matt. 8:11, 12: "And I tell you that many will come from the east and from the west and will take their seats with Abraham and Isaac and Jacob in the Kingdom of Heaven, while the natural heirs of the Kingdom will be driven out into the darkness outside. There will be weeping and gnashing of teeth."

Matt. 9:35: "And Jesus went round all the towns and villages, teaching in their synagogues and proclaiming the Gospel of the Kingdom."

Matt. 13:10: "To you [disciples] it is granted to know the secrets of the Kingdom of Heaven; to them it is not."

Matt. 13:19: "When a man hears the Message concerning the Kingdom..."

Matt. 6:33: "Seek first God's Kingdom and righteousness."

Matt. 13:41: "The Son of Man will send his angels, and they will gather out of his Kingdom all causes of sin and all who violate his laws; and these they will throw into the fiery furnace."

Matt. 13:43: "Then the righteous will shine like the sun in their Father's Kingdom. Listen, everyone who has ears."

Matt. 6:9, 10: "In this manner therefore pray, 'May Thy Kingdom come.'"

Matt. 19:24: "It is easier for a camel to go through the eye of a needle than for a rich man to enter the Kingdom of God."

Matt. 20:21: "Command," she replied, "that these my two sons may sit one at your right hand and one at your left in your Kingdom."

Matt. 26:29: "I tell you I will never again drink the fruit of the vine till the day that I drink the new wine with you in my Father's Kingdom."

Matt. 24:14: "And this Gospel of the Kingdom will be proclaimed throughout the whole world to set the evidence before the nations; and then the end will come."

Luke 4:43: "I must proclaim the Gospel of the Kingdom of God to the other towns also, because for this purpose I was sent."

Luke 8:1: "Shortly after this he visited town after town, and village after village, proclaiming the Gospel Message of the Kingdom of God."

Luke 9:2: "He sent them out to proclaim the Kingdom of God and to cure the sick."

Luke 9:11: "And receiving them kindly he talked to them about the Kingdom of God."

Luke 9:60: "'Leave the dead,' said Jesus, 'to bury their dead; but you go and announce far and wide the Kingdom of God.'"

Luke 12:32: "Do not be afraid, little flock: it is your Father's good pleasure to give you the Kingdom."

Luke 21:31: "So also, when you see these things happening [the events surrounding the return of Jesus to the earth], you may be sure that the Kingdom of God is about to come."

Luke 22:28-30: "You, however, have remained with me in my trials; and I covenant to give to you, as my Father has covenanted with me, a Kingdom, so that you may eat and drink at my table in my Kingdom, and sit on thrones to govern the twelve tribes of Israel."

These quotations will suffice to underline the fact that the Kingdom of God is indeed the main focus of the ministry and mission of Jesus. The Kingdom is overwhelming in its importance. It is decisive for the meaning of Christianity, the key which unlocks the teaching of the New Testament.

Jesus inaugurated his ministry in Galilee by calling on the public to "Repent and believe the Good News of the Kingdom of God" (Mark 1:14, 15). With this resounding command the risen Jesus continues to speak to men and women everywhere. The challenge is as urgent today as it was when first issued by Jesus: Change your minds and your lives and believe in the Good News message of salvation, the message about the Kingdom of God which Jesus and the Apostles always proclaimed.

In our next lesson we will investigate the meaning of the key phrase "Kingdom of God." This will clarify the foundation of our faith in God and in Jesus. For the moment we invite readers to commit themselves to the Gospel as Jesus preached it, and to a search for an understanding of Jesus' key concept. He announced God's immortality program by inviting everyone everywhere to believe and obey the Gospel of the Kingdom. God wants everyone to be saved and come to the knowledge of the Truth (the true Gospel) (1 Tim. 2:4).

"The Kingdom of God is the Christian answer to the most vital question that man has to solve, the question of the purpose of his being."[17]

---

[17] A. Robertson, *Regnum Dei*, Bampton Lectures, 1901, p. vii.

Lesson 2
Believing the Gospel Message
About the Kingdom of God

Master Texts:

"The God of Heaven will set up **a Kingdom** which will never be destroyed...It will break in pieces and consume all these [previous] kingdoms and it will stand forever" (Dan. 2:44).

"In mercy will the throne be established and he [the Messiah] will sit upon it in the tabernacle of David, judging and seeking judgment" (Isa. 16:5).

"At that time they will call **Jerusalem the throne of the Lord** and all the nations will be gathered to it, to Jerusalem, for the name of the Lord; nor will they walk any more after the stubbornness of their evil heart" (Jer. 3:17).

"Then the sovereignty, the dominion and the greatness of **all the kingdoms under the whole heaven** will be given to the people of the saints of the Highest One. Their Kingdom will be an everlasting Kingdom and all dominions will serve and obey them" (Dan. 7:27).

"Behold, the days are coming," says the Lord, "when I will raise up for David a righteous branch [the Messiah] and **he will reign as king** and deal wisely, and will execute justice and righteousness in the land. In his days Judah will be saved, and Israel will dwell securely. And this is the name by which he will be called: 'The Lord is our righteousness'" (Jer. 23:5, 6).

When Jesus embarked on his intensive evangelistic campaign in Galilee in about 27 AD, he challenged his audience to "repent and believe in the Gospel of the Kingdom of God" (see Mark 1:14, 15). His summons to a radical change of heart was based on the fact that God was one day going to usher in the worldwide Kingdom promised by Daniel and all the prophets — the Kingdom promised to the descendant of David (2 Sam. 7). Intelligent belief in that **promise of the Kingdom** is to be the disciple's first step.

We are to be prepared for the Kingdom, ready to enter it when it comes. The nature of Jesus' activity was not like what we today would call preaching a sermon. It was that of a herald making a public announcement on behalf of the one God of Israel. The thrust of the message was that each individual should undertake a radical redirection of his life in face of the certainty of **the coming Kingdom of God**. This was, and still is, the essence of the Christian Gospel. How can it be otherwise, when it is the Gospel Message which comes from the lips of Christ himself? Christianity is based on the teaching of the Christ. It is founded upon the Great Commission in Matthew 28:19, 20 where Jesus instructed his followers to take his Gospel to all the nations, and baptize converts in water. What Jesus requires is that we believe in God's great Kingdom program and become part of the "team" which announces it wherever we can.

To be part of the Kingdom program and to be fully in it when it comes, means that we *believe* in faith that God is going to bring the Kingdom when Jesus returns.

It is a matter of common sense to recognize that by using the term "**Kingdom of God**" Jesus would have evoked in the minds of his audience thoughts of a divine worldwide **government on earth**, with its **capital at Jerusalem**. This is what the Kingdom of God would certainly have meant to his contemporaries. The writings of the prophets, which Jesus as a Jew recognized as the divinely authorized words of God, had unanimously promised the arrival of a new **era of world peace and prosperity**. The book of Daniel is typical. It had spoken of a time coming when "the sovereignty and kingship and the splendors of all the kingdoms under heaven will be given to the people of the saints of the Most High" (Dan. 7:27, Jerusalem Bible). This **ideal government, or Kingdom**, or **empire** would rule forever on earth. God's people would be victorious in a renewed earth. Peace would extend across the globe.

The fact is that the term "Kingdom of God" unambiguously refers firstly to a divine world government on earth, to be introduced, as all the prophets had foretold, by a supernatural upheaval. The expectation of **a new order on earth** was the national hope of Israel at the time when Jesus began to preach. That this was so can be demonstrated by examining the writings of the prophets, as well as the literature which followed the closing of the Old Testament canon. Thus to announce the coming of the Kingdom involved both a threat and a promise. To those who responded to the Message by believing it and reordering their lives accordingly, there was a promise of gaining a place in the glories of the future Divine Rule. To the rest the Kingdom would threaten destruction, as God executed judgment upon any not found worthy of entering the Kingdom when it came. This theme governs the whole New Testament. Jesus promised two destinies: entrance into the Kingdom for those who obey Jesus, and destruction for those who refuse his Gospel of the Kingdom Message. This theme underlies the whole New Testament, from Matthew to Revelation.

The Christianity of Jesus was not meant to become obsolete after he left the earth! His half-brother Jude urged people even at the end of the first century that they should urgently "contend for the faith once and for all delivered to God's holy people" (Jude 3).

Barriers to Believing the Gospel

The association of the Kingdom of God with a spectacular divine intervention leading to the establishment of a **New World Order** has proven to be an embarrassment to much of the theology of the past 1600 years. Various techniques have been employed to eliminate from Jesus' teaching this central notion of the Kingdom of God as a real government to be imposed upon our world. However, the vision of the prophets which Jesus came to confirm (Rom. 15:8) is unmistakably clear. And there is ample evidence in the New Testament to show that Jesus shared with his contemporaries the hope for an actual "exterior," "concrete" Kingdom in which he and his followers would enjoy positions of authority. What, for example, could be more explicit than the Savior's promise to the faithful Christians:

> To those who prove victorious, and keep working for me until the end, I will give the authority over the pagans which I myself have been given by my Father, to rule them with an iron scepter and shatter them like earthenware...Those who prove victorious I will allow to share my throne, just as I was victorious myself and took my place with my Father on His throne (Rev. 2:26; 3:21, Jerusalem Bible).

These assurances were given to the Church as the "message of the Son of God, the faithful and true witness" (Rev. 2:18; 3:14). (A true witness means a true Gospel preacher.) They proceed directly from Jesus to his Church. As is well known, they reflect accurately the Jewish (and New Testament Christian) hope for world dominion under the promised Messiah and his faithful people, just as Daniel had predicted. In the same book of Revelation we find an angelic chorus singing of the wonders of God's plan. Their hymn is in praise of the Messiah, the executive of the divine plan:

> You are worthy to take the scroll and break the seals of it, because you were sacrificed, and with your blood you bought men for God of every race, language, people and nation and made them a line of kings and priests to serve our God and rule the world (Rev. 5:9, 10, Jerusalem Bible).

The tendency to want to collapse these plain statements and render them less "offensive" is widespread, but it must be consciously overcome. In order to make Jesus more "religious" and less political, many have tried to think only of a present "reign" of the Church or a "reign" of Christ "in the heart," but this is evidently not what these Kingdom texts say. The rulership promised to the believer will be granted only **after he has become victorious through the trials of the present life.** He will share the Kingdom with Jesus at the (future) **resurrection**, just as Jesus gained his position of authority on the Father's throne only at his resurrection. Jesus, too, had to undergo trial and tribulation before God approved him as the future world governor.

Commentators on these passages frequently attempt to keep such promises at arms length. They seem to want to distance themselves from anything so "Jewish," even sometimes labeling these biblical texts "unchristian" or "crude." This would mean that Jesus was unchristian and that he was a non-Messianic Messiah!

Another way of avoiding this uncomfortable material is to categorize it as "apocalyptic"[1] literature, as though classifying it might make it less offensive! It is indeed Christian apocalyptic, coming to us as the Revelation (Apocalypse) granted to Christ by God (Rev. 1:1). This does not mean, however, that it is any less a

---

[1]Describing a catastrophic divine intervention, introducing a new era and a new government on earth.

reflection of the mind of Jesus than any other of his sayings recorded in the New Testament. If to some the promise of "power over the nations" seems too political, it may be because the nature of the Kingdom of God has not been grasped. What is political is not therefore necessarily unspiritual. Nothing could be a greater spiritual blessing than to have Jesus as King of the Kingdom of God functioning in Jerusalem and across the world.

Deeply ingrained habits of thought have long caused us to think that things "spiritual" are divorced from real political structures functioning on earth. Such thinking is the result of centuries of Greek, Platonic thinking. Jesus was not a Platonist and Paul warned against the extreme dangers of philosophy (Col. 2:8). The Hebrew outlook which Jesus shared does not, however, operate in those dualistic terms. Nor, therefore, must we, if we wish to be in tune with the historical and risen Jesus. If we try to "spiritualize" or allegorize the plain statements of the Bible about the future, we simply dissolve plain information and make it mean whatever pleases *us*. This is the opposite of following the mind and will of God and Jesus. We cannot risk making up our Christianity in terms which seem to us spiritually or politically "correct."

Jesus had earlier spoken at the Last Supper of his intention to share rulership with his disciples in the Kingdom. He assured them of a place of honor as ministers of state in a new government. This, in fact, was the essential point of the New Covenant: "You are the ones who have stood by me in my trials; and just as my Father has covenanted a Kingdom to me, I covenant with you the right to eat and drink with me in my Kingdom, and you will sit on thrones governing[2] the twelve tribes of Israel" (Luke 22:28-30).

Precisely the same political reward had been promised to the Apostles on an earlier occasion, with a special note of the time when the Messianic government would come into power: "And Jesus said to them, 'Truly, I say to you, that you who have followed me, in the New World when the Son of Man will sit on his glorious throne, you also will sit upon twelve thrones, governing the twelve tribes of Israel'" (Matt. 19:28).

Formidable barriers have been erected over the centuries against our grasping the fundamental concept presented to us by

---

[2]The word "judge" means in this context "administer" or "govern." Note that in Hebrew thinking kings were "judges," i.e., rulers.

Jesus in **his "Good News (Gospel) about the Kingdom of God."** By removing the Kingdom from its biblical context, it has been possible to "reinterpret" it (a sophisticated way of abandoning the original meaning!) and replace it with our own more acceptable "kingdom in the hearts of men." Thus a new version of the Gospel of Jesus has replaced his original message. Jesus' name has been added to our "good causes," while the Good News about the Messianic Kingdom, understood as Jesus meant it, has often been discarded by churchgoers and preachers.

This, tragically, has been the history of the development of the central Christian idea — **"the Gospel of the Kingdom and the things concerning Jesus"** (Acts 8:12; 28:23, 31). Out of deference for Jesus, as God's Messiah, and in obedience to his original challenge to belief in **the Good News of the Kingdom** (Mark 1:14, 15), we must insist on defining the Kingdom according to its biblical setting. Can intelligent response to the Gospel mean anything less?

The Background to the Kingdom of God

The announcement that the Kingdom of God was "at hand" (Mark 1:14), and that men should respond by believing the Good News about the Kingdom (Mark 1:15), challenged Jesus' audiences to understand that their national hopes were to be realized. Jesus did not say *when* the Kingdom of God would arrive. The announcement that it was "at hand" meant, as it had long before meant in the same words used by the prophets, speaking of the Day of the Lord, that men should prepare for its arrival with the greatest urgency. After all, any of us might die before the Kingdom arrives. The next second (to us) after we fall asleep in death we will face the future Kingdom. When we are dead we have no knowledge of anything (Ecc. 9:5, 10), including the passage of time. We will awake from the sleep of death at the time of the future resurrection (Dan. 12:2; 1 Cor. 15:23).

The concept of the Kingdom of God had a rich history in the recorded messages of the prophets of Israel, whose work Jesus expressly said he came not to destroy (Matt. 5:17). The announcement of the Kingdom by Jesus would call attention to the certain fulfillment of those predictions: The establishment on earth of a Divine Government presided over by the ideal King of Israel, the Messiah.

That Israel was looking forward to an era of world peace under the government of the Messiah cannot reasonably be doubted. The fact is documented in hundreds of standard works on the Bible and the history of the Jewish religion. An expert on the literature of the prophets states what is clear to any who has read their writings:

> For many centuries the Jews had believed that some day in the not distant future their God, the Creator of the Universe, would manifest Himself and glorify His Name and His people Israel in the sight of all mankind. This is the essential substance of the Messianic Hope.

In view of this hope the attitude of the early Christians can be stated as follows:

> Their minds were always filled with a sense of expectancy, a sense of an impending change of tremendous import in which Jesus would occupy a central and conspicuous position in the capacity of Messiah, and they, as his chosen disciples, would share in his glory.[1]

Needless to say, the Christians' hopes were directed towards the return of Jesus in power and glory to inaugurate the great era of his Kingdom.

Another Old Testament scholar notes that the prophet Daniel "equates the coming kingdom with the golden age and envisages it as being established here on earth as the final phase of history."[2] The Kingdom would mean a restructuring of human society under a Divine Government operating in a renewed earth.

One has only to glance at the subject headings given by the translators of the Jerusalem Bible to catch the flavor of the Old Testament background to Jesus' proclamation of the Kingdom of God. In the writings of the great prophet Isaiah we learn of an era of "everlasting peace" (Isa. 2:1-4); "a future restoration" (Isa. 4:4-6); "The Coming of the Virtuous King" (Isa. 33:17-24); "The Liberation of Israel" (Isa. 43:1-7); "The Glorious Resurrection of Jerusalem" (Isa. 60).

In Jeremiah we read of "Zion in the Messianic Age" (Jer. 3:14-18); "The Conversion of the Nations" (Jer. 16:19-21); "The Future King" (Jer. 23:1-8); "Promises of the Recovery of the Northern Kingdom of Israel" (Jer. 30); "Promise of Restoration for Judah"

---

[1] H.D. Hamilton, D.D., *The People of God*, Vol. II, pp. 19, 20.
[2] D.S. Russell, *Apocalyptic, Ancient and Modern*, p. 26.

(Jer. 31:23-26); "Jerusalem Magnificently Rebuilt" (Jer. 31:38-40); "The Institutions of the Future" (Jer. 33:14-26). Ezekiel gives us a description of "Judah and Israel in One Kingdom" (Ezek. 37:15-28); Hosea speaks of "The Repentance and Reconciliation of Israel: A Promise of Future Happiness" (Hosea 14:2-9); Joel foresees "The Glorious Future of Israel" (Joel 4:18-21); Amos writes warmly about "Prospects of Restoration and Idyllic Prosperity" (Amos 9:11-15); Obadiah describes the political triumph of the Kingdom of God (Obad. 21; cp. Micah 4:1-5); finally, Zechariah provides a vivid picture of "Messianic Salvation" (Zech. 8:1-17); "The Messiah" (Zech. 9:9-10); "The Restoration of Israel" (Zech. 9:11-17). He concludes with a description of "The Splendor of Jerusalem" (Zech. 14:1-21).

No one who has pondered this stirring vision of the future can possibly miss its point. With one accord the prophets of Israel proclaimed that there is coming on earth an era of peace and permanent security for all nations under the supervision of God's chosen agent, the promised son of David. What Irving Zeitlin writes of Isaiah summarizes the Jewish hope of God's Kingdom on earth:

> The prophet looks forward to the end of this era and to ushering in the new, wherein arrogance, oppression, war and idolatry will all vanish together. Only after Israel has been cleansed of her haughtiness will she truly become God's people, and carry his word to the other nations. "For out of Zion will go forth the law, and the word of the Lord from Jerusalem."[3]

A distinguished Oxford professor of the Old Testament noted in his commentary on Daniel that: "Isaiah and Micah picture the Messianic age as beginning immediately after the troubles were past — to which their nation was exposed at the hands of **the Assyrian** (Isa. 11:1-10; see 28-34; 30:19-26, see v. 31; 31:7, 32:1-8, see 31:8; Micah 5:4-7)." We learn here the identity of the future final enemy of Israel.

We must here register our protest against the extraordinary idea that this vision of the future was fulfilled during the historical ministry of Jesus, or before or since. It should be obvious to all that the nations have not beaten their swords into farm instruments and

---

[3] *Ancient Judaism*, p. 228.

that Jesus as King-Messiah has not yet visibly taken up his position as ruler of the nations on the restored throne of David (Luke 1:32, 33). When did Jesus ever in the past deliver Israel from the Assyrian (see Micah 5:5-7)? Micah presents a prophecy for the future.

The Promise of Good Things to Come

The prophets' forecast of a future golden age is so essential to our understanding of the Christian Gospel that we must examine the words of the prophets in detail. When Jesus commanded repentance and belief in the Good News about the Kingdom of God (Mark 1:14-15), his message contained far more than the promise of forgiveness of personal sins. He demanded belief in the God of history and intelligent **faith in His plan** destined to find its climax in the establishment of the Kingdom of God on earth. We are commanded to "repent," i.e., change our entire outlook, and *believe the Good News of the Kingdom* — believe in the plan that God is working out for the benefit of us as individuals and for the world, through Jesus.

An obedient response to the Good News about the Kingdom obviously entails an understanding of the meaning of the word "Kingdom." One cannot believe Good News about something which one does not understand! What, then, is this Good News? A number of fundamental texts lie behind Jesus' use of the term "Kingdom of God." On these the expectation of the Kingdom of God is built. We must insist that the Good News embraced information about **a coming World Government**, with Jesus as its chief executive, and how we must respond by preparing ourselves for its arrival. Though terms like "government" and "executive" may have negative connotations for us who have witnessed the misuse of authority, nevertheless the biblical promise is of justice and peace on earth under the benign rule of the Messiah. And who does not long for peace and justice in the affairs of man?

The Kingdom Promised to David and His Descendant

Of critical importance for Jesus and his audience (and no less for us) was the celebrated promise made to King David that the Kingdom of Israel would one day become permanently secure, when his distinguished descendant took over the reins of power:

This is what you must say to my servant David: "...I will give you fame as great as the fame of the greatest on earth. I will provide a place for my people Israel; I will plant them there and they will never be disturbed again; nor will the wicked continue to oppress them as they did, in the days when I appointed judges over Israel; I will give them rest from all their enemies. Yahweh will make you great; Yahweh will make you a House. And when your days are complete and you lie down with your fathers, I will raise up your descendant after you, who will come forth from you, and I will establish his Kingdom. He will build a house for My name, and I will establish the throne of his Kingdom forever. I will be **a father** to him and he will be a **son** to me...and your house and your Kingdom will endure before you forever; your throne will be established forever" (2 Sam. 7:8-16, about 1000 BC).

This remarkable divine oracle, provided for David by the prophet Nathan, represents a veritable goldmine of information. It contains many of the essential ingredients of New Testament theology relating to the person and work of Jesus. It is indispensable as a guide to Jesus' Good News Message about the Kingdom of God.

It is important for us to know how the Jewish people had understood this promise of national glory, to be realized in the promised Messiah and his Kingdom. Based on the hope of the restored kingdom of David, the following excerpts from the "Psalms of Solomon," dating from about 50 years before the birth of Jesus, depict the Messianic empire of the future. These Psalms are not themselves part of the official canon of Scripture. They draw their inspiration, however, directly from numerous Messianic passages in the Old Testament Psalms and the prophets, and particularly from 2 Samuel 7, Psalms 72, 89, 132:

Lord, you chose David to be king over Israel and swore to him about his descendant forever, that his kingdom should not fail before you...See, Lord, and raise up for them their king, the son of David, to rule over your servant Israel, in the time known to you, O God. Undergird him with strength to destroy the unrighteous rulers, to purge Jerusalem from Gentiles who trample her to destruction; in wisdom and righteousness to drive out the sinners from the inheritance; to smash the arrogance of sinners like a potter's jar; to shatter all their substance like an iron rod; to destroy the unlawful nations with the word of his mouth; at his warning the nations will flee from his presence; and he will condemn sinners by the thought of their heart. He will gather a holy people whom he will lead in righteousness and he will judge the tribes of the people that have been made holy by the Lord their God. He will not tolerate unrighteousness to pause among them, and any person who knows wickedness will not live with them. For he will know that they are all children of their God. He will distribute them upon the land according to their tribes...and he will have Gentile nations serving under his yoke and he will glorify the Lord in a place prominent above the whole earth. And he will purge Jerusalem and make it holy as it was even from the beginning, for nations to come from the ends of the earth to see his glory, to bring as gifts her children who had been driven out, and to see the glory of the Lord with which God has glorified her.

There will be no unrighteous among them in his [Messiah's] days, for all will be holy, and their King will be the Lord Messiah. For he will not rely on horse and rider and bow, nor will he collect gold and silver for war. Nor will he build up hope in a multitude for a day of war. The Lord himself is his king, the hope of the one who has a strong hope in God...

O Lord, your mercy is upon the works of your hands forever. You show your goodness to Israel with a rich gift. Your eyes are watching over them and none of them will be in need. Your ears listen to the hopeful prayer of the poor, your compassionate judgments are over the whole world, and your love is for the descendants of Abraham, an Israelite. Your discipline for us is as for a first-born son, an only child, to divert the perceptive person from unintentional sins. May God cleanse Israel for the day of mercy in blessing, for the appointed day when his Messiah will reign. Blessed are those who are born in those days, to see the good things of the Lord which he will do for the coming generation; which will be under the rod of discipline of the Lord Messiah, in the fear of his God, in wisdom of spirit, and of righteousness and of strength, to direct people in righteous acts, in the fear of God, to set them all in the fear of the Lord, a good generation living in the fear of God, in the days of mercy (from Psalms of Solomon 17, 18).

These psalms capture the essence of the Messianic hope presented by the Old Testament and current at the time when Jesus began to announce the Kingdom of God. They show a striking affinity also with passages in Luke's gospel (1:32; 2:11), the book of Revelation (11:15-18; 19:15-16) and other New Testament texts.

The Vision of the King and Kingdom

A leading exponent of the Gospel of the Kingdom of God was the sixth-century BC prophet Daniel. In a series of remarkable visions he had predicted that "the God of Heaven will set up a Kingdom which will never be destroyed and that kingdom will not be left to another people. It will crush and put an end to all these kingdoms, but it will itself endure forever" (Dan. 2:44).

The Kingdom of God was destined to replace hostile world empires pictured by the great image of Daniel chapter 2. According to the prophet, whose message we are challenged to believe, "the great God has made known to the king [Nebuchadnezzar] what will take place in the future [in Hebrew, *be acharit hayamim,* i.e., in Messianic times]; so the dream is true and its interpretation trustworthy" (Dan. 2:45). Along with the promise of the Kingdom goes the assurance that it will be ruled by the "Son of Man" (Jesus' favorite title for himself, but including his followers who make up "the body of Christ"), whose "dominion is an everlasting dominion which will not pass away; and his Kingdom is one which will not be destroyed" (Dan. 7:14). The right to rule was to be conferred on the Son of Man, assisted by his Saints (Dan. 7:27), to whom would be given "dominion, glory and a Kingdom, that all peoples, nations and men of every language might serve them" (Dan. 7:27, RSV).

The bright future is nowhere more vividly depicted than in the words of the prophet Isaiah. His vision is of:

days to come [when] the mountain of the Temple of Yahweh will tower above the mountains and be lifted higher than the hills. All the nations will stream to it;

people without number will come to it; and they will say:
"Come, let us go up to the mountain of Yahweh, to the
Temple of the God of Jacob, that he may teach us his ways
so that we may walk in his paths; since the law will go out
from Zion, and the oracle of Yahweh from Jerusalem." He
will wield authority over the nations and adjudicate
between many peoples; these will hammer their swords
into ploughshares, their spears into sickles. Nation will not
lift sword against nation; there will be no more training for
war. O House of Jacob, come let us walk in the light of
Yahweh (Isa. 2:1-5, Jerusalem Bible).

When that new age dawns, "those who are left of Zion and
remain of Jerusalem will be called holy and those left in Jerusalem,
noted down for survival" (Isa. 4:3). Following the cleansing of the
Temple area, when "the Lord has washed away the filth of the
daughter of Zion and cleansed Jerusalem of the blood shed in her"
(Isa. 4:4), "Yahweh will come and rest on the whole stretch of
Mount Zion and on those who are gathered there, a cloud by day,
and smoke, and by night the brightness of a flaring fire. For, over
all, the glory of Yahweh will be a canopy and a tent to give shade
by day from the heat, refuge and shelter from the storm and the
rain" (Isa. 4:6).

The miraculous nature of the predicted Kingdom is matched by
the supernatural conception of the Messiah: "The maiden will be
with child and will give birth to a son whom she will call
Immanuel" (Isa. 7:14). Matthew sees in the miraculous conception
of Jesus the ultimate fulfillment of the oracle delivered by Isaiah
700 years earlier. Of Mary's miraculous pregnancy he reports
simply that "all this took place to fulfill the words spoken by the
Lord through the prophet" (Matt. 1:22). "The one begotten
[brought into existence] in her is from the holy spirit" (Matt. 1:20).

Inseparable from the greatness of the future Kingdom is the
majesty of the promised King:

For there is a child born to us, a son given to us and
dominion is laid on his shoulders; and this is the name they
give him: Wonder Counselor, Mighty God,[3] Father[4] of the

---

[3]Mighty God, according to the standard Hebrew Lexicon, means
"Divine Hero." The Messiah was to reflect the very glory of God, his
Father (Luke 1:35 gives the basis of this father-son relationship).

Coming Age [so the Greek version of the Hebrew text], Prince of Peace. Wide is his dominion in a peace that has no end, for the throne of David and for his royal power, which he establishes and makes secure in justice and integrity, from this time onward and forever. The jealous love of Yahweh Sabaoth [the Lord of the armies of heaven] will do this (Isa. 9:6, 7).

When the promised national hero of Israel appears, further words of Isaiah find fulfillment:

A shoot springs from the stock of Jesse, a scion thrusts from his roots: on him the spirit of Yahweh rests, a spirit of wisdom and insight, a spirit of counsel and power, a spirit of knowledge and of the fear of Yahweh. (The fear of Yahweh is his breath.) He does not judge by appearances; he gives no verdict on hearsay, but judges the wretched with integrity, and with equity gives a verdict for the poor of the land. His word is a rod that strikes the ruthless; his sentences bring death to the wicked. Integrity is the loincloth around his waist, faithfulness the belt about his hips (Isa. 11:1-5).

Under the just rule of the future King even nature will reflect a corresponding harmony:

The wolf lives with the lamb; the panther lies down with the kid; calf and cub feed together with a little boy to lead them. The cow and the bear make friends; their young lie down together. The lion eats straw like an ox. The infant plays over the cobra's hole; into the viper's lair the young child puts his hand. They do not hurt nor harm on all my holy mountain, for the country is filled with knowledge of Yahweh as the waters swell the sea (Isa. 11:6-9).

As in Daniel's vision the peaceful Kingdom will be established on the ruins of former evil governments:

Once the oppression is over, and the destroyer is no more, and those now trampling the country under foot have gone away, the throne will be made secure in gentleness, and on

---

[4]The Messiah, of course, is not God, the Father. But the Messiah is the parent of the Coming Age of the Kingdom. He is preparing for that Kingdom now and he will be in charge of all its affairs.

it there will sit, in all fidelity, within the tent of David, a judge careful for justice and eager for integrity (Isa. 16:5). The triumph of the Kingdom will mean the banishment of all hostile forces: "That Day, Yahweh will punish above, the armies of the sky, below, the kings of the earth; they will be herded together, shut up in a dungeon, confined in a prison and, after long years, punished" (Isa. 24:21, 22). At that point the glorious Kingdom will appear: "The moon will hide her face, the sun be ashamed, for Yahweh Sabaoth [Lord of the armies of heaven] will be king on Mount Zion, in Jerusalem" (Isa. 24:23).

The time will come for the fulfillment of God's great plan for the earth: "Behold, a king will reign righteously, and princes will rule justly. And each will be like a refuge from the wind, and a shelter from the storm, like streams of water in a dry country, like the shade of a huge rock in a parched land" (Isa. 32:1, 2).

With this complex of ideas providing the indispensable background of Jesus' watchword, the Kingdom of God, we are in a position to react with understanding to his first recorded command: "Repent and believe the Good News [about the Kingdom of God]" (Mark 1:14, 15).

The Christian Hope as an Essential Part of the Gospel

Upon his arrival in Galilee, Jesus launched his campaign on behalf of the Good News about the Kingdom of God. His use of the familiar term "Kingdom of God" stimulated hopes for peace on earth, based on all the prophets had said. Jesus presented himself as the ultimate "theocrat," the one who for the first time could guarantee world peace and prosperity.

If the phrase "Kingdom of God" has ceased to have definite meaning for many, perhaps we should substitute "**Future Divine Messianic Government on Earth**," for this is the concept underlying the entire mission of Jesus. The idea does not originate with Jesus. Rather, he came "to confirm the promises given to the fathers" (Rom. 15:8). As the one appointed to rule in the Kingdom, he continues to summon the public to respond to the Good News in advance of the arrival of the Kingdom. The present is a time of urgent preparation for the dawning of the Kingdom. We must learn to live in a manner fitting our call to the Kingdom. The invitation to respond intelligently to the Good News continues to go out, as the Church faithfully obeys her commission to "**proclaim this**

Good News about the Kingdom in the whole world" (Matt. 24:14). When the world has been fairly warned, the end of the age will come (Matt. 24:14). Only then will the New Age of the divine Kingdom on earth be introduced.

In a world saturated with gospels claiming the name of Christ, it is urgently necessary to insist on the fact that the genuine Christian Gospel — the one proclaimed by Jesus himself — is the Gospel of the Kingdom. Our Christian documents yield that fact above all others:

Jesus came into Galilee proclaiming the Gospel of God and saying, "The time is fulfilled, and the Kingdom of God is at hand; repent and believe the Gospel" (Mark 1:14, 15).

"I must proclaim the Good News of the Kingdom of God: That is the reason for which I was sent" (Luke 4:43).

"This Gospel of the Kingdom will be proclaimed throughout the world" (Matt. 24:14).

The Same Gospel Yesterday, Today, Until the Kingdom Comes
"Theology" has devised a number of techniques for avoiding the obvious. Strangely, as we saw in lesson one, it has dropped the all-important phrase "Gospel of the Kingdom." It has substituted a gospel which speaks only of the death and resurrection of Jesus, and not of his Kingdom. It has attempted this by side-stepping the definitive evidence of Matthew, Mark and Luke relating to Jesus' ceaseless preaching of the Kingdom (Luke 4:43, etc., long before he said a word about his death and resurrection! See Luke 18:29-34.) It has also bypassed the explicit information given by Luke in the book of Acts describing the activity of the Church after the resurrection of Jesus. Luke makes every effort to prevent us from ever forgetting that intelligent belief in the Kingdom of God is the first step towards embracing biblical Christianity:

"When they believed Philip as he proclaimed the Good News about the Kingdom of God and the name of Jesus Christ, they were being baptized, both men and women" (Acts 8:12).

This is Luke's deliberately chosen formula for describing the content of the message of salvation. He repeats it at crucial junctures in his narrative (Acts 1:3, 6; 19:8; 20:25; 28:23, 31). He even reserves it for his final word about the Christian mission under Paul in Rome: He was **"proclaiming the Kingdom of God and teaching those things which concern the Lord Jesus**

Christ, with all confidence, no man forbidding him" (Acts 28:31). Not only does the Savior receive here his full official title, "the Lord Jesus Messiah"; his own Gospel of the Kingdom is given official recognition as the Message now going to Gentiles. It is exactly the same Message which some of the Jews had rejected, when Paul had **"expounded and testified the Kingdom of God, persuading them concerning Jesus, both out of the Law of Moses and out of the Prophets, from morning till evening"** (Acts 28:23). Not surprisingly, the Message of the Kingdom is none other than the one always proclaimed by Jesus himself. Hebrews 2:3 defines the Message of salvation as the Gospel originally announced by Jesus himself. And Romans 16:25 equates Paul's Gospel with the Gospel heralded by Jesus.

Can anyone resist the conclusion that the Kingdom of God is the primary ingredient (in addition, of course, to "the things concerning Jesus") in the Gospel according to the Bible? The Gospel of the Kingdom is the principal concern of Jesus throughout his ministry and it is the customary Message of the spirit-filled Christians in Acts, who authorize baptism (as Jesus had insisted, Mark 16:15, 16; Matt. 28:19, 20) only when their audience has professed faith in **the Good News (Gospel) of the Kingdom and the Name of Jesus Messiah** (Acts 8:12; 19:8; 28:23, 31).

It is a remarkable fact that churches no longer use the apostolic formula of faith required of candidates for baptism (Acts 8:12), that of belief in **"the Kingdom of God and the things concerning the name of Jesus"** (cp. Acts 28:23, 31). Would not the use of this early creed, with its primary emphasis on the Kingdom, help to ensure that Jesus' own Christian Gospel would never be forgotten?

In lesson three we will pursue our examination of the meaning of the Kingdom of God from its background in the prophets. This will enable us to understand **the Message of Jesus** in its biblical environment and ward off all attempts to uproot it from its heritage in Old Testament prophecy. At all costs the Gospel Message must be defended against the many substitute messages by which it is constantly threatened. The Gospel of Jesus is certainly not the "gospel of consumerism." Nor is it the "the gospel of heaven," as a place for disembodied souls.

"His teaching is the Gospel — 'the Good News' — of the Kingdom."[4]

---

[4] A. Robinson, *Regnum Dei*, Bampton Lectures, 1901, p. 62.

Lesson 3
The Basis for Believing
the Christian Gospel of the Kingdom

Master Texts:
"For a child will be born to us, a son will be given to us; and the government will rest on his shoulders...There will be no end to the increase of his government or of peace on the throne of David and over his kingdom, to establish it and uphold it with justice and righteousness from then on and forevermore. The zeal of the Lord of hosts will accomplish this" (Isa. 9:6, 7).

"How beautiful on the mountains are the feet of one who brings **good news**, who heralds peace, brings happiness, proclaims salvation, and tells Zion, 'Your God is King'" (Isa. 52:7).

"I must proclaim **the Good News of the Kingdom of God** in other cities also; that is the reason for which I was sent" (Luke 4:43).

From the recorded ministry of Jesus Christ we have seen that his evangelistic activity centered upon a public proclamation: The announcement that **the Kingdom of God** was to be inaugurated on earth, and that men and women should respond to **this Good News of the Kingdom** by believing the Message and changing their minds and their lives accordingly (Mark 1:14, 15). In this way, they would be ready to enter the Kingdom of God when it arrived with the Second Coming of Jesus. We are still waiting for the coming of that Kingdom. Joseph of Arimathea, a Christian disciple, was waiting for it after the ministry of Jesus on earth was complete (Mark 15:43). He did not imagine that the Kingdom had already come!

We maintain that since this was the Gospel Message always presented by Jesus, it is by definition the Christian Gospel. No wonder, then, that the early church required its prospective candidates for baptism to believe in "**the Kingdom of God and the name of Jesus Christ**" (Acts 8:12; cp. Acts 28:23, 31). Jesus has not changed (Heb. 13:8) nor has his Gospel Message of the

Kingdom, which continues to demand an urgent response from all who hear it. All Christians, if they are to be involved in the work of God (1 Cor. 15:58), should be active in some capacity as teachers or supporters of the Kingdom of God Gospel as Jesus taught it (see for example Luke 8:3). They should be coworkers for the Kingdom (Col. 4:11). But they should take plenty of time to prepare before they teach it publicly. The Gospel can be talked about in many different situations. The important thing is that the Message is spread (Luke 9:60). Matthew 5:5 — "Blessed are the meek for they will inherit the earth/Kingdom of God" — is a good place to start. Converts should be encouraged **to give up their talk of "going to heaven," "when I get to heaven," "so and so has gone to a better place," etc.** and start following the language of Jesus about **entering and inheriting the Kingdom when Jesus comes back**. This is good discipleship. People who talk constantly of "going to heaven" do not sound at all like Jesus.

We have also pointed out that the Good News about the Kingdom has its roots in the prophecies of the Old Testament. These announced the coming of **a golden age on earth**, following a decisive, catastrophic intervention by God called the Day of the Lord, or "the great and terrible Day of the Lord." God's intention is to establish a just government throughout the world under the supervision of His chosen agent, the Messiah (Christ). (See particularly Dan. 2:44; 7:18, 22, 27.)

In Lesson 1 we quoted at length from experts on the theology of the Bible who agree that the Kingdom Message was the heart and soul of all that Jesus came to preach and teach. This cardinal fact may be grasped by any reader of the New Testament, particularly in view of Jesus' all-embracing purpose statement: "**I must proclaim the Good News of the Kingdom of God to other cities also; that is the reason for which I was sent**" (Luke 4:43).

In contrast to the unmistakable prominence given in the Bible to the Kingdom of God, we noticed the remarkable silence on the subject of the Gospel of the Kingdom on the part of the churches calling themselves Christian. According to their leading spokesmen, past and present, *the Kingdom of God has never held a central position in their Gospel message*, or in their creeds. Their writings and tracts dealing with evangelism continue to say little or nothing about the Kingdom. We are amazed at this fact, as they also appear to be. The situation seems to call for an urgent reexamination of the biblical documents, in order to determine what we are supposed to believe as Christians, on this the most critical of subjects — the Gospel Message. The Gospel is the divine Message for our salvation! We must understand it properly. Christianity is a response to the Gospel preaching of Jesus and thus obedience to Jesus as Lord Messiah (Luke 2:11).

Our suspicion is that, following apostolic times, the original faith became submerged under a deluge of alien ideas introduced mainly by Gentiles, who had little understanding of the Old Testament roots of Jesus' announcement about the Kingdom. Gradually, the concept of the Kingdom lost its meaning as **a real government** to be brought to power on earth in the future, and it became a "kingdom in the heart" — a religious ideal, often the creation of man's own aspirations and dreams. In this way the dynamic proclamation of **a coming crisis in world history** was largely replaced by a more "comfortable" gospel claiming to deal with "personal" salvation or social improvement. Some of the essential facts of the Message proclaimed by the Apostles were retained — the death, burial and resurrection of Jesus. Nevertheless, the primary factor in the Gospel, the necessity of understanding and **believing in the coming Kingdom** (Mark 1:14, 15; Acts 8:12; 28:23, 31), was dropped. Vague promises of "heaven" at death replaced the promise of the **Golden Age of the Kingdom of God on earth to be introduced by the return of Jesus**.

This depleted, abbreviated and distorted version of the Gospel has become popular because:

1. **The Old Testament roots of the Gospel about the Kingdom** are ignored.

2. The unambiguous testimony of Matthew, Mark and Luke to what **Jesus preached** as the Gospel is disregarded. Luther and Calvin and in our time C.S. Lewis and evangelists generally are responsible for the failure to preach the Gospel firstly from the Gospel words of Jesus.

3) The plain statements in Acts about the Church's continued proclamation of the **Kingdom of God as the heart of the Gospel** are bypassed (Acts 8:12; 19:8; 20:25; 23:28, 31).

4) An anti-Jewish tendency has caused the Gospel of Jesus to seem too "Jewish" and Messianic.

The Christian documents demonstrate, beyond any argument, that Jesus preached the Gospel *of the Kingdom of God*. Not only this, he did not initially say anything about his own death and resurrection (Luke 18:31-34). **This must prove conclusively that the Message about the Kingdom contains information** *other than* **the death and resurrection of the Savior.** This point is so crucial to our whole argument that we must emphasize it further. Jesus proclaimed the Gospel of the Kingdom in the company of the twelve Apostles: "Now after this he made his way through towns and villages preaching and proclaiming the Good News of the Kingdom of God. With him went the twelve" (Luke 8:1). Later, "he called the twelve together and gave them power and authority over all demons and to cure diseases, and he sent them out **to proclaim the Kingdom of God** and to heal" (Luke 9:1-2).

At this stage the disciples had no knowledge of the death and resurrection of Jesus. This is proved by their subsequent reaction to Jesus' announcement of his impending arrest and crucifixion:

> Then taking the twelve aside he said to them, "Now we are going up to Jerusalem, and everything which is written by the prophets about the Son of Man is to come true. For he will be handed over to the pagans and will be mocked, maltreated and spat on, and when they have scourged him, they will put him to death; and on the third day he will rise again." But **they could make nothing of this**; what he had said was quite obscure to them; they had no idea what it meant (Luke 18:31-34).

Even immediately after the resurrection the disciples still did not understand it. And yet they had been preaching the Gospel of the Kingdom in the company of Jesus. "They did not yet understand the Scripture that he must rise from the dead" (John 20:9). This was after the death and resurrection of Jesus had occurred.

Now if, as is commonly said, the Gospel consists of information about the death and resurrection of Jesus only, how is it that both Jesus and the twelve *proclaimed the Gospel without reference to the Savior's death and resurrection?* The answer is clear. The Gospel of the Kingdom was announced before Jesus died (Mark 1:14, 15; Matt. 4:23; 9:35; Luke 4:43; Luke 8:1, etc.) and, as the book of Acts informs us, after the resurrection (Acts

1:3; 1:6; 8:12; 19:8; 20:25; 28:23, 31). In Acts, however, we find *added to the Gospel about the Kingdom*, the new facts about the death and resurrection of Jesus, which had now become history. The result is a **Gospel message about the Kingdom of God and the name of Jesus Christ (Acts 8:12; 28:23, 31)**. The Kingdom message remains as the primary component of the Gospel. Jesus' death and resurrection are additional, indispensable subjects for belief.

More Hebrew Background

A modern commentator remarks that the Kingdom of God "for Jesus' first hearers...was not the empty or nebulous term it often is today. The concept had a long history and an extensive background in the Old Testament."[1] Since the Kingdom is the main subject of the Gospel of salvation, it must follow that the Christian Gospel itself has become an "empty or nebulous" thing for modern audiences! Hence the urgent need **to define the heart of the Gospel from its Old Testament heritage and from the words of Jesus**. There can obviously be no faith-response to Jesus' initial call for repentance and **belief in the Kingdom** (Mark 1:14, 15) as long as the Kingdom remains a nebulous idea. Faith must have an object and that object is the Message of the Kingdom as well as Jesus himself. You cannot fairly separate Jesus from his Message. That is why Jesus says: "Whoever loses his life for **me and the Gospel**...Whoever is ashamed of **me and my words**" (Mark 8:35, 38). And the Gospel was and is always the Gospel of the Kingdom of God.

The nation of Israel had long been convinced of its high destiny in the purposes of God. As part of the covenant between the nation and its God, Israel was to enjoy a position of special privilege: "If you obey My voice and hold fast to My covenant, you of all the nations will be My very own, for all the earth is Mine. I will count you **a kingdom of priests**, a consecrated nation. These are the words you are to speak to the sons of Israel" (Exodus 19:5-6).

Israel as a whole had repeatedly failed to live up to her high calling. Nevertheless, the promise of world supremacy was reserved for a faithful remnant destined to inherit the future

---

[1] Hugh Anderson, *New Century Bible, The Gospel of Mark*, p. 84.

Kingdom of God. The invitation to kingship was repeated through the prophet Isaiah:

> Pay attention, come to me; listen and your soul will live. With you I will make an everlasting **covenant** out of the favors promised to David. See, I have made of you **a witness** to the peoples, a leader and **a master of the nations**. See, you will summon a nation you never knew, those unknown will come hurrying to you, for the sake of Yahweh, your God, of the Holy One of Israel who will glorify you (Isa. 55:3-5, Jerusalem Bible).

In the New Testament the prospect of **royal position** in the Kingdom is offered to the **New Israel of the Church** (Gal. 6:16; Phil. 3:3), gathered from both Jews and Gentiles. We have already referred to Jesus' own assurance to the faithful Church:

> Those who prove victorious, I will allow **to share my throne**, just as I was victorious myself and took my place with my Father on His throne...To those who prove victorious, and keep **working for me** until the end, I will give the authority over the pagans which I myself have been given by my Father, to rule them with an iron scepter and shatter them like earthenware (Rev. 3:21; 2:26, 27).

This prospect gave rise to the Christian "slogan" found in 2 Timothy 2:12: "If we suffer with him, **we will also reign as kings with him**." The faithful of all the ages and of all nations are destined to "rule as kings on the earth" (Rev. 5:10). That is their royal future and they must prepare now for this very high honor.

In Revelation 2:26 (above), Jesus is quoting the celebrated Messianic Psalm 2, one of many which describe the glories of the future Kingdom of God. It will be initiated by a decisive intervention by God, sending His Messiah to crush political rebellion and establish a **new government in Jerusalem**. The fact that appeal is made to this Psalm in the book of Revelation shows that the traditional Messianic hope was taken over into Christianity, with full approval of Jesus himself:

> Why this uproar among the nations? Why this impotent muttering of pagans — kings on earth rising in revolt, princes plotting against Yahweh and His Anointed [Messiah]. "Now let us break their fetters! Now let us throw off their yoke!" The One whose throne is in heaven sits laughing; Yahweh derides them. Then angrily he

addresses them; in a rage he strikes them with panic, "This is my King installed by me on Zion, my holy mountain." "Let me proclaim Yahweh's decree; he has told me, 'You are my Son, today I have become your father. Ask and I will **give the nations for your heritage, the ends of the earth for your domain**. With iron scepter you will break them, shatter them like potter's ware'" [cited by Jesus in Rev. 2:26]. So, now, you kings, learn wisdom, earthly rulers, be warned: Serve Yahweh, fear him, tremble and kiss his feet, or he will be angry and you will perish, for his anger is very quick to blaze. Happy all who take shelter in him (Psalm 2, Jerusalem Bible).

The promise of "the ends of the earth for your domain" is reflected in Jesus' own claim to the "authority which I myself have been given by my Father" (Rev. 2:26). The same theme is taken up by the angelic chorus when they sing of the faithful who "**will rule as kings on the earth**" (Rev. 5:10) and in the famous millennial passage which foresees the saints ruling with the Messiah for a thousand years (Rev. 20:4). This Kingdom of the saints belongs to the **future age** of the millennial rule of Christ. Jesus referred to that era as "**that [famous] age**" (Luke 20:35). It is the age of the future Kingdom of God on a renewed earth and it is entered by those who have responded now to the Gospel of the Kingdom, have been baptized in water in obedience to Acts 2:38, 8:12, etc. and continue in faith until Jesus returns. (If they fall asleep in death before Jesus returns, Jesus will resurrect them to take part in the Kingdom. See Dan. 12:2, 13; 1 Cor. 15:23, etc.)

The Loss of the Messianic Element in the Gospel

The attempts of commentators to avoid this Messianic material are a monument to man's effort to construct his own "de-Messianized" versions of Christianity. The crux of the problem is that man does not *want* God to impose His rule on the earth. Much less does he like to think of Jesus shattering the nations and ruling them with a rod of iron. The original Messianic version of Christianity, preached and taught by Jesus and the Apostles, has therefore been dismantled. Its Messianic framework has been removed. What remains as "Christianity" is barely recognizable as the faith of the New Testament. The name of Jesus has been attached to a system of religion markedly different from the original faith. Promises of an ethereal "heaven" are a far cry from Jesus' constant invitation to men and women to seek the Kingdom of God and "**inherit the earth**" (Matt. 5:5).

The New Testament has as its supreme goal the establishment, by divine intervention, of world peace under the government of the coming Messiah. The "revised" version of the faith promises a salvation for the individual in a realm far removed from the earth. Jesus, however, offered his followers positions of responsibility in a future New World Order — the Kingdom of God. Belief in that New World Order was, and is, the first step in intelligent faith in the Gospel. "The Kingdom of God is at hand; **repent and believe in the Good News**" (Mark 1:14, 15).

The loss of Christianity's central point may be likened to a team hoping to go to the moon. They decide that they need a launching pad and a spaceship in order to realize their dream. After they have acquired the necessary equipment for the journey, they forget what it was they needed the equipment for. Their interest in the pad and the spacecraft remains, but the trip to the moon is forgotten. Churchgoers have likewise almost no idea of their future and destiny. This leads to an impoverishment of the faith and disconnects them from the words of Jesus and the Bible.

In New Testament Christianity the hope of a place in the future Kingdom of God provides the stimulus to the whole Christian venture. The death and resurrection of Jesus make possible the believer's hope for a place in that Kingdom. Grasping the nature of that hope is the first step to be taken by the disciple. Belief in Jesus provides the way to the goal and guarantees its ultimate realization.

In contemporary presentations of the "gospel," people are being asked to "believe in Jesus," "give their heart to Jesus," "ask Jesus into their lives," etc. But there is no clear idea of what Jesus stands for. **Audiences are not exposed to Jesus' Message about the Kingdom**, which he preached long before he spoke of his death and resurrection. The situation is comparable to a political campaign in which a candidate appeals for support before the voters know what his manifesto is. It is impossible to express **intelligent faith in Jesus unless one understands what Jesus meant by his "news about the Kingdom"** — the Gospel. This will explain why Luke, in Acts, so precisely summarizes the process by which converts are to be initiated into the faith: "When they believed Philip as he proclaimed the **Good News about the**

Kingdom of God and the Name of Jesus Christ, they were baptized, both men and women" (Acts 8:12). The challenge to believe in the Good News about the Kingdom of God (Mark 1:14, 15) remained at the heart of Christian preaching after the resurrection of Jesus. It is urgently needed today as the indispensable guide to evangelism according to the apostolic method. How can we relate to Jesus without understanding his own passion for the Kingdom of God? When Jesus said that he was commissioned to proclaim the Kingdom of God (Luke 4:43), he set an example for all believers. Can we say that we are also "sent to proclaim the Kingdom"? We should be able to follow Jesus confidently in this respect.

In the Bible, people did not just "receive the Lord." They received the message of Jesus (John 17:8; Acts 8:12, etc.). "Receiving Jesus" in the Bible means "believing in his Name" (John 1:12). Jesus' Name means the Gospel revelation which he brought for our salvation. There is no believing in Jesus without believing in Jesus' words. **We must not only believe in Jesus. We must believe what Jesus believed (see John 5:47). Christianity means having "the faith of Jesus" as well as faith in him.**

Jesus himself gave a final warning in John 12:48: "He who rejects me and does not receive my sayings has one who will judge him. The word I spoke is what will judge him on the last day." If rejecting Jesus means not "receiving his sayings," obviously **"accepting Jesus" means accepting his sayings.** But where would you find this simple information in contemporary tracts offering "salvation"?

More on the Gospel of the Kingdom in the Prophets

A large portion of the message of the prophets is devoted to descriptions of the Coming Kingdom of God. There is not the slightest doubt as to the meaning of these glowing accounts of the Messiah's future worldwide empire:

> To us a child is born, to us a Son is given and the government will be upon his shoulder...Of the increase of his government and of peace there will be no end, upon the **throne of David, and over his Kingdom**, to establish it and to uphold it with justice and with righteousness from this time forth and for evermore (Isa. 9:6, 7, RSV).

The appointed ruler will be characterized by "the spirit of wisdom and understanding, the spirit of counsel and might, the spirit of knowledge and the fear of the Lord. And his delight will be in the fear of the Lord" (Isa. 11:2, 3, RSV). With him, "princes will rule in justice" (Isa. 32:1). The consequences of the Messiah's perfect government will be seen in nature itself:

> The wilderness and the dry land will be glad, the desert will rejoice and blossom; like the crocus it will blossom abundantly, and rejoice with joy and singing. The glory of Lebanon will be given to it, the majesty of Carmel and Sharon. They will see the glory of the Lord, the majesty of our God...Then the eyes of the blind will be opened, and the ears of the deaf unstopped; then will the lame man leap like a hart, and the tongue of the dumb sing for joy, for waters will break forth in the wilderness, and streams in the desert; the burning land will become a pool, and the thirsty ground springs of water...And the ransomed of the Lord will return, and come to Zion with singing; everlasting joy will be upon their heads; they will obtain joy and gladness, and sorrow and sighing will flee away (Isa. 35:1-10).

In Isaiah 40:10 the language of the Gospel is closely associated with a time in the future when "the Lord God comes with might and his arm **rules for him.**" A verse earlier we read of one **"evangelizing Zion and bringing the Gospel to Jerusalem"** (40:9). The association of the two ideas of "Gospel" and "rule" leads naturally to the concept of the New Testament **"Gospel of the Kingdom of God."** Whenever the biblical text speaks of God becoming King, the Jewish commentaries translate the Hebrew verb "rule" by a noun: "The Kingdom of God will be revealed" (Jewish Targum, i.e., commentary, on Isa. 40:10). So also in Exodus 15:18, "the Lord will reign forever and ever" means that "the Kingdom of the Lord endures forever and ever."

The Old Testament roots of the Kingdom of God must always be taken into account when we confront the Kingdom in the Gospel Message of Jesus. Uprooted from its Hebrew background the Kingdom is indeed a vague term in the minds of many Bible readers. There is a grave risk of placing a meaning on this central Gospel term which will not be the meaning attached to it by Jesus and the Apostles. The result will inevitably be a loss of vital, saving information.

Exactly the same connection between the Gospel and the Kingdom is found in Isaiah 52:7: "How beautiful on the mountains are the feet of him who brings **good tidings**, who publishes peace, who brings good tidings of good, who publishes salvation, who says to Zion, 'Your **God reigns**.'" The context speaks of a public manifestation of the Lord: "The Lord has bared his holy arm before the eyes of all the nations; and all the ends of the earth will see the salvation of our God" (Isa. 52:10). This refers to the Second Coming of Jesus to establish his Kingdom on earth.

These critically important passages, along with the description of the Kingdom of God replacing the empires of the world in Daniel 2:44, convey a clear picture of the Kingdom as a coming **reign or government of God on earth**, to be introduced by a supernatural intervention. It is belief in this stupendous event which Jesus demands with his summons to "Repent and believe the Gospel [of the Kingdom of God]" (Mark 1:14, 15). By so doing we affirm our faith in what God has promised to do. This is the essence of faith and hope. We align ourselves with God's plan by believing in what God is working out on earth through Jesus.

To add to our picture of the Kingdom, we quote further from Isaiah's vision of the bright future:

> For behold, I create new heavens and a new earth; and the former things will not be remembered or come to mind. But be glad and rejoice forever in that which I create; for behold, I create Jerusalem a rejoicing, and her people a joy. I will rejoice in Jerusalem, and be glad in my people; no more will be heard in it the sound of weeping and the cry of distress. No more will there be in it an infant that lives but a few days, or an old man who does not fill out his days, for the child will die a hundred years old, and the sinner a hundred years old will be accursed. They will build houses and inhabit them; they will plant vineyards and eat their fruit. They will not build and another inhabit; they will not plant and another eat; for like the days of a tree will the days of my people be, and my chosen will long enjoy the work of their hands. They will not labor in vain, or bear children for calamity; for they will be the offspring of the blessed of the Lord, and their children

with them. Before they call I will answer; while they are yet speaking I will hear. The wolf and the lamb will feed together, the lion will eat straw like the ox, and dust will be the serpent's food. They will not hurt or destroy in all my holy mountain, says the Lord (Isa. 65:17-25, RSV).

The Gospel of the Kingdom

Throughout the ministry of the Apostles the essential Message of salvation is the "Gospel of the Kingdom and the Name of Jesus Christ" (Acts 8:12). The same message may appear under different names, as "the Gospel of God," "the Gospel of Christ," "the Gospel of Grace," or "the Gospel of Peace." Statistically, by far the most frequent designation of the Gospel is "the Gospel of the Kingdom," as can be seen from the following survey. It should never be forgotten that the Message proclaimed by Jesus himself, the twelve, and the seventy, before the crucifixion, centered on the Kingdom of God. However, the same Message of the Kingdom continued to form the heart of the proclamation after the death and resurrection of Jesus. The evidence from Matthew, Mark, Luke and Acts leaves no room for doubt about the content of the Christian Gospel:

Matt. 4:17: "From that time Jesus began to preach, saying, 'Repent, for the Kingdom of Heaven is at hand.'" (John the Baptist issued the same challenge to repentance and belief in the Gospel of the Kingdom in Matt. 3:2.)

Matt. 4:23: "And he went about all Galilee, teaching in their synagogues and preaching the Gospel of the Kingdom and healing every disease and every infirmity among the people."

Matt. 9:35: "And Jesus went about all the cities and villages, teaching in their synagogues and preaching the Gospel of the Kingdom, and healing every disease and every infirmity."

Matt. 13:19: "When anyone hears the Message of the Kingdom and does not understand it, the evil one comes and snatches away what was sown in his heart."

Matt. 24:14: "And this Gospel of the Kingdom will be preached throughout the whole world, as a testimony to all nations; and then the end will come."

This information demonstrates beyond dispute that the substance of the Gospel Message was, and is, the Kingdom of God.

It is the same Gospel of the Kingdom which remains the saving message until the end of the age (Matt. 24:14).

Mark's Gospel contains 14 occurrences of the term "Kingdom of God." Like Matthew, Mark understands the Gospel of the Kingdom to be the essential saving message: "Now after John was arrested, Jesus came into Galilee, preaching the Gospel of God, and saying, 'The time is fulfilled, and the Kingdom of God is at hand. **Repent and believe the Gospel'**" (Mark 1:14, 15). **Christianity, as taught by Jesus, begins with belief in the Gospel Message about the Kingdom**. Spreading the Gospel meant an extensive proclamation of the Good News about the Kingdom: "Let us go somewhere else to the towns nearby, in order that I make my proclamation; for that is what I was commissioned for" (Mark 1:38).

Luke makes it unmistakably clear that the Good News concerns the Kingdom of God. Fourteen times (Luke 4:43; 8:1; 9:2, 11, 60; 10:9, 11; 16:16; Acts 1:3; 8:12; 19:8; 20:25; 28:23, 31, cited below) he defines the Gospel as the Gospel of the Kingdom:

Luke 4:43: "I must proclaim the Gospel of the Kingdom of God to the other cities also; that is the reason I was sent."

Luke 8:1: "Soon afterwards he went on through cities and villages, preaching and bringing the Gospel of the Kingdom of God."

Luke 9:2: "And he sent them out to proclaim the Kingdom of God."

Luke 9:11: "He welcomed them and spoke to them of the Kingdom of God."

Luke 9:60: "As for you, go and proclaim the Kingdom of God."

Luke 10:9, 11: "Say to them, 'The Kingdom of God has come near to you.'"

Luke 16:16: "The law and the prophets were until John; since then **the Gospel of the Kingdom of God is preached** and everyone is forcing his way into it" (perhaps better translated: "Everyone is solemnly urged to enter it").

Acts 1:3: "He spoke to them of the Kingdom of God [for forty days]."

Acts 8:12: "When they believed Philip as he preached the Gospel about the Kingdom of God and the Name of Jesus, they were baptized, both men and women."

Acts 19:8: "And [Paul] entered the synagogue and for three months spoke boldly, arguing and pleading about the Kingdom of God."

Acts 20:25: "I know that all you among whom I have gone about proclaiming the Kingdom will see my face no more."

Acts 28:23: "And he expounded the matter to them from morning to evening, testifying to the Kingdom of God and trying to convince them about Jesus both from the law of Moses and the prophets."

Acts 28:30, 31: "And he lived there two whole years at his own expense, and welcomed all who came to him, preaching the Kingdom of God and teaching about the Lord Jesus Christ quite openly and unhindered."

In Acts 20:24 Paul summarizes his ministry to the Ephesians as testifying "to the gospel of the grace of God." This he immediately identifies with "preaching about the Kingdom of God" (v. 25). As a recent study of Luke's understanding of the Kingdom rightly states, **"Preaching about the Kingdom sums up the ministry of Jesus, the apostles, disciples and Paul."**[2] The same author says that **"the Christian message can be summarized in the phrase 'Kingdom of God.'"**[3] However, to judge by hundreds of tracts and religious books offering the "gospel," one would never think that the Kingdom of God was the heart of the message, or even part of it at all! The phrases "Kingdom of God" and "Gospel of the Kingdom" are almost entirely missing.

A Suppression of Information?

There is a marked absence of the phrase "Kingdom of God" in places where we would most expect it to be found. A prominent leader of the ecumenical movement, who served as Associate General Secretary of the World Council of Churches, remarks that:

> The Kingdom of God was the central theme of the preaching of Jesus as we find it in the New Testament... And yet it cannot be said that it has been the central theme in the great classical traditions of Christendom. It is not

---

[2] Robert O'Toole, S.J., in *The Kingdom of God in 20th-Century Interpretation*, ed. Wendell Willis, p. 153.
[3] *Ibid.*

mentioned in the Apostles' Creed. The Nicene Creed says of Christ that "his kingdom will have no end," but does not use the phrase Kingdom of God. The main traditions stemming from the Reformation have spoken of "preaching the gospel" or "preaching Christ," *but seldom of "preaching the Kingdom."*[4]

A recent tract issued by the Billy Graham Evangelistic Association bears the title, "What Is the Gospel?" The writer steers clear of the phrase "Gospel of the Kingdom," but tells us that the Gospel is "the Gospel of God," "the Gospel of Christ," "the Gospel of our salvation," and "the Gospel of peace." Mention is made also of the phrase "Gospel of the grace of God" (Acts 20:24), **but, amazingly, the instructive, explanatory phrase which occurs in the very next verse (Acts 20:25) is entirely omitted. Paul here defines the "Gospel of the grace of God" as "the proclamation of the Kingdom"!**

The International Standard Bible Dictionary discusses the term "Gospel," and explains that the term refers to the message which Christ and his Apostles announced. It then points out that:

in some places it is called "the gospel of God" (Mark 1:14; Rom. 1:1; 1 Thess. 2:2, 9; 1 Tim. 1:11). In others it is called "the gospel of Christ" (Mark 1:1; Rom. 1:16; 15:19; 1 Cor. 9:12, 18; Gal. 1:7). In another it is called "the gospel of the grace of God" (Acts 20:24); in another "the gospel of peace" (Eph. 6:15); the gospel of your salvation (Eph. 1:13); and yet another "the glorious gospel" (2 Cor. 4:4, AV).[5]

Despite the fact that the Gospel is directly connected to the term Kingdom, as "the Good News of the Kingdom of God," in some 20 places in Matthew, Mark and Luke, **the dictionary omits entirely to tell us of the phrase** "Gospel of the Kingdom." This extraordinary silence about the Kingdom of God is characteristic of so much that is known as Christian writing (see Lesson 1).

Before proceeding with our examination of the Kingdom of God in the prophets (in Lesson 4), we complete our analysis of the content of the Gospel as preached by the apostolic church in Acts. In Acts 8, Luke uses several parallel phrases to describe the

---

[4] Leslie Newbegin, *Sign of the Kingdom*, p. vii, emphasis added.
[5] p. 1281.

evangelistic activity of the Church. They were "preaching the Message as Good News" (literally, "evangelizing the word," v. 4); Philip "**proclaimed the Christ** to them" (v. 5). Samaria thus "received the **Message of God**" (v. 14). After "they had testified and spoken the Message of the Lord, they returned to Jerusalem, **preaching the Gospel** to many villages of the Samaritans" (v. 25). At the center of this account, however, Luke provides the most comprehensive description of the content of the saving Message. With a carefully worded formula, he lets us know exactly what "**proclaiming the Christ**" or "**proclaiming the Message**" or "**preaching the Gospel**" mean. It is "**preaching the Gospel of [i.e., about, Greek *peri*] the Kingdom of God and the Name of Jesus Christ**" (**Acts 8:12**). This is Luke's fullest summary of the Gospel. He repeats it at two other critically important points in his narrative (Acts 28:23, 31). It defines his other "shorthand" statements and ought to serve as a rallying point for all proclamations of the Gospel. Quite extraordinarily, these texts receive almost no mention in literature defining the Gospel. If they were taken seriously, current "gospels" would be exposed as defective. Another important fact would emerge. The Apostles were no less insistent upon the Kingdom of God as the center of their Message than Jesus had been. They were following their Master faithfully. But can the same be said of evangelism today?

Without an understanding of the phrase "Gospel of the Kingdom," there can be no intelligent response to Jesus' first command. We are required to "**repent and believe the Good News about the Kingdom of God**" (Mark 1:14, 15). All subsequent preaching in the New Testament should be referred to this basic thesis statement about the Gospel of salvation. Cut loose from Jesus' appeal for **belief in the Gospel of the Kingdom**, preaching exposes itself to the menace of a distorted and thus "another gospel." That such a distortion has occurred will not be hard to see. One has only to listen to preachers of "the gospel" to recognize that whatever else they may preach, it is not the Kingdom of God. This can only mean that the principal element of Jesus' proclamation has been silenced. Such a "muzzling" of the Savior, in the name of the Savior, remains the baffling and disturbing feature of contemporary preaching.

"*The Kingdom of God is the central point in Christ's teaching...The fundamental teachings of Jesus naturally group themselves round this central theme.*"[6]

---

[6] *Dictionary of Christ and the Apostles,* Vol. 1, p. 486.

Lesson 4
Intelligent Response to the Good News about the Kingdom

Master Texts:

"Now it will come about that in the last days, the mountain of the house of the Lord will be established as the chief of the mountains, and will be raised above the hills; and all the nations will stream to it. And many peoples will come and say, 'Come, let us go up to the house of the mountain of the Lord, to the house of the God of Jacob; that he may teach us concerning his ways, and that we may walk in his paths.' For instruction will go from Zion, and the word of the Lord from Jerusalem. And he will settle disputes between the nations, and will render decisions for many peoples; and they will hammer their swords into ploughshares, and their spears into pruning hooks. Nation will not lift up sword against nation, and never again will they learn war" (Isa. 2:1-4).

"And in the days of those kings [represented by Daniel's image] the God of heaven will set up a Kingdom which will never be destroyed, and that Kingdom will not be left to another people; it will crush and put an end to all these kingdoms, but it will itself endure forever" (Dan. 2:44).

"He will be great and will be called the Son of the Most High; and the Lord God will give him the throne of his father David [2 Sam. 7:14-16], and he will rule over the house of Jacob forever" (Luke 1:32, 33).

The author of a series of explanatory sermons on "Essential Christianity" asked in 1894:

> Have you seriously pondered the fact that Jesus Christ **was always preaching "the Kingdom of God**," and that in the model prayer which he gave us, he taught us to pray always that his **Kingdom** might come (Matt. 6:10)? In the present day men are always talking about the "Church"...In view of this modern practice, is it not startling to be reminded that in the model prayer there is no reference at

all to the "Church," whilst the reference to the "Kingdom" is prominent and pronounced...? So far as the record goes, Christ referred to the Church only twice...On the other hand, he speaks of the Kingdom not less than one hundred and twelve times.

The same author went on to point out that:

one of the most mischievous and fatal mistakes ever made in Christian history was the mistake of St. Augustine, who identified the Kingdom of God with the Church...But the Church is no more the Kingdom of God than the British army is the British Empire. **It is high time for all Christians to ponder the long-lost teaching of Christ with respect to the Kingdom of God.**[1]

It has been our contention that a loss of clarity regarding the Kingdom of God must directly affect our comprehension of Jesus' Gospel Message — the Christian Gospel. The Kingdom of God is, as we have seen, the principal subject of all that Jesus taught (Luke 4:43, etc.). There can, therefore, be no question of our responding to his call for repentance and belief in the Gospel Message about the Kingdom if we do not know what he meant by the Kingdom of God. Any appeal for us to accept "the Gospel," when no reference to the Kingdom of God appears, must be defective, since it omits an essential part of the saving Message offered by Jesus and the Apostles for belief (Mark 1:14, 15; Luke 4:43; Matt. 4:17; Acts 8:12; 28:23, 31).

If perhaps we have vaguely imagined the Kingdom to be a synonym for the Church, the community of the faithful, we will have to examine the biblical evidence to see if the Kingdom can possibly be confined to a reign of God in the present time, either in our hearts or in the body of believers as a whole. If we have been talking about "heaven" as the goal of the Christian, we will have to begin to speak instead, as Jesus always did, of the Kingdom of God.

The author we cited above went on to tell us about the roots of Jesus' conception of the Kingdom:

I think there can be no doubt where Jesus Christ found and nourished his doctrine of the Kingdom. He found it in the

---

[1] Hugh Price Hughes, M.A., *Essential Christianity*, pp. 57-59, emphasis added.

book of Daniel, and especially in Daniel 7. There are many evidences that the book of Daniel was one of the favorite books of Jesus Christ, one of the books which he diligently and deeply studied during the years of peaceful obscurity in Nazareth before his stormy public ministry began. He makes several references to Daniel, and when the book of Daniel is once understood, it throws quite a flood of light upon the numerous parables in which our Lord described the Kingdom...He declared again and again that the Kingdom was the first object of his life to establish, and, he asserted, it ought to be the first object of our lives to promote. He summed up all our duties in the ever-memorable command to "seek first the Kingdom of God and His righteousness" (Matt. 6:33).[2]

Taking our cue from the book of Daniel, we may easily establish the fact that the Kingdom of God (or Kingdom of Heaven) is a real, external empire. Not only this, it is to be an empire which will seize power suddenly and dramatically from the world's governments which precede it; and it will be administered by "the Son of Man" (Dan. 7:13, 14) and "the saints" (Dan. 7:27). On no account, from the evidence of Daniel, could it be an invisible reign established only in the hearts of believers. Its **political dimension** as well as its location **on earth** is unmistakably clear. It is equally obvious that the Kingdom of God described by Daniel has not yet appeared.

"And in the days of these kings, the God of Heaven will establish a Kingdom [in the New Testament, the Kingdom of God or Kingdom of Heaven] which will never be destroyed, and that Kingdom will not be left for another people; it will crush and put an end to all these kingdoms, but it will itself endure forever" (Dan. 2:44). In the next verse the impact of the Kingdom is likened to a stone crushing the "iron, the bronze, the clay, the silver and the gold" of former world empires. The certainty of this shattering event is based on what "the great God has made known to the king" and what "will take place in the future. The dream is true, and its interpretation is trustworthy" (Dan. 2:45).

To him [the Son of Man — Jesus' favorite self-title] was given dominion, glory and a kingdom, that all the peoples,

---

[2] *Ibid.*, p. 59.

nations, and men of every language might serve him. His dominion is an everlasting dominion which will not pass away; and his Kingdom is one which will not be destroyed...Then the sovereignty and the dominion and the greatness of all the kingdoms under the whole heaven will be given to the people of the saints of the Most High. Their Kingdom will be an everlasting Kingdom and all dominions will serve and obey them (Dan. 7:14, 27, RSV).

The Kingdom of God is evidently an empire, exercising sway over all nations. It will come to power on the earth ("under the whole heaven") and its establishment will be by a catastrophe, an international upheaval resulting in a complete political reorganization. The administration of the Kingdom will be in the hands of "the Son of Man" and "the saints." A recurring theme of the New Testament (but infrequently preached) is that Jesus and his followers will be the executives of the new World Government — the Kingdom of God (Matt. 19:28; Luke 22:28-30; 1 Cor. 6:2; 2 Tim. 2:12; Rev. 2:26; 3:21; 5:10; 20:4). To be a saint in the New Testament is to be one appointed to rule with the Messiah in the coming Kingdom.

Jesus' Announcement of a Coming Crisis

In the light of this background information, Jesus' public proclamation of the nearness of the Kingdom of God must be understood as a warning about a great future crisis in history. The stupendous event foreseen not only by Daniel, but by the other Hebrew prophets, demanded an immediate repentance and reformation of lifestyle. The point of the call for repentance, "for the Kingdom of God is at hand" (Mark 1:14, 15), was simply that a place in the Kingdom would be granted only to those found living in faithful obedience to God. The threatening element in the proclamation of the Gospel can be seen from John the Baptist's appeal for a "U-turn" in conduct, private and national, because the Kingdom of God was "at hand" (Matt. 3:2). Referring to Jesus, John says: "His winnowing fork is in his hand, and he will thoroughly clear his threshing floor; and he will gather his wheat into the barn, but he will burn up the chaff with unquenchable fire" (Matt. 3:12). Matthew describes this Message in exactly the same words as he summarizes the teaching of Jesus. Both agents of God's word, John and Jesus, called for repentance, "for the

Kingdom of God is at hand" (Matt. 3:2; 4:17). The Message contained both a threat and a promise — sudden death as the appalling consequence of persistent unrepentance, and the glory of the Kingdom for those who had heeded the Message and prepared themselves accordingly. This simple theme governs the entire New Testament. There are two possible destinies for human beings — "the barn or the bonfire." Either one enters the Kingdom or one is destroyed. Hence the critical warning element in the Christian Gospel.

Underlying the call for repentance was the well-known concept of the "Day of the Lord" predicted by the Old Testament prophets. This day of terrible divine wrath is equated in the New Testament with the Second Coming of Jesus to establish the promised Kingdom. Thus in the well-known parable of the tares, the good seed are:

> the sons [disciples] of the Kingdom and the tares are the sons of the evil one; and the enemy who sowed them is the Devil, and the harvest is the end of the age; and the reapers are the angels. Therefore, just as the tares are gathered up and burned with fire, so will it be **at the end of the age**. The Son of Man will send forth his angels, and they will gather out of his Kingdom all stumbling blocks, and those who commit lawlessness, and will cast them into the furnace of fire; in that place there will be weeping and gnashing of teeth. Then the righteous will shine forth **in the Kingdom** of their Father. He who has ears to hear let him hear (Matt. 13:38-43).

It is crucial to note that the coming of the Kingdom of God, in which the righteous are to "shine forth as the sun," is placed **at the end of the age**. At the same time as the appearance of the Kingdom, the wicked will be "cast into the furnace of fire." "The Kingdom of their Father" (i.e., the Kingdom of God), in which the righteous appear in glory, is evidently a new order introduced by a judgment at which the wicked perish. The Kingdom in these texts is certainly not a kingdom of the present time, much less a "rule of God in the heart." It has yet to appear at "the end of the age." All of this fits admirably with the Kingdom described by Daniel 2 and 7, and it is evident that Jesus derived his teaching from that book.

These simple facts are confirmed by the context in Daniel from which Jesus' reference to the shining forth of the righteous is taken. The words are part of Daniel's prediction of the resurrection of the dead (Dan. 12:2-3). It is when "many of those who are sleeping in the dust of the ground awake to everlasting life" that the righteous "will shine brightly like the brightness of the expanse of heaven" in the Kingdom of God (Dan. 12:3). We note that the righteous according to Jesus (Matt. 13:43) are "those who cause many to gain understanding and make many righteous" (Dan. 12:3). It is "by his knowledge that the Servant makes many righteous" (Isa. 53:11). These are most important texts describing the Christian life. Knowledge of God's Kingdom plan is an essential basis for the Christian life.

The Kingdom Expected by Jesus' Contemporaries
The Kingdom of God eagerly anticipated by Jesus' fellow countrymen was undoubtedly a New World Order affecting not just a handful of disciples, but the entire earth. The "Day of the Lord," which was to introduce it, would be a cataclysm like the flood because of its destructive power. Yet beyond the awful judgment, a renewed, regenerated earth was to emerge, and sane, peaceful government would ensure a golden age for all permitted to survive into the new Kingdom. Unlike many modern audiences, those who heard Jesus proclaim the Kingdom would have been fully aware of what the prophets had said about the coming great turning point in history:

> The mortal will be humbled, and brought low...Get among the rocks, hide in the dust, at the sight of the terror of Yahweh, at the brilliance of his majesty, when he arises to make the earth quake. Human pride will lower its eyes, the arrogance of men will be humbled, Yahweh alone will be exalted on that day. Yes, that day will be the day of Yahweh Sabaoth [the Lord of the armies of heaven] against all pride and arrogance, against all that is great, to bring it down...Human pride will be humbled, the arrogance of men will be brought low. Yahweh alone will be exalted on that day, and all idols thrown down. Go into the hollows and the rocks, into the caverns of the earth, at the sight of the terror of Yahweh, at the brilliance of his majesty, when he arises to make the earth quake. That day man will fling to the moles and the bats the idols of silver

and the idols of gold that he made for worship (Isa. 2:9-20, Jerusalem Bible).

The hope of a new era of peace on earth, following the fearful Day of the Lord, may be grasped by simply reading what the prophets say. The expectation about the Kingdom, current when Jesus launched his campaign for repentance and belief in the Good News, has been clearly documented by historian and theologian alike. The facts they present provide an indispensable guide to the meaning of Jesus' favorite phrase, "the Kingdom of God." Unless that term is firmly rooted in its first-century Hebrew environment, it becomes quite impossible to know what Jesus requires of us with his call for "repentance and belief in the Gospel about the Kingdom" (Mark 1:14, 15; cp. Acts 1:3; 1:6; 19:8; 20:25; 28:23, 31). Detached from its context, the Kingdom of God has been redefined, with almost total disregard for its biblical meaning, in various different ways acceptable to our own religious ideas and ideals. It is quite wrong, however, to attribute these to Jesus or call them his Gospel. The loss of a proper historical sense for defining the Christian Gospel of the Kingdom lies at the heart of all our theological confusion and division.

One distinguished historian of Christianity describes the historical setting necessary for grasping the impact made by Jesus and John the Baptist's announcement of the Kingdom:

> The expectation of a great deliverance...and of a golden age of righteousness and peace and prosperity, kept alive by the lessons from Scripture which were read and expounded in the synagogues...gave birth from time to time to prophets, who announced that the great moment was come.[3]

With their proclamation, both Jesus and John were calling upon men and women to prepare for the coming divine intervention, the Day of the Lord, which in the New Testament is the equivalent of the expected arrival of the Kingdom. The teaching of Jesus and the Apostles is dominated throughout by the expectation of the coming judgment and the consequent inauguration of the New World Order. Every word of their exhortations is directed towards preparing us for the great event.

---

[3] G.F. Moore, *History of Religions*, p. 107.

The whole New Testament is a manual of instruction for those preparing to rule with Jesus in the coming Kingdom. Apostolic preaching of the Gospel of the Kingdom of God, the Christian Gospel, presupposes an understanding of this Hebrew view of history. Our problem is that audiences are now constantly asked to accept "the Gospel" in ignorance of the Hebrew frame of reference within which Jesus taught. This results in a misunderstanding which can only be corrected when potential converts are taught the basic "vocabulary" of the New Testament. It is no solution to reduce the Gospel to a Message only about the death and resurrection of Jesus. **These events, most certainly, guarantee the future establishment of the Kingdom**; but the Kingdom remains the Kingdom foreseen by the prophets. We are still to pray for its coming (Matt. 6:10). And it is the heart of the Gospel of salvation (Acts 8:12; 28:23, 31; Matt. 13:19; Luke 8:12).

The Longstanding Aversion to the Jewishness of Jesus
Commentators often display their dislike of Jesus, the Christ, when they are confronted with the Savior's Messianic outlook. We can most easily illustrate this antipathy to the Messianic Kingdom (and thus to the Gospel of the Kingdom) by citing a school of thought which denies that the book of Revelation derives its inspiration from Jesus Christ. To scholars of this persuasion, the Revelation was written by one who:

> lives on the learned results of past ages. He has studied books and digested books. He has drawn his great eschatological [relating to the future] system from them...This very human wisdom he produces as if it were God's word, and he tries to conceal from himself his insight into the real origin of the book by making as loud assertions of its divine origin as possible...Thereby his work becomes a memorial of the decay of prophecy...The final act of the drama is described by him in two stages...First of all, after the battle of the Messiah, there is the thousand years' reign of Christ and the martyrs...This is indeed the official Jewish eschatology...We have here the most entire reversion conceivable to the old familiar national Jewish language. The Christian people takes the place of the Jewish, and takes over its contempt for the Gentiles...For such Christians the whole transformation

which Jesus effected of the conception of the Kingdom of God has been in vain.[4] So much for the Jesus of the book of Revelation! According to our quotation, he is just an ignorant Jew. Unfortunately those who belong to this school of thought begin by misunderstanding Jesus and his Message of the Kingdom. They then accuse Jesus (in the Revelation) of contradicting their misconception! It appears that unbelief carries with it an inevitable penalty: "If you will not believe, neither will you understand" (Isa. 7:9, LXX). It is possible to be given over into the power of our own sin.

We cite further evidence of the fact that Jesus' Message in the book of Revelation, and thus his whole Messianic outlook, has been rejected by many.

One book requires notice by reason of its peculiar character and of its influence on Christian eschatology [teaching about the future], namely the Revelation of John...Most of the visions contain so little that is specifically Christian [although given by Jesus Christ!] that it has been seriously questioned whether they were not appropriated entire from Jewish sources with only a superficial adaptation to Christian use. Whatever degree of literary originality may be allowed the author, the matter is Jewish throughout. The resurrection of the saints to enjoy the thousand-year reign of the Messiah; the war of Gog and Magog at the end of the millennium, and their destruction; the general resurrection and the last judgment; the new Jerusalem descending from heaven in all its glitter of gold, even to the river of life and the trees bearing monthly crops of new fruit and medicinal leaves, are the trite ideas and imagery of Jewish eschatology...with its corporeal resurrection and its millennial reign. [These were] brought over into the church, and found acceptance...among ignorant Christians. In the second century millenarian eschatology [belief that the saints will rule with Christ for a thousand years] was orthodoxy in Asia Minor and the wide regions which took their theology from that source; it is the faith of Irenaeus. It has survived

---

[4] Paul Wernle, *The Beginnings of Christianity*, 1903, Vol. I, pp. 364, 372-374, emphasis added.

through all the vicissitudes of theology, and over and over again, has broken out in epidemics of enthusiasm.[5]

We may applaud this excellent summary of what the book of Revelation expects in the future, while marveling at the cavalier fashion in which the great Truths of the New Testament are dismissed as non-Christian and Jesus' vision is dismissed as "trite."

It is a little-known fact that the "founding fathers" of large sections of Protestant Christianity also found the Message of Jesus recorded in the Revelation unacceptable:

> Luther at first (Preface in Translation of New Testament, 1522) expressed a strong aversion to the book [of Revelation], declaring that to him it had every mark of being neither prophetic nor apostolic...He cannot see that it was the work of the Holy Spirit. Moreover, he does not like the commands and threats which the writer makes about his book (22:18, 19), and the promise of blessedness to those who keep what is written in it (1:3; 22:7), when no one knows what that is, to say nothing of keeping it, and there are many nobler books to be kept. Moreover, many Fathers rejected the book..."Finally everyone thinks of it whatever his spirit imparts. My spirit cannot adapt itself to this book, and a sufficient reason why I do not esteem it highly is that Christ is neither taught nor recognized in it, which is what an Apostle ought before all things to do."
>
> Later (1534) Luther finds a possibility of Christian usefulness in the book...but he still thought it a hidden, dumb prophecy unless interpreted, and upon the interpretation no certainty had been reached after many efforts...He remained doubtful about its apostolicity, and (in 1545) printed it with Hebrews, James and Jude as an appendix to his New Testament, not numbered in the index...Zwingli [a leading Reformer] regarded Revelation as "not a Biblical book," and even Calvin, with his high view of inspiration, does not comment on 2 and 3 John and Revelation.[6]

---

[5] G.F. Moore, *History of Religions*, pp. 144, 145, emphasis added.

[6] "Revelation," *Hastings Dictionary of the Bible*, Vol. IV, p. 241.

Readers should reflect on the remarkable fact that churches have continued to give their allegiance to Calvin and Luther, despite the former's hesitancy about the Apocalypse and the latter's obvious refusal to heed the warnings of Jesus given in the Revelation:

> I testify to everyone who hears the words of the prophecy of this book, if anyone adds to these things, God will add to him the plagues written in the book; and if anyone takes away from the words of the prophecy, God will take away his part out of the book of life, and out of the holy city, and from the things which are written in this book (Rev. 22:18, 19). Blessed is he who keeps the sayings of the prophecy of this book. Blessed is he who reads and they who hear the words of this prophecy and keep the things which are written in it: for the time is at hand (Rev. 1:3).

This hardly sounds as if the book could be safely relegated to an appendix!

The book of Revelation, as is well recognized, draws together the strands of Old Testament prophecy and describes the establishment of the Kingdom of God on earth at the Second Coming of Jesus. It is the fitting climax to the expectations of both Old and New Testament, depicting the triumph of the Kingdom of God over a hostile world.

The Kingdom of God announced by Jesus will finally come to power on earth when the seventh angel sounds:

> **The kingdoms of this world [note that none of the present nations are the Kingdom of God now] have become the kingdoms of our Lord and of His Messiah; and he will reign forever and ever...We give you thanks, O Lord God Almighty, who is, and was and is to come; because you have assumed power and have** *begun to reign.* **[Cp. Ps. 97:1 and 99:1, "The Lord has** *begun to reign.***"]** And the nations were angry and your wrath has come, and the time of the dead that they should be judged, and that you should give reward to your servants the prophets, and to the saints, and to those who fear your name, small and great; and should destroy those who destroy the earth (Rev. 11:15-18).

This is the Kingdom of God announced in the Gospel Message, and the Kingdom for which Christians are to pray, "Thy

Kingdom come!" It is not widely recognized that in so praying, Christians anticipate the overthrow of human governments, in order that peace and harmony may prevail across the globe. One fact is unmistakably clear in the New Testament: the Kingdom of God will come only as a result of a divine intervention bringing to an end the "present evil age" (Gal. 1:4).

An Anti-Messianic Tendency

The rejection of the book of Revelation points to a deeply rooted anti-Messianic tendency in much traditional theology. When commentators assess the Revelation as unchristian, attempt to remove it from the canon of Scripture, or "reinterpret" it to avoid its "Jewish" millennial prophecy, they display their dislike of the Jesus whose all-consuming concern was to bring peace to the earth and justice for all through his Kingdom.

The real Jesus never abandoned the prophets' hope for Messianic government on earth. He knew, however, that the triumph of the Kingdom must await his Second Coming in glory. Thus in the New Testament the Day of the Lord is expected to arrive when Jesus returns "in flaming fire taking vengeance on those who do not know God" (2 Thess. 1:7). Then the Kingdom will come; then the hopes of all the ages will reach fulfillment; then only can the agonized cry, "How long, O Lord?" find its answer. It is to this Messianic future that the New Testament strains in verse after verse. (Someone has calculated that the Second Coming is mentioned over 300 times in the New Testament. The number is much higher when synonyms for the return of Jesus are taken into account.) Once, however, the tension line between the believer and the bright future in the Kingdom is slackened, the vitality of the faith is lost and the point of discipleship is destroyed. At present, churchgoers often lack that essential drive to reach the promised Kingdom. They have not been told what that Kingdom is. So many of their mentors seem to have no coherent view of the Christian future. There is a blank throughout the last chapter of their book, needing to be filled with all the riches of the Biblical hope for the reign of Christ on earth.

A Future with No Substance

The prospect of the coming reign of Christ and the faithful on earth is part and parcel of the Gospel Message, inextricably linked with the sacrificial death of Jesus and his resurrection (Acts 8:12; 28:23, 31). Tragically many who claim to be Christians disparage the Hope of the coming Kingdom by treating it as disposable, a relic of a primitive mentality which we, with our vastly superior scientific outlook, could not think of embracing. In so doing they place the Christian doctrine of the Kingdom under a fog. The Christian future is reduced to a meaningless non-event, rather than a stupendous climax in history for which all are commanded to prepare. The fact that not everyone will survive until the coming of Jesus in power is no excuse for neglecting the teaching about the Messiah's return. The date of that return is known to no one. Those believers who have died before the end of the age will take part in the glory of the Kingdom through resurrection (1 Thess. 4:13; 1 Cor. 15:23, Rev. 11:15-18).

The following inquiry was addressed to a representative of the clergy in a Presbyterian magazine. The response illustrates the unwillingness of many to face the stark reality of Jesus' warnings about the future:

Q. Why are there so few sermons in our churches on the second coming? Is this part of our belief or not?

A. Not all Christians think alike on matters of theology, but it would be hard for someone to feel at home in our tradition, who did not understand God as the One who has come, who is present (Christ is risen) and who is yet to come in whatever form the future winds up taking. To literalize the second coming is to ruin both its beauty and its significance. To ignore it is to avoid what may be the most important part of the Gospel we know about since the past and the present, relatively speaking, are brief, while tomorrow borders on the forever.

An appropriate reaction to this answer appeared in a later issue of the magazine:

I compliment the Rev.____ for his illusive non-answer to what I am sure was a serious question concerning the second coming of Jesus Christ. If I understand his answer, he said, in effect, "We don't all agree. But if you want to be comfortable in our fellowship, you will need to agree that Jesus is coming again, but not really — for if you actually believe in the second coming you will ruin both its beauty and its significance. Yet you can't ignore it because it is in the future." Why not a simple answer? Why not admit that those who cannot receive the Bible literally must spiritualize the second coming because it is too large a segment of the New Testament to be ignored?

This approach to the New Testament doctrine about the future is typical of much of what has gone under the name of Christian teaching over many centuries. It has been hard for many to detect the trick being played with words, when an outright rejection of the biblical doctrine of the Kingdom is veiled by impressive "theological" language. What much traditional theology has done to the Second Coming should not be graced with the term "spiritualize." It has evaporated the return of Christ. The whole vision of the prophets and the whole Gospel of the Kingdom is in jeopardy if its dominant future element is removed. Even the Gospel proposed by many evangelicals suffers from the same absence of any future reference. Here is how they define evangelism:

> To evangelize is to spread the good news that Jesus Christ died for our sins, and was raised from the dead according to the Scriptures, and that as reigning Lord he now offers the forgiveness of sins and the liberating gift of the spirit to all who repent and believe.[7]

This appears to us to lack essential elements of the Gospel as Jesus taught it. Jesus preached the Gospel about the Kingdom and only later added information about his death and resurrection. Jesus spoke of responding to the Gospel Message of the Kingdom as the essential first step for salvation and immortality. He taught that the seed of immortality was found in the Gospel of the Kingdom of God (see Matt. 13:19; Luke 8:12; 1 Pet. 1:21-25).

The Future Kingdom of the Gospel

The urgent demand by Jesus to "repent and believe the Good News of the Kingdom" (Mark 1:14, 15. Why doesn't Gospel preaching begin with this verse?) implies an understanding of the term "Kingdom of God." While Jesus' leading phrase remains unclear, the Gospel itself is obscured. Perhaps it is this uncertainty over the meaning of Jesus' proclamation about the Kingdom that

---

[7] The Lausanne Covenant, International Congress on World Evangelization, Lausanne, Switzerland, July, 1974.

has caused evangelicals to drop all reference to the Kingdom of God in their definition of the Gospel, and to rely on what they think is a full account of the saving Message: the death, burial and resurrection of Jesus. It is customary to appeal to Paul's words in 1 Corinthians 15:1-5:

> Now I make known to you, brethren, the gospel which I preached to you, which also you received, in which also you stand, by which also you are being saved, if you hold fast the message which I preached to you, unless you believed in vain. For I delivered to you as of first importance [literally "among the first," NASV margin] what I also received, that Christ died for our sins, according to the Scriptures, and that he was buried, and that he was raised on the third day according to the Scriptures, and that he appeared to Cephas and then to the twelve...Whether then it was I or they, so we preached and so you believed.

An important key to understanding Paul's fine statement about his own Gospel Message is found in the little phrase *en protois*, "amongst things of primary importance" (v. 3). The point is that it was the resurrection of Jesus which some of the Corinthians were beginning to doubt: "How do some among you say there is no resurrection of the dead?" (1 Cor. 15:12). In response to *this particular crisis of belief*, Paul reminds his audience that the death and resurrection of Jesus are of absolutely fundamental significance in the Christian Gospel. Without the death of Jesus to gain forgiveness for all of us, and without his return from death to life through resurrection, there can be no hope of salvation in the coming Kingdom.

It is a dangerous mistake, however, to argue from this text that the facts about Jesus' death and resurrection formed the whole Message of the Gospel. Paul is careful to say that these central facts were preached "amongst things of primary importance" (v. 3). This, however, was not the entire Gospel. There were other things also, of equal importance in the Gospel, namely the announcement about the Kingdom of God (Acts 8:12; 19:8; 20:25; 28:23, 31). We recall that Jesus had proclaimed the Kingdom long before he spoke of his death and resurrection (Luke 4:43; cp. Luke 18:31-34) — a fact which proves that the Kingdom of God is not a synonym for the death and resurrection of Christ.

Furthermore, it is evident that Paul was not here directly addressing the subject of the Kingdom of God as a future event coinciding with the return of Jesus. The Corinthians had accepted that belief as part of the Gospel of salvation. Thus Paul is able to elaborate on the doctrine of the Kingdom only a few verses later. Having just mentioned the future coming of Jesus (v. 23), he speaks of the Kingdom over which Jesus will preside at his coming (vv. 25-27). That Kingdom, it should be carefully noted, is the Kingdom into which "flesh and blood" cannot enter, for "the perishable cannot inherit the imperishable" (v. 50). In order to enter the Kingdom of God, Christians must be summoned from death at the last trumpet and be changed, in the twinkling of an eye, into immortal persons (vv. 51, 52). These verses confirm, once again, the fact that the Kingdom of God comes into power at the Second Coming.

The Kingdom has a principal place in the New Testament Gospel Message in addition, of course, to the equally essential preaching of the death and resurrection of the Savior. It is a serious mishandling of the Bible to place 1 Corinthians 15:1-5 in conflict with the massive evidence for the central importance of the Kingdom of God in the pre- and post-resurrection proclamation (Luke 4:43; Mark 1:14, 15; Matt. 4:17; Acts 8:12; 19:8; 20:25; 28:23, 31, etc.). Once again we must emphasize the importance of Acts 8:12 (echoed in Acts 28:23, 31) as Luke's comprehensive summary statement about the Gospel Message: "When they believed Philip as he preached the Good News about the Kingdom of God and the Name of Jesus Christ, they were being baptized, both men and women" (cp. Matt. 13:19; Luke 8:12).

Contemporary Statements About the Gospel
A definition of the Gospel was offered by the Lausanne Conference on Evangelism in 1974 (cited above). It speaks of the forgiveness of sins through the death of Jesus, of his resurrection and of his present reign in heaven. **It says nothing, however, about the Kingdom of God as the goal of the Christian believer.** The future dimension of salvation, so prominent in the New Testament, is absent. This absence of the Kingdom appears to cut the Gospel Message in half, stripping it of its strong emphasis of God's plan to send His Son **back to the earth to reign with his followers in the Messianic government** promised by the

prophets. The New Testament Gospel does not deal only with the past and the present, but with the past, present and future. One may, however, search contemporary statements of the gospel message (tracts, books and appeals on radio and television) in vain for any reference to the future activity of Jesus Christ. Yet Jesus' focus in the Gospel directs us towards the ultimate goal, the gaining of a place not "in heaven," but in the Kingdom of God on earth (Dan. 7:27). It would be difficult to see how the Christian objective could have been more plainly defined than in the following verses: "Blessed are the meek, for they will inherit the earth" (Matt. 5:5). "You have made them to be a Kingdom and priests to our God, and they will reign on the earth" (Rev. 5:10).

The Gospel Hope
       The loss of the Kingdom of God from the Christian Gospel stems from the loss of the biblical view about the future which formed so vital a part of original Christianity. For centuries churchgoers have been persuaded that the ultimate goal of their commitment to Christ is to "go to heaven" when they die. This notion is fundamentally unbiblical. It undermines the need for the coming of the Kingdom of God on earth at the return of Jesus. In the New Testament, hope (the second of the trio of Christian virtues, faith, hope and love) is directed towards the glorious Messianic future. "Hope may be defined as desire of future good, accompanied by faith in its realization...**Faith** has regard equally to past, present and future, **while no doubt in Scripture referring mainly to the future. Hope is directed only to the future.**"[8]
       A clear hope was instilled into the mind of the believer when he heard the Gospel message about the Kingdom: "We heard of your faith in Christ Jesus, and the love which you have for all the saints, *because of* the hope laid up for you in heaven, of which you previously heard in the word of truth, the gospel...just as you learned it from Epaphras" (Col. 1:4-7). "In Christ, also, after listening to the message of the truth, the gospel of your salvation — having also believed, you were sealed with the holy spirit of promise, which is given us as a downpayment of our inheritance" (Eph. 1:13, 14). A few verses later Paul prays that "the eyes of your heart may be enlightened, so that you may know what is the

---

[8] "Hope," *Hastings Dictionary of the Bible*, Vol. I, p. 583.

hope of his calling, what is the wealth of the glory of his **inheritance** in the saints" (Eph. 1:18). It is critically important for believers to know that they are invited to rule with Messiah on earth in the coming New Order.

In these verses it becomes clear that the future hope was part of Paul's Gospel. Apostolic evangelism went beyond the promise of the forgiveness of sins and faith in Jesus' death and resurrection. It put before the convert the promise of inheriting the Kingdom of God at the return of Christ. A Gospel message, therefore, which is not pledged to the future fact of God's coming intervention to overthrow all human government and grant the Kingdom to the Church, is not the Gospel of the New Testament. The hope which the Colossians learned when they heard the Gospel is of such significance that Paul speaks of their love and faith which "spring from the hope" (NIV). It is "because of the hope" (Col. 1:5, NASV) prepared for them in heaven that the Colossians are to develop faith and love in the spirit. We should note that their hope of inheriting the Kingdom of God is "laid up in heaven." This is typical of the Jewish belief that all the good things of the future are already prepared in heaven for the faithful, waiting to be revealed on earth at the coming of the Messiah (see 1 Pet. 1:4, 5). It remains, therefore, a fact that Christian hope is directed, not towards "going to heaven" at death, but "inheriting the earth" (Matt. 5:5), and ruling in it (Rev. 5:10) when Christ returns. The Kingdom is prepared in heaven. But it will appear on the earth when Jesus returns.

We are not going to leave the earth for heaven! The exact opposite: Jesus is going to leave heaven and come back to the earth.

In the light of these facts, we suggest that the Lausanne Convention's definition of evangelism needs modification as follows:

> To evangelize is to spread the Good News that God has planned as the goal of history to establish His Kingdom on the earth when Jesus returns; that Jesus now offers forgiveness through faith in his Kingdom Gospel and his atoning death and resurrection. For all those who believe the Gospel message and obey him (Acts 5:32) he grants the promise of his spirit now as a "down-payment" to empower them in the present life in preparation for

positions of rulership with Christ in the Kingdom to be inaugurated at his return.

In this way the apostolic orientation towards the future Kingdom is incorporated into the Gospel, reflecting the New Testament pattern.

The Urgent Need to Recover the Gospel Framework

The Message of Jesus is set within a Jewish, Old Testament framework (which Jesus did not come to overthrow! Matt. 5:17). He came to bring the ultimate meaning to the Law, not just to repeat it in the letter. Unlike many modern Bible readers, Jesus believed the message of the prophets and, with them, longed for the fulfillment of their united vision of a coming Kingdom of peace. The appeal to us likewise to believe the prophets is built into Jesus' Gospel Message. We are urged to repent and believe the Gospel of the Kingdom (Mark 1:14, 15). This is where New Testament Gospel preaching begins. It is a call for belief in God's plan, not only to give His Son as the sacrificial lamb to die for the sins of the world, but also to send him back to reign in his Kingdom (Acts 3:21; 2 Tim. 4:1).

Christianity, in New Testament terms, is a challenge to prepare now for participation in the Kingdom which will be introduced by a supernatural upheaval when Jesus returns. Let the scientifically-minded read the New Testament with this simple scheme in mind, testing the evidence, and the Scriptures will be become clear. But once the Kingdom of God is "reinterpreted" (a thoroughly deceptive way of rejecting it while pretending not to!) to mean only a religious ideal now, with a promise of "heaven at death," the clarity of the New Testament is lost. *One simply cannot remove the Jewish apocalyptic framework in which the Christian Gospel is set without collapsing the whole Message.* The absence of the word "Kingdom" from modern presentations of "the Gospel" witnesses to the loss of essential saving information. As a learned scholar of the Church of England remarked, "When the Greek and Roman mind in turn, instead of the Hebrew mind, came to dominate the Church, there occurred a disaster in belief and practice from which we have never recovered, either in doctrine or in practice."[9]

---

[9] Canon H. Goudge, "The Calling of the Jews," in *Essays on Judaism and Christianity.*

Recovery will begin when Jesus' and Paul's Gospel Message of the Kingdom is reinstated.

> *That the central theme of the teaching of Jesus is the announcement of the Kingdom of God is beyond dispute...The Good Tidings, the Gospel, is precisely that the Kingdom of God is at hand: there is no doubt on this point...The Gospel is to the Kingdom what an invitation is to a feast.*[10]

---

[10] Charles Guignebert, Professor of the History of Christianity, *Jesus*, pp. 325, 326.

Lesson 5
The Kingdom of God — God's Plan
in World History

Master Texts:

"God said to Abraham...'Look all around you from where you are toward the north and the south, toward the east and the west. All the land within sight I will give to you and your descendants forever...Come travel through the length and breadth of the land, for I mean to give it to you'" (Gen. 13:14-17).

"God said to Abraham, 'Here now is my covenant with you: you will become the father of a multitude of nations. You will no longer be called Abram, your name will be Abraham...I will make you into nations, and your issue will be kings. I will establish my covenant between myself and you, and your descendants after you, generation after generation, a covenant in perpetuity, to be your God and the God of your descendants after you. I will give to you and your descendants after you the land you are living in, the whole land of Canaan, to own in perpetuity, and I will be your God" (Gen. 17:3-8).

"And the Scripture, foreseeing that God would justify the Gentiles by faith, preached the Gospel beforehand to Abraham, saying, 'All the nations will be blessed in you'" (Gal. 3:8).

"If you [Israel] obey my voice and hold fast to my covenant, you of all the nations will be my very own, for all the earth is mine. I will count you a kingdom of priests, a consecrated nation" (Ex. 19:5- 6).

"If you are a Christian, then you count as descendants of Abraham and you are heirs of the promises [made to Abraham]" (Gal. 3:29).

Kingship and possession of the land of Palestine formed the basis of God's covenant between Himself and the chosen people, represented initially by Abraham. The royal function of Israel depended, however, on their obedience. How far they succeeded in living up to the high ideal demanded of them is documented in the

Old Testament history of the Israelites. It was often a story of failure to meet God's standard, David being the exceptional example (despite some lapses) of rulership exercised in cooperation with God. The prophets of Israel were also fine models of obedience to God and service in His great Kingdom plan.

As we have seen, Israel's national hope, kept burning even in times of oppression by their enemies, was that the ultimate ideal King, the Messiah, would eventually bring about the golden age of world peace so vividly predicted by the prophets. With the dawning of that great day, the Kingdom of God would come. We know that prayers for the advent of the Kingdom were being offered continuously in the synagogue at the time when Jesus began to preach. It is impossible not to notice the close affinity of this prayer with "the Lord's prayer": "Magnified and sanctified be his great name in the world which he has created according to his will. May he establish his Kingdom in your lifetime and in your days and in the lifetime of all the house of Israel, even speedily and at a near time."

As a distinguished German theologian says, "the true background to Jesus' teaching is to be found in...Jewish thought concerning God as ruler, and upon his Kingdom as the manifestation of his kingly activity."[1]

> Weiss claims that this is the dominant emphasis in the Old Testament, and he shows that such an emphasis carries with it the thought of conflict with a worldly or human kingship. The conception is that God will demonstrate his kingship by an act of judgment against the worldly kingship. Against this background we can see that it was natural for the prophets...when they proclaimed the great crisis that was to come, to do this in the form of a proclamation of the coming of a mighty act of God as king. The hope expressed in [the prophets] is for the coming of a mighty kingly activity of God whereby his people would be redeemed, his enemies and theirs destroyed, and the present evil state of things [cp. Gal. 1:4, "this present evil age"] totally and forever reversed...It is

---

[1] John Weiss, *Jesus' Preaching of the Kingdom of God*, 1892.

this hope which lies behind Jesus' usage of the term Kingdom of God.[2]

Man Destined to Be Ruler

The subject of the Christian Gospel, the Kingdom of God, has its roots deep in the Hebrew Scriptures (somewhat unfortunately known to us as "the Old Testament," since many professing Christians think of "old" as practically equivalent to "discarded"). It is well to remember that Paul referred to the Old Testament as the "sacred writings which are able to give you [Christians] the wisdom which leads to salvation through faith which is in Messiah Jesus" (2 Tim. 3:15). To be a Christian, therefore, we must acquire the wisdom and understanding found in the sacred revelations of the Hebrew part of our Scriptures.

The very first command given to man was to "rule...over all the earth" (Gen. 1:26). We see here the start of the golden thread of the Kingdom which runs throughout the Bible from Genesis to Revelation. Adam was assigned a position as God's vice-regent. Made in the image and likeness of God (Gen. 1:26), man is a "facsimile" of God, a representation which corresponds to a model. The word "image" means "a hewn or carved statue such as an idol," a sculpture. Both "'image' and 'likeness' are expressions which...point back from man to God...God shows himself as the 'prototype' and 'original' of man."[3]

The psalmist sings of the exalted position conferred upon man by God: "What is man, that you are mindful of him? And the son of man, that you visit him? For you have made him but little lower than God, and crowned him with glory and honor. You make him to have dominion over the works of your hands; you have put all things under his feet" (Ps. 8:4-6). Honor and majesty are the attributes of a king (Ps. 96: 6, 10, 13: "Clothed with honor and majesty, God is coming to rule the world"). Man, therefore, is created to be God's representative ruler on earth. The problem is that "we do not yet see all things subjected to him" (Heb. 2:8). But man is once again going to rule the world properly when Jesus comes back as the promised second Adam.

---

[2] Norman Perrin, *The Kingdom of God in the Teaching of Jesus*, p. 19, discussing the work of John Weiss.

[3] Friedrich Horst, "Face to Face," *Interpretation*, July, 1950, p. 260.

The Hope for Just Government on Earth

The tension between the "present evil state of things" (Gal. 1:4) and the hope of the coming Kingdom of God gives a sense of excitement and drama to the whole Bible. A coherent "plot" runs throughout the Scriptures. Adam is created with a divine office. He "sells out" to Satan after being outwitted by the cunning of the Devil (the arch-villain of the drama). The first pair thus "vote for" the evil ruler, and this tendency to submit to Satan is perpetuated in subsequent generations. The accumulating rebellion reaches a crisis in Genesis 6, where evil angelic beings ("sons of God," cp. Ps. 29:1; 89:6; Dan. 3:25; Job 38:7; Job 1:6; 2:1) interfere with the human genetic system to produce a race of giants. This terrible condition on earth calls for a world catastrophe at the Flood, in which only eight persons survive the judgment. The descendants of Noah do no better than their predecessors. A second race of tyrants is born of the hybrid angelic-human "marriages" (Gen. 6:4; Num. 13:33; see also Jude 6; 2 Pet. 2:4).

The divine solution for rescuing man from his apparently incorrigible wickedness lies in the promise of the "seed of Abraham" (Christ, Gal. 3:16). The hope for ultimate deliverance from Satanic governments (2 Cor. 4:4: Satan is the "god of this age") will be fulfilled only when the "seed of the woman" (Gen. 3:15) puts an end forever to our present (evil) world systems. This will happen when ownership of the earth passes to its rightful heirs, Christ and his faithful followers. Dominion over the earth was destined for man in Genesis. That rule will become a reality when the second Adam — man as he was intended to be — takes over the "kingdoms of this world" (Rev. 11:15) and "rules in the midst of his enemies" (Ps. 110:2). With the Messiah at that inauguration of a new world government will be "those who volunteer freely in the day of [Messiah's] power" (Ps. 110:3). His freshly invigorated people, enjoying new life as resurrected, immortal beings, will assist Jesus in his task of establishing the new society on earth. (All contemporary "New Age" movements and groups promoting the dominion of the Church *prior to* the return of Christ are dangerous perversions of the biblical scheme for bringing peace to the world.)

Abraham, the Land and Kingship

The promise of the land (Gen. 13:14-17, above) as a possession was made to Abraham on condition that he give up everything in obedience to God (Gen. 12:1-4). Abraham, "the father of the faithful," is the "model Christian," demonstrating his faith in the unseen God. He is commended for his confidence that despite every evidence to the contrary (Rom. 4:18), he would indeed be the "father" of the promised Messiah. His inheritance included the Kingdom of God which was nothing less than the promised land, extended beyond the boundaries of Palestine to the far corners of the earth: "For the promise to Abraham or to his seed that he would be heir of the world was not through the law but through the righteousness of faith" (Rom. 4:13).

The paraphrase given by the *International Critical Commentary* on Romans gives the sense exactly:

> The promise made to Abraham and his descendants of worldwide Messianic rule, as it was not dependent on circumcision, so also was not dependent on Law, but on a righteousness that was a product of faith. If this worldwide inheritance really depended on any legal system, and if it was limited to those who were under such a system, there would be no place left for faith or promise.[4]

"The worldwide Messianic rule" is a synonym for the Kingdom of God, which is the principal theme of the Christian Gospel (Luke 4:43; Mark 1:14, 15; Acts 8:12; 19:8; 20:25; 28:23, 31, etc.). It must follow that Jesus and the Apostles announced "the worldwide Messianic rule" when they proclaimed the Gospel. It is a rule waiting to be publicly manifested at the Second Coming. All attempts to force it into the present (except in the sense that the power and spirit of the future Kingdom are already active in advance because Jesus now sits at the right hand of the Father) are dislocations of the biblical scheme and account for the massive confusion which exists on the subject of the Kingdom (and thus about Christianity itself). We are to pray "Thy Kingdom come." This means that the Kingdom has not yet come!

Acts 7:5 states simply that Abraham, during his lifetime, did not receive "a square foot" of his inheritance, yet God promised him that he would receive it: "God promised that He would it give

---

[4] p. 109.

it to him and to his descendants after him." Heb. 11:8-13 should be read carefully:

> By faith Abraham, when he was called, went out to *a place* which he was to receive for an inheritance...By faith he lived in *the land of promise*, as in a foreign land, dwelling in tents with Isaac and Jacob, fellow heirs of the same promise...All these died in faith without receiving the promises...They were looking for the city which is to come (Heb. 11:8-13; 13:14). (Note that the city is coming to the earth: the patriarchs did not go to it!)

It should be most carefully noted that the patriarchs lived in *the place which was promised to them* (Heb. 11:8, 9) — the place which they would one day inherit. That place was not a "realm beyond the skies" but a land situated on the earth. It is the earth which is destined to be ruled by God's people. The grand central theme of all Scripture is the promise that ideal government will be brought to the earth when Jesus, as Messiah, seed of Abraham and David (Matt. 1:1), returns to rule. It is time for Bible readers to "hear" and grasp the significance of their calling as "children of Abraham," "coheirs" and prospective "co-rulers" with the Messiah:

Matt. 5:5: "Blessed are the gentle, for they will inherit the earth."

Rev. 5:10: "You have made them to be a Kingdom and priests to our God and they will reign on the earth."

Rev. 20:4: "They came to life [in resurrection] and ruled as kings with Messiah for a thousand years."

2 Tim. 2:12: "If we suffer with him we will reign as kings with him."

1 Cor. 3:21: "All things belong to you."

Heb. 2:5: "God has not subjected to angels the inhabited earth of the future, which is our theme [but he has subjected it to Jesus and his followers]."

Ps. 115:16: "The heavens are the heavens of the Lord, but the earth he has given to the children of men."

Rev. 2:26: "He who overcomes will rule the nations." Luke 19:17: "Take charge of ten cities." Matt. 25:23: "Rule over many things."

Ps. 112:1, 2; 111:6; 113:7, 8: "How blessed is the man who fears the Lord...His descendants will be mighty on earth...He has made known to his people the power of his works by giving them the heritage of the nations...He raises the poor from the ash heap to make them sit with princes, with the princes of his people."

1 Thess. 2:12: "Walk in a manner worthy of God who is calling you into His own Kingdom and glory."

Emphasis should be placed on the fact that it is the "gentle" who are destined for this bright future. Those believers who continue to threaten their enemies and fellow believers in other lands with nuclear extinction should question whether they belong to the category of which Jesus speaks. Even King David was disqualified from building the temple because as a man of war he had taken the lives of others (1 Chron. 28:3). There is an important lesson here for the Christian Church.

The "sermon on the mount" sets out the qualities of character and behavior required in those who hope to inherit the Kingdom. Obedience through the spirit is demanded by Jesus: "Everyone who hears these words of mine and acts on them will be like a wise man who built his house on a rock" (Matt. 7:24).

A popular form of so-called "dispensationalist" theology menacingly declares that the "sermon on the mount is not church Truth precisely."[5] It would be hard to think of a more glaring contradiction of the words of Jesus than this. We must state plainly that the "sermon on the mount" is precisely truth for the Christian Church, truth without which it is impossible to enter the Kingdom. John the Apostle was well aware of teaching which claimed to be "Christian" while it denied what Jesus taught: "If anybody does not keep within the teaching of Christ but goes beyond it, he cannot have God with him; only those who keep to what he taught can have the Father and the Son with them" (2 John 9).

In this connection the words of a Quaker leader, writing in 1676, may help put the point clearly:

> Whoever can reconcile this, "Resist not evil" with "Resist evil by force"; again, "Give also thy other cheek," with "spoil them, make a prey of them, pursue them with fire and sword"; or "Pray for those who persecute you" with "Persecute them by fines, imprisonment, and death itself." Whoever can find a means to reconcile those things, may be supposed also to have found a way to reconcile God

---

[5] John Walvoord, *Commentary on Matthew.*

with the Devil, Christ with Anti-Christ, light with darkness and good with evil.[6]

The Kingdom of God Seen by the Prophets

In previous lessons we have quoted extensively from the Hebrew prophets to show that they spoke constantly of a coming time of peace for mankind under the supervision of the Messiah, God's chosen King. The great turning point in history will occur when Jesus "returns in the same way as he departed to heaven" (Acts 1:11). Every word of the New Testament is designed to exhort us to maximum effort, as we prepare for the event destined to effect the greatest ever change in world politics.

Ezekiel writes of a time when God will:

> take the sons of Israel from the nations where they have gone. I will gather them together from everywhere and bring them home to their own soil. I will make them into one nation in my own land and on the mountains of Israel, and one King is to be King of them all; they will no longer from two nations, nor be two separate kingdoms. They will no longer defile themselves with their idols and their filthy practices and all their sins. I will rescue them from all the betrayals they have been guilty of; I will cleanse them; they will be my people and I will be their God. My servant David will reign over them, one shepherd for all; they will follow my observances, respect my laws and practice them. They will live in the land that I gave my servant Jacob, the land in which your ancestors lived. They will live in it, they, their children, their children's children, forever. David, my servant, is to be their prince forever. I will make a covenant of peace, an eternal covenant with them. I will resettle them and increase them. I will settle my sanctuary among them forever (Ezek. 37:21-26).

> Mountains of Israel, you will grow branches and bear fruit for my people, who will soon return. Yes, I am coming to you. I have turned to you. You will be tilled and sown. I will multiply the men who live on you, the whole House of Israel, yes, all. The cities will be lived in again and the ruins rebuilt. I will multiply the men and the

---

[6] Robert Barclay.

animals that live on you; there will be many of them and they will be fertile. I will repopulate you as you were before; I will make you more prosperous than you were before, and so you will learn that I am Yahweh. Thanks to me, men will tread your soil again, my people Israel. They will have you for their own domain, and never again will you rob them of their children...I will never again let you hear the insults of the nations; you will never again have to hear the taunts of the foreigners...It is the Lord Yahweh who speaks (Ezek. 36:8-15, Jerusalem Bible).

Hosea's vision of the glorious future of Israel is no less inspiring and clear. First God urges the people to repent:

Israel, come back to Yahweh your God; your iniquity was the cause of your downfall. Provide yourself with words and come back to Yahweh. Say to Him, "Take all iniquity away so that we may have happiness again and offer you our words of praise. Assyria cannot save us; we will not ride horses any more, or say 'our God' to what our own hands have made, for you are the one in whom orphans find compassion." I will heal their disloyalty. I will love them with all my heart, for my anger has turned from them. I will fall like dew on Israel. He will bloom like the lily, and thrust out roots like the poplar; his shoots will spread far; he will have the beauty of the olive and the fragrance of Lebanon. They will come back to live in my shade; they will grow corn that flourishes; they will cultivate vines as renowned as the wine of Helbon. What has Ephraim to do with idols any more when it is I who hear his prayer and care for him? I am like a cypress ever green. All your faithfulness comes from me. Let the wise man understand these words. Let the intelligent man grasp their meaning. For the ways of Yahweh are straight, and virtuous men walk in them, but sinners stumble (Hosea 14:1-10, Jerusalem Bible).

When that day comes, the mountains will run with new wine and the hills flow with milk, and all the river beds of Judah will run with water. A fountain will spring from the house of Yahweh to water the wadi of Acacias. Egypt will become a desolation, Edom a desert waste on account of the violence done to the sons of Judah whose innocent blood they shed in their country. But Judah will be inhabited forever, Jerusalem from age to age. "I will avenge their blood and let none go unpunished," and Yahweh will make his home in Zion (Joel 3:18-21).

These promises will find fulfillment after the great Day of the Lord described in the previous verses (Joel 3:15-17).

The destiny of Israel is similarly mapped out by Amos:

Yet I am not going to destroy the House of Jacob [Israel] completely — it is Yahweh who speaks. For now I will issue orders and shake the House of Israel among the nations, as you shake a sieve so that not one pebble can fall to the ground. All the sinners of my people are going to perish by the sword, all those who say, "No misfortune will ever touch us or even come anywhere near us." That day [following Jesus' intervention at the Day of the Lord] I will re-erect the tottering hut of David, make good the gaps in it, restore its ruins and rebuild it as it was in the days of old, so that they can conquer the remnant of Edom and all the nations that belonged to me. It is Yahweh who speaks, and he will carry this out. The days are coming now — it is Yahweh who speaks — when harvest will follow directly after ploughing, the treading of grapes soon after sowing, when the mountains will run with new wine and the hills all flow with it. I mean to restore the fortunes of my people Israel; they will rebuild the ruined cities and live in them, plant vineyards and drink their wine, dig gardens and eat their produce. I will plant them in their own country, never to be rooted up again out of the land I have given them, says Yahweh your God (Amos 9:8-15, Jerusalem Bible)

The Restoration of All Things

The powerful sermon delivered by Peter shortly after the day of Pentecost ended with a typical challenge to repentance. The formula of evangelism is no less appropriate for our time:

Now you must repent and turn to God, so that your sins may be wiped out, and so the Lord may bring in the times of refreshment. He will send you the Messiah He has predestined, that is Jesus, whom heaven must keep until the universal restoration comes which God proclaimed, speaking through his holy prophets (Acts 3:19-21). The key word "restoration" conjures up for his audience the whole complex of promised blessings of the Messianic age to come. Only a short time earlier the disciples, who were fully-fledged exponents of the Gospel of the Kingdom of God (Acts 1:3), had inquired with obvious excitement: "Is this the time when you are going to restore the Kingdom to Israel?" (Acts 1:6).

The time for the great restoration was not revealed, for Jesus himself had declared his ignorance (he really did not know, Mark 13:32 — a fact which should put an end to any claims that he was omniscient!) about the calendar date of his return to inaugurate the Kingdom. The fact of the coming restored Kingdom was, of course, never in doubt. The exact time was not part of God's revelation, though signs of the impending world transformation were given in detail by Jesus (Matt. 24), basing his predictions on already existing forecasts of Daniel.

Jesus had spoken daily of the "Life of the Age to Come" (inadequately rendered in our versions "everlasting life" or "eternal life," showing signs of a Greek paganizing influence and a loss of the vision of the Kingdom). In the New World of the Kingdom the Apostles are to enjoy positions as ministers of state in the Messianic rule (Matt. 19:28). In Acts 3:21 Peter assures the nation, and those of us who become part of the new "Israel of God" — the Church (Gal. 6:16), that the whole world will experience the universal renewal when the Messiah, who is temporarily retained in heaven, returns to take over the reins of power. Had not Jesus declared that he was born to be King?

"Yes, I am a King. I was born for this; I came into the world for this: to bear witness to the Truth, and all who are on the side of Truth listen to my voice" (John 18:37). This is John's parallel to Luke 4:43, where Jesus described his whole purpose as being the preaching of the Gospel of the Kingdom. Before Pilate he stated that bearing witness to his position as King of the Kingdom was the reason for his whole mission. The preaching of the Kingdom and of Jesus as King is "the truth."

The Kingdom of God and the Kingdom of Satan

The Kingdom of which Jesus spoke is "not of this world" (John 18:36). A powerful propaganda campaign has for too long prevented ordinary Bible readers from "hearing" the meaning of the phrase "not of this world." Tragically they have been persuaded to believe that Jesus' Kingdom will never be located on planet earth! With a single verse many seem to want to contradict the vision of all the prophets (and many New Testament texts), describing the coming of the Kingdom of God to this earth. Jesus meant that his Kingdom does not have its origin in the present evil system — "the world." The reason for this is simple. Satan is the ruler or "prince" (acting only within the limits prescribed by God) of all governmental systems organized prior to the coming of the Kingdom at Jesus' return. That is fundamental to Biblical Christianity and declared over and over again in the New Testament:

Satan said: "I will give you all this power and the glory of these kingdoms, for it has been committed to me and I give it to anyone I choose. Worship me, then, and it will all be yours" (Luke 4:6, 7).

"The god of this world has blinded the minds of unbelievers" (2 Cor. 4:4).

"The whole world lies in the power of the Evil One" (1 John 5:19).

"The primeval Serpent, known as the Devil and Satan, deceives the whole world" (Rev. 12:9).

"[The Christian's battle] is against the Sovereignties and the Powers who originate the darkness of this world, the spiritual army of evil in the heavens" (Eph. 6:12).

The nature of the deceptive tyranny of Satan is far more subtle than many recognize. It extends deep into the field of "religion," in which "counterfeit apostles, dishonest workmen, are disguised as apostles of Christ. There is nothing unexpected about that; if Satan himself goes disguised as an angel of light, there is no need to be surprised when his servants, too, disguise themselves as servants of righteousness" (2 Cor. 11:13-15).

The Hope of Life in the Promised Land

The New Testament is saturated with the hope that Jesus will return to relieve the world of its mounting pressures and problems. Because "the love of many will grow cold" as the end of the age approaches (Matt. 24:12), there is a greater urgency than ever for penetrating Bible study and consequent Christian behavior based on the teaching of Jesus.

To sustain the faithful in their darkest hour God has given the assurance of "the joy which was set before Jesus" (Heb. 12:2). This was the hope of a life of immortality to be enjoyed in the Kingdom of God, the promised land. How little the importance of the land is understood by modern readers of the New Testament! Pagan notions about an immortal soul which departs to heaven at death have all but destroyed the biblical hope of resurrection into the promised inheritance of the new earth.

A leading scholar describes the fundamental importance of the land in Biblical faith:

> In the original promise to Abraham, the content of the promise consists of progeny, blessing and the land...Further, Israel is to become a great nation. Thus the promise is made to foretell the rise of the Davidic empire...The covenant of Yahweh with David at his installation at Hebron (2 Kings 5:1ff) reflects the Abrahamic covenant...The promise of the land to Abraham was absorbed in the Abrahamic covenant...The divine promise to Abraham was the bedrock on which all subsequent history rests...The whole of the hexateuch [first six books of the Bible] in all its vast complexity was governed by the theme of the fulfillment of the promise to Abraham in the settlement of Canaan. The chief purpose of this work was to present in all its biblical and theological significance *this one leading conception*, in relation to which all the other conceptions of the hexateuch assume an ancillary role. Of all the promises made to the patriarchs it was that of *the land* which was most prominent and decisive...For the hexateuch *the land is the promised land* and that inviolably...The Pentateuch [first five books of the Bible] remained the bedrock of revelation for the Jews. *The promise of the land* is embedded in it. Disobedience to the commandments of Yahweh, through intermarriage with the inhabitants of the land [of Canaan] would inexorably incur the withdrawal of Yahweh's support and the loss of the land.
>
> One thing seems clear: concern with the land and hope for the land emerges at many places in the Old Testament

outside the hexateuch. While the promise was regarded as fulfilled in the settlement [see Acts 7:17 — the promise to Abraham was partly fulfilled] that settlement was not regarded as a complete settlement [see Acts 7:5 — Abraham never received the promise of the land]...Promises which have been fulfilled in history are not thereby exhausted of their content, but remain as promises on a different level...The promise of the land was proclaimed ever anew, even after its fulfillment...Promise and fulfillment inform much of the Old Testament, and the tradition, however changed, continued to contain the hope of *life in the land*.[7]

Jesus, whose teaching is rooted in the Old Testament, did not for one moment abandon the hope of a renewed earth. Indeed his whole purpose was to stir men and women to reorientate their lives now in preparation for the coming of the promised land of the Kingdom of God. This is the challenge of the Christian Gospel, which promises that the "meek will inherit the land" (Psalm 37:11, cited in Matt. 5:5).

A single united theme binds every part of Scripture together. Its central structure is the mandate of rulership given to man (Gen. 1:26), renewed to Abraham, Isaac and Jacob (Gen. 12ff.), confirmed in the house of David (2 Sam. 7), and reaching its climax in the promised Messiah, Jesus. Little wonder, then, that Matthew presents Jesus as "son of David, son of Abraham" (Matt. 1:1). Nor is it surprising that Luke builds his two treatises (Luke and Acts) round the promise of "the Kingdom and the things concerning Jesus" (Luke 1:32-35; Acts 8:12; 28:30, 31). The biblical story concerns the issue of dominion. Who is to be in charge of the earth? Man's inability to create a righteous society on earth can be remedied only by his acceptance of the rule of Jesus, first in our lives now, and finally as a world government coming to power at the return of the Messiah.

Such, in short, is the Good News of the Kingdom of God, the Christian Gospel. Entry into fellowship with the One God of Israel through His Son, the Messiah, begins with belief in the Gospel of the Kingdom as well as the acceptance of the atoning death of

---

[7] W.D. Davies, *The Gospel and the Land*, 1974, pp. 19-25, 36, emphasis added.

Jesus to blot out our sins. Repentance involves belief in and commitment to the Biblical revelation about God's plan in history revealed from Genesis to the Apocalypse (Revelation). This includes, as is well known, the substitutionary death of Jesus for our forgiveness. Jesus died in our place. Baptism follows intelligent belief in the Good News (Acts 8:12). Subsequently, we must persist to the end, in hope of our inheritance of the earth (Matt. 5:5) which is the same exactly as the inheritance of the Kingdom of God (2 Pet. 1:11). That inheritance lies definitely in the future. It cannot be received until the return of Jesus.

In our next lesson we hope to demonstrate that the Kingdom of God in the Bible is first and foremost the Kingdom destined to arrive at the future coming of Jesus. Only secondarily, and in a different sense, may it be said that the Kingdom is already present. Much confusion could have been avoided had we taken as axiomatic the statement of Luke 21:31: "When you see all these things [cataclysms connected with the end of the age] happening, know that the Kingdom of God is about to come" (Good News Bible).

> *It was the beautiful dream of Hebrew prophecy that in the latter days the Kingdom of God or the Kingdom of the Messiah should overlap the bounds of human empires, and ultimately cover the whole earth...Prophecy was never weary of telling of the Golden Age she saw in the far future, when the shadows would lift and the new Dawn would steal over the whole world...It is not unlikely that the term Kingdom of God was one of the current phrases of the times, a golden casket holding within it the dream of a restored Hebraism.*[8]

---

[8] Henry Burton, *St. Luke*, pp. 251, 251.

Lesson 6
The Kingdom of God — An Event of the Future

Master Texts:

"There will be weeping and gnashing of teeth there when you see Abraham and Isaac and Jacob and all the prophets in the Kingdom of God, but yourselves being cast out. And they will come from the east and west, and from north and south, and will recline at the table in the Kingdom of God" (Luke 13:28, 29).

"Truly I say to you, I will never again drink of the fruit of the vine until that day when I drink it new in the Kingdom of God" (Mark 14:25).

"For I say to you, I will not drink of the fruit of the vine from now on until the Kingdom of God comes" (Luke 22:18).

"When you see [these cataclysmic events of the end of the age] recognize that the Kingdom of God is near" (Luke 21:31).

"Thy Kingdom come!" (Matt. 6:10).

"In that day," declares the Lord, "I will assemble the lame and gather the outcasts, those whom I have afflicted. I will make the lame a remnant and the outcasts a strong nation. And the Lord will reign over them in Mount Zion from now on and forever. As for you, tower of the flock, hill of the daughter of Zion, to you it will come — even the former dominion will come, the Kingdom of the daughter of Jerusalem" (Micah 4:6-8).

Our discussion in previous lessons has centered around the fundamental concept of the Kingdom of God, the theme of the Christian Good News. It is easy to demonstrate from Scripture that **Jesus built his whole mission and ministry around the Kingdom idea.** It is therefore disconcerting, to say the least, that modern evangelism has little to say about the Kingdom. It appears that the Gospel itself is in jeopardy when the Kingdom is absent from the Message. The honest seeker for Truth will find this startling difference between what Jesus and the Apostles taught as the Good News and what is now presented as the Gospel, a stimulus to dig further in the quest for the precious information that leads to salvation.

It is commonly agreed by commentators on the New Testament that the Kingdom of God has a present and future reference in the teaching of Jesus. Attempts to define the Kingdom more precisely are plagued by a tendency to focus almost exclusively on the present aspect of the Kingdom. The future Kingdom is usually dismissed with a vague reference to its "consummation."

The future dimension of the Kingdom is the primary one in the New Testament. No text says that Christians have inherited the Kingdom of God. That cannot happen until Jesus comes back. The Kingdom is the goal of all Christian effort. The spirit of the Kingdom, the preaching and promise of the Kingdom are present whenever the Kingdom Gospel is believed. But the Kingdom as the empire of Jesus on earth is in the future. We can have June's weather in April, but confusion would reign if we said April is really June.

It is impossible to grasp the meaning of Jesus' favorite term "Kingdom of God" unless we pay full attention to the overwhelming volume of references to the Kingdom as **an event of the future**.[1] It appears to be a dislike of this essential New Testament fact which causes Bible readers to fix almost exclusively upon Luke 17:20, 21 as their favorite Kingdom text:

> Now having been questioned by the Pharisees as to when the Kingdom of God was coming, he answered them and said, "The Kingdom of God is not coming with signs to be observed; nor will they say, 'Look, here it is,' or 'There it is!' For behold, the Kingdom of God is in your midst."

Reading this text to the exclusion of scores of verses which describe the Kingdom as a future event associated with the Second Coming, one might conclude that the Kingdom was first and foremost present in its King, Jesus, or, following the King James Version of Luke 17:21, that it is "within you," i.e., in your heart. The King James is almost certainly mistranslated here, since Jesus never spoke elsewhere of the Kingdom as internal, in the human heart.

---

[1] See our article "The Kingdom of God: Present or Future?" at www.restorationfellowship.org

If the immediately following context of Luke 17:20, 21 is taken into account, it becomes clear that the coming of the Son of Man (which Luke elsewhere says is the coming of the Kingdom of God — Luke 21:31) will be "just like lightning, when it flashes out of one part of the sky, shines to the other part of the sky...On the day that Lot went out from Sodom it rained fire and brimstone from heaven and destroyed them all. It will be just the same on the day that the Son of Man is revealed" (vv. 24, 29, 30). In a later chapter Luke reports Jesus as saying:

> And there will be signs in the sun and moon and stars, and upon the earth dismay among nations, in perplexity at the roaring of the sea and the waves, men fainting from fear and the expectation of the things which are coming upon the world; for the powers of the heavens will be shaken. And then they will see the Son of Man coming in a cloud with power and great glory...When you see these things happening, recognize that the Kingdom of God is near (Luke 21:25-31).

With this evidence before us, it is utterly impossible to confine the Kingdom of God to the presence of the Messiah in Palestine in the first century, much less to a religious ideal established in the heart.

Jesus may well have said, as modern translations confirm, that he as King was "among them," and they were failing to recognize the Kingdom as represented by him. Other scholars claim that Luke 17:21 means that the Kingdom, when it comes, will be visible universally and not something hidden.

The Kingdom of God for Luke and the other New Testament writers is primarily the rule of God to be imposed upon a wicked world by the powerful intervention of Jesus at the end of the age. If we do not reckon with this fundamental Old and New Testament fact, we strip the teaching of Jesus of its motivating dynamic — the need for us all to prepare now for the great day. We must all face the Messiah, and give an account of our deeds, either through resurrection or survival until his coming.

Has the Kingdom Come?

It is important that we examine the massive evidence for the Kingdom of God as a new stage of world history **to be introduced at Jesus' return**. To speak of this as the "consummation" of the

Kingdom is misleading. The New Testament says that *the present evil age* is going to be "consummated" (i.e., come to its end, Matt. 24:3) when Jesus returns. The Kingdom of God will at that time be manifested publicly. It will then be inaugurated as the governing body of the New Age. Since the Kingdom comes into power only when Jesus comes back, it is confusing to say that it has already come. Its coming lies in the future.

We are to pray continuously "Your Kingdom come!" (Matt. 6:10; Luke 11:2). We must guard against watering down the significance of this petition by making it mean something like "may your Kingdom grow," "may your kingdom spread" or "may your kingdom be perfected." For Jesus and the disciples the Kingdom **has not yet come**. Christians are to long for its coming and pray for it to be established so that God's "will may be done on earth." The petition contains the perfect definition of the Kingdom. It is a state of affairs on earth when God's ways will be followed. That state of affairs, however, cannot possibly be realized worldwide until the banishment of Satan from his present position as "god of this age" (2 Cor. 4:4). The deposing of Satan must, in the divine plan, await the return of the Messiah. Such is the worldview which permeates the whole New Testament.

The Lord's prayer is directed to the coming of the Kingdom in the future. We are to hallow God's name. We are to treat with awe and reverence His whole Kingdom plan in Jesus. God's name refers to the whole revelation of Himself He has granted us in Scripture. Our first priority in prayer is to request the coming of the Kingdom when Jesus returns. The Kingdom is then described as a new heaven and earth, when God's will is done on earth and also in heaven. It may be that the request for "daily bread" means bread "for the morrow" of the future Kingdom. We need spiritual sustenance now to continue on the journey of faith towards the Kingdom. The prayer ends with a request to be delivered from the time of trial preceding the Kingdom and from "the evil one," a reference probably to the Devil rather than to evil in general.

The attempts of professing Christians to bring in the Kingdom before the predetermined time must end in failure. Jesus operated always within the consciousness of what "must be" in God's purposes. Christendom, as a whole, has ignored the divine program and has even attempted (since the time of Constantine) to establish itself as the Kingdom of God ruling now, sometimes in partnership with the secular state. **Such a thing is utterly impossible within the world view of the New Testament**. Satan is at present the "ruler of this world system." Nations are at present definitely not Christian, definitely not the Kingdom of God. Linking arms with Satan in an effort to turn his kingdoms into the kingdoms of God is fraught with disaster. Those who take this path simply become "friends of the world" and in consequence "enemies of God" (James 4:4). "What have I to do with judging [i.e., administering] outsiders?" says Paul (1 Cor. 5:12). Christian administration is now confined to the body of believers: "Do you not administer those who are within the Church?" (1 Cor. 5:12).

Systems of belief that attempt to introduce the Kingdom of God politically now — so called dominion theology — do not represent Jesus' teaching about the Kingdom.

The Coming of the Kingdom

Certainly in the New Testament the Kingdom has not yet "come." Speaking shortly before his death, the Lord Messiah did not expect to drink again of the wine of the Passover cup until the Kingdom had come: "For I say to you, I will not drink of the fruit of the vine from now on until the Kingdom comes" (Luke 22:18).

Moreover, Joseph of Arimathea, who was a disciple of Jesus (Matt. 27:57), was **waiting for the Kingdom of God to come**, after the crucifixion and after the historical ministry of Jesus: "And behold a man named Joseph, who was a member of the council, a good and righteous man (he had not consented to their plan and action), a man from Arimathea, a city of the Jews, who was *waiting for* the Kingdom of God..." (Luke 23:50, 51; Mark 15:43).

Cleopas speaks for the disciples when, after the resurrection of Jesus, he expresses their hope, now apparently frustrated, that "it was Jesus who was going to redeem Israel" (Luke 24:21). The redemption of Israel was linked in their minds with the coming of the Kingdom in power. That event still lay in the future.

Confirmation of Luke's understanding that the Kingdom had not come with the ministry of Jesus is found in Luke 21:31. The dramatic events which will lead up to the return of the Son of Man in power and glory herald the coming of the Kingdom of God: "When you see all these things happening, know that the Kingdom of God is about to come" (Luke 21:31, Good News Bible).

The Nobleman in the Parable in Luke 19

The critically important parable in Luke 19 similarly places the Kingdom of God in the future and associates it with the coming of Jesus to reign. The nobleman (Jesus) is to depart to a far country (i.e., to the Father in heaven) to receive his authority to rule, and then to return as king to initiate the Kingdom. This information is given by Jesus to correct the misunderstanding that the Kingdom was to be "manifested *immediately*" (Luke 19:11). According to Jesus, there is no question that the Kingdom will appear, but not in the immediate future (cp. Acts 1:6; 3:21).

It is instructive to note that it was Jesus' proximity to Jerusalem at the time which prompted the excitement that the Kingdom would come into power then. In its historical setting, this is exactly the kind of Kingdom we should expect. Its capital would be Jerusalem, the seat of Messianic government ("the city of the great king," Matt. 5:35), just as all the prophets had envisaged it. Jesus says nothing, then or at any time, to suggest that their conception of the Kingdom was fundamentally wrong (or "crude" — the disparaging term sometimes used by commentators). It is only *the time of the arrival* of the Kingdom which needs to be clarified. No precise chronological data is offered here or anywhere in the Bible to allow setting of dates. Much harm has been done to the New Testament doctrine of the Second Coming by those who succumb to the illusion that the date of the great event may be known in advance. (An enormous confusion was caused by the Jehovah's Witnesses who set 1914 as the date for the second coming, and when Jesus did not come then, dodged the consequences of their miscalculation by saying that Jesus came invisibly! Seventh-day Adventists proposed an unbiblical notion that 1844 marked a special entry of Jesus into "the second apartment of the heavenly sanctuary.")

The parable of Luke 19 makes two important points about the Kingdom of God. Firstly, the Kingdom had not yet arrived, late in the ministry of Christ. Secondly, it will appear in power and visibly when Christ returns from the "far country" at the end of an unspecified period of absence. When the Messiah returns he will reward his faithful followers by putting them in charge of urban populations (v. 17) and executing those of his enemies who "did not want me to reign over them" (v. 27). The Kingdom thus described is certainly not confined to a reign of Jesus "in the hearts of men." It has authority to confer power on those who followed the Messiah and the right to banish the incorrigibly wicked by execution. (The execution of others *now* by those claiming to be Christians would be unthinkable by the standards of the New Testament. This has not prevented some Christians from killing their Christian opponents. The case of Calvin's execution of Servetus over a doctrinal issue is the classic example of failure to understand the command to love. *The Church has absolutely no right to take the lives of others in the present age.*)

In every case where the *coming* of the Kingdom is described, an event of the future is meant. (We leave for the moment the occasional verse which implies the presence of the Kingdom, in a different sense, in the ministry of Jesus.)

"In the Kingdom"

We should now examine a group of sayings which describe a situation where people are said to be "in the Kingdom of God." Is this in the present or the future?

The phrase "in the Kingdom" is first found in Matthew 8:11, where Jesus says that many will come and recline with Abraham, Isaac and Jacob "in the Kingdom," while others will be refused entry into the Messianic banquet. The event is perhaps the celebration promised by Isaiah 25:6-8. There will be a "feast prepared in this mountain [Jerusalem]" at which the faithful will rejoice with Jesus. Further reference is made to this great occasion when Jesus announces, at the Last Supper, that he will no more drink of the wine of the Passover until he drinks it new "in the Kingdom of God" (Matt. 26:29, Luke 22:18). Jesus obviously expects to celebrate with the disciples "in the Kingdom" when the "Kingdom comes" (Luke 22:18).

The Kingdom is evidently future when James and John request from Jesus prominent positions with him "in your Kingdom" (Matt. 20:21). This is a request for recognition in the future reign of Messiah. Although the petition cannot be granted, Christ confirms the reality of the future Kingdom, and its nature as a real government, by stating that the highest offices in it will be assigned to those whom God chooses (Matt. 20:23). Similarly, Matthew 19:28 places the inauguration of the Kingdom in the New Age or New World (Moffat and NIV). It is then that Christ "sits on his throne of glory," that is, "when the Son of Man comes in his glory" (Matt. 25:31), and his authority to govern is shared with his Apostles. At the same time the righteous "shine forth in the Kingdom of their Father" (Matt. 13:43, quoting Dan. 12:3). This event occurs at the "end of the age" (Matt. 13:40), a time when the wicked will be cast "into a furnace of fire" (Matt. 13:42).

A composite version of Matthew's and Luke's description of the Kingdom leaves no room for doubt that the Kingdom of God is a world government associated with the return of Jesus:

> "I tell you positively," Jesus replied, "in the reborn world, when the Son of Man takes his seat on the throne of state, you too will be seated on twelve thrones, governing the twelve tribes of Israel. You are those who have stayed with me through all my trials, and just as my Father has promised me [covenanted me] His Kingdom, so do I now promise you that you will eat and drink at my table in my Kingdom and you will sit on thrones governing the twelve tribes of Israel" (Matt. 19:28; Luke 22:28-30).[2]

We can easily establish when the disciples expected to rule with Christ in the New World. With crystal clarity Matthew tells us quite precisely when it is that Jesus is to sit on his throne of glory: "When the Son of Man will come in his glory and all the holy angels with him, then will he sit upon the throne of his glory...Then will the King say....inherit the Kingdom" (Matt. 25:31, 34).

At the risk of repetition we give the following combined version of Jesus' important sayings about the future. This information provides a clear picture of God's plan for the introduction of the Kingdom: "In the reborn world, when the Son of Man takes his seat on his throne of glory [that is, 'when the Son of Man comes in his glory,' Matt. 25:31], you too will be seated on twelve thrones [eating and drinking at my table in my Kingdom, Luke 22:30] governing the twelve tribes of Israel." This state of affairs has never happened, proving that the Kingdom has not yet come.

Entering and Inheriting the Kingdom

When the center of systematic theology is founded on the recorded words of Jesus, the Kingdom of God will be seen as the sum total of biblical Christianity. Unless we strip the Kingdom of

---

[2] *Authentic New Testament*, translation by Hugh Schonfield.

its historical significance and invent new meanings for it, we will have little difficulty grasping its essential character as a real world government to be prepared for now, and awaiting manifestation at the Second Coming. Within this Messianic framework, the New Testament tells a coherent story. Without it, the New Testament can be (and has been) bent to suit almost any ideology.

The concept of entry into the Kingdom or inheriting the Kingdom of God appears throughout the New Testament. When is this to occur? We find an unequivocal answer in Matthew 25, where the blessed are invited to "inherit the Kingdom prepared for you from the foundation of the world" (v. 34). This will happen "when the Son of Man comes in his glory and sits on his glorious throne" (v. 31). Evidently the inheritance is to be acquired in the future at the return of Jesus. Elsewhere in Matthew, Mark and Luke entry into the Kingdom is equated with entry into "Life" or "the Life of the New Age" (or as we might say, "New Age Life," which has nothing whatsoever to do with popular movements under that title!).

Mark places entry into "Life" at a time when the wicked living at the coming of Christ will "go into Gehenna, into the unquenchable fire" (Mark 9:43). Entrance into "Life" or "the Life of the Coming Age" (in our versions inaccurately translated "everlasting" or "eternal life") is exactly the same as entrance into the Kingdom of God:

"Teacher, what good thing must I do to obtain eternal life?...If you wish to **enter life**, keep the commandments...Truly I say to you, it is hard for a rich man to **enter the Kingdom of Heaven**...It is easier for a camel to go through the eye of a needle than for a rich man to **enter the Kingdom of God**" (Kingdom of Heaven = Kingdom of God). "Who then can **be saved?**" (entering the Kingdom = being saved). "In the new world, you will sit on thrones to **govern the twelve tribes of Israel**" (being saved = ruling with Christ in the Kingdom). "Everyone who has left houses...for my sake will inherit **eternal life**," i.e. Life in the Coming Age of the Kingdom — the concept is based on the prediction in Daniel 12:2 (Matt. 19:16, 17, 23, 24, 25, 28, 29).

This basic "vocabulary" controls the New Testament. The Christian inheritance is always placed in the future. In one verse only (Col. 1:13) Paul speaks of the transfer of Christians into the Kingdom of God as already a fact. This is not untypical of Paul's thinking, since all the realities of the future may be tasted in the present. The Kingdom exists now in heaven where Jesus is preparing to establish it on earth. A single verse should not, however, be used to contradict the predominant evidence of Matthew, Mark, and Luke, nor the clear statements of Paul elsewhere in which he places Christian inheritance of and entry into the Kingdom in the future.

> The phrase "Kingdom of God" is *used normally* in St. Paul of that Messianic Kingdom which is to be the reward and goal of the Christian life...Hence it comes to mean the principles or ideas on which that kingdom is founded, which are already exhibited in this world.[3]

In Romans 14:17 Paul speaks of the Kingdom being "righteousness, peace, and joy in the holy spirit." This should not be taken to contradict his sayings elsewhere which place the inheritance of the Kingdom at the Second Coming. Though Christians have already been transferred out of the Kingdom of darkness (Col. 1:13), only a few verses later Paul says, "You will receive the reward of the inheritance" (Col. 3:24).

The Kingdom Is Mainly Future

It is important that we emphasize that the arrival of the Kingdom of God in the New Testament is predominantly a future event, leading to **a New World Order on earth**. The following plain statements from leading authorities provide a necessary corrective to the widely-held view that the Kingdom is mainly in the present:

> In the New Testament the Kingdom of God is conceived, **first of all, as something in the future** (Mark 9:1, 47; 14:25; Matt. 13:41-43; 20:21; Luke 22:16, 18; 1 Cor. 15:50, et al.) which comes from God (Mark 9:1; Matt. 6:10; Luke 17:20; 19:11). Therefore it is something man can only wait for (Mark 15:43), seek (Matt. 6:33; cf. Luke 12:32), and inherit (1 Cor. 6:9ff; Gal. 5:21; James 2:5), but he is not able to create it by himself.[4]

---

[3] *International Critical Commentary* on Romans 14:17.

[4] Eduard Schweitzer, *The Good News According to Mark*, p. 45, emphasis added.

Would that this clear statement had been taken to heart by every commentator!

The objective analysis of the Kingdom of God in Matthew, provided by the *Dictionary of Christ and the Gospels*, ought to serve as a much-needed guide to all our thinking about the Kingdom:

> The Kingdom — the central subject of Christ's doctrine. With this he began his ministry (Matt. 4:17) and wherever he went he taught it as Good News (4:23). The Kingdom he taught was coming, **but not in his lifetime**. After his ascension he would come as Son of Man on the clouds of heaven (16:17; 19:28; 24:30) and would sit on the throne of his glory...**Then the twelve Apostles should sit on twelve thrones judging the twelve tribes of Israel**. In the meantime he himself must suffer and die and be raised from the dead. How else could he come on the clouds of heaven? And **the disciples were to preach the Good News of the coming Kingdom (10:7; 24:14) among all nations making disciples by baptism (28:19).** The body of disciples thus gained would naturally form a society bound by common aims. Hence the disciples of the Kingdom would form a new spiritual Israel (21:43).[5]

The same authority goes on to say:

> In view of the needs of this new Israel of Christ's disciples, who were to await his coming on the clouds of heaven, it is natural that a large part of the teaching recorded in the Gospel should concern *the qualifications required in those who hoped to enter the Kingdom when it came*...Thus the parables convey some lesson about the nature of the Kingdom and the period of preparation for it. It should be sufficiently obvious that if we ask what meaning the parables had for the editor of the first gospel, the answer must be that he chose them because...they taught lessons about the Kingdom of God *in the sense in which that phrase is used everywhere in the Gospel of the Kingdom which was to come, when the Son of Man came upon the clouds of heaven*. Thus the parable of the sower illustrates the varying reception met with by the Good

---

[5] Vol. II, p. 145, emphasis added.

News of the Kingdom as it is preached amongst men. That of the tares also deals not with the Kingdom itself, but with the period of preparation for it. At the end of the age, the Son of Man will come to inaugurate his Kingdom...*There is nothing here nor elsewhere in this Gospel to suggest that the scene of the Kingdom is other than the present world renewed, restored and purified.*

The last sentence of our quotation makes the excellent point that Matthew does not expect believers to "go to heaven" but that Jesus will come back to rule with them on a renewed earth. The perceptive reader of the New Testament will note the amazing difference between the biblical view of the Kingdom and what in post-biblical times was substituted for it: a departure of the faithful at death to a realm removed from the earth.

The complaints of commentators about the unscriptural idea that Christians "go to heaven when they die" seem to have fallen on deaf ears. Cherished tradition remains unshaken by the celebrated Henry Alford's remarks:

> The words "great is your reward in the heavens" must not be taken as having any bearing on the future habitation of the glorified saints...The local question is to be decided by wholly different testimonies of Scripture — by the general tenor of prophecy and the analogies of the divine dealings; and **all of these point unmistakably to this earth purified and renewed and not to the heavens in any ordinary sense of the term, as the eternal habitation of the blessed.**[6]

"The Kingdom he taught was coming, but not in his lifetime." "In the New Testament the Kingdom of God is conceived, first of all, as something in the future" (cited above). So say leading analysts of the gospel records. We may add a further statement from a recognized authority on Luke:

> It cannot really be disputed that Luke means by the Kingdom a future entity. The spiritualizing interpretation according to which *the Kingdom is present in the Spirit and in the Church is* **completely misleading**...It is the message of the Kingdom that is present, which in Luke is

---

[6] *Commentary on the Greek New Testament*, Vol. I, pp. 35, 36, emphasis added.

distinguished from the Kingdom itself. He knows nothing of an immanent [i.e. already present] development on the basis of the preaching of the Kingdom.[7]

It cannot be too strongly emphasized that the Kingdom of God, the heart of the Christian Gospel, is chiefly the Kingdom which is yet to assume power over the nations when Jesus returns. The Kingdom as in some sense present in the ministry of the Church has been vastly exaggerated in proportion to the Kingdom as future. Certainly the Message of the Kingdom is to be proclaimed now, and certainly the conduct fitting candidates for the Kingdom must be demonstrated by Christians now (1 Thess. 2:12), but the Kingdom, properly speaking, is the Kingdom to be established when Jesus returns.

In confirmation of this central key to reading the New Testament with understanding, we add the statements of two further well-recognized authorities:

There is nothing in Matthew, Mark, and Luke antagonistic to the eschatological [i.e., future] view of the Kingdom. The Kingdom is not present in any sense not reconcilable with the fact that it is also and *mainly future*...The references to the Kingdom are prevailingly of futuristic implication...Jesus did not dissociate himself from the traditional view that the end would come in the form of a catastrophic transformation, culminating in the Advent of Messiah himself, who would come from heaven...He seems everywhere to set his seal to this view...He steadfastly contemplated a final wonder of destruction and reconstruction which would be the perfect establishment of the Kingdom of God on earth.[8]

The Grimm-Thayer Lexicon discusses the word "Kingdom" in the New Testament and makes the following important point:

By far more frequently [than the use of the Kingdom as present] the Kingdom of Heaven [or God] is spoken of as a future blessing, since its consummate establishment is to be looked for on Christ's solemn return from the skies, the

---

[7] Hans Conzelmann, *The Theology of St. Luke*, p. 122, emphasis added.

[8] "Eschatology," *Dictionary of Christ and the Gospels*, emphasis added.

dead being called to life again and the ills and wrongs which burden the present state of things being done away.[9]

The Kingdom in the Rest of the New Testament

If we examine the evidence outside Matthew, Mark, and Luke, we find that the writers consistently use the term "Kingdom of God" to denote the future reward and objective of the present Christian life. *The Theological Wordbook of the Bible*, among many other authorities, confirms this fact quite simply:

> God's reign is still to be established...It is generally in this [future] sense that the expression Kingdom of God is used in the New Testament outside the Gospels...The Kingdom of God is the dominant theme of the recorded teaching of Jesus...The Christian inheritance is identified with the Kingdom of God, the earth, eternal life, salvation, the grace of life, glory (cp. Mark 10:37, "glory" = Matt. 20:21, "Kingdom"), a place (i.e., Canaan), the world...Kingdom of God is the most characteristic description of the inheritance...For Christians the inheritance is future...The inheritance is the object of hope...Christians are heirs presumptive; their entering into their inheritance is still to come.[10]

Clear references to the future Kingdom are found in the following texts:

Acts 14:22: "It is through much tribulation that we must enter the Kingdom of God."

1 Cor. 6:9: "Do you not understand that the wicked will not inherit the Kingdom of God?"

Gal. 5:21: "People who indulge in such practices will never inherit the Kingdom of God."

Eph. 5:5: "Be sure of this: no one guilty of sexual vice, or impurity or lust (which is as bad as idolatry) has any inheritance in the Kingdom of Christ and God."

James 2:5: "Listen, my brothers, has not God chosen the poor of this world to be rich in faith and to inherit the Kingdom which He has promised to those who love Him?"

---

[9] "*basileia*" (Kingdom), *Thayer's Lexicon*, p. 97.
[10] pp. 113, 121.

2 Pet. 1:11: By developing Christian qualities of character now, "there will be supplied to you entrance into the eternal Kingdom of our Lord and Savior, Jesus Christ."

Heb. 12:26, 28: "Once again I will make heaven and earth quake...Therefore let us give thanks that we receive an unshakable Kingdom."

1 Cor. 15:50: "Flesh and blood [i.e. human beings in their present constitution] cannot inherit the Kingdom of God," i.e. a transformation of our present bodies into spiritual bodies is required for inheritance of the Kingdom. This will happen at the Second Coming (1 Cor. 15:50, 51).

Rev. 11:15: "The kingdoms of this world have become the Kingdom of our God and of His Messiah" (at the Second Coming).

Contrary to so much contemporary preaching, the Gospel of the Kingdom remains throughout the New Testament the Message of salvation. Not only this — by Kingdom, the New Testament writers do not mean an abstract rule of God in the heart now. Nor do they mean the visible body of Christians, the Church. What they do mean is the government which will intervene to produce the peace and harmony on earth for which man strives so hopelessly.

That this is a basic fact of our Bible is attested by distinguished names in contemporary scholarship, though the same conclusion may be reached by anyone conducting his own careful Bible study:

"The preaching of the Kingdom in Acts obviously refers to the Kingdom of God which will begin with the Parousia [Second Coming of Christ]."[11]

"Nothing obviously distinguishes the term 'Kingdom of God' in Acts from such apocalyptic [i.e. future and dramatic] use it has in the gospels; for example one enters it through much tribulation (Acts 14:22)."[12]

"Luke's understanding of the Kingdom is that it is still in the future and it will mean the restoration of Israel."[13]

"In Acts the term 'Kingdom of God' is used only of a future event." "Luke's theology anticipated a restored Israel"[14] (i.e., a real, external Kingdom on the earth in the future, Acts 1:6).

---

[11] E. Haenchen, *Acts of the Apostles*, 1971, p. 141, fn. 2.

[12] H.J. Cadbury, *Acts and Eschatology*, p. 311.

[13] Kevin Giles, *Reformed Theological Review*, Sept.-Dec., 1981.

[14] E. Earle Ellis, *New Century Bible Commentary* on Luke, p. 13.

A final quotation correctly summarizes the New Testament evidence for the Good News about a future Kingdom of God on earth. What Luke describes as apostolic belief and teaching is a far cry from what is presented as the gospel in our day:

Acts includes many familiar elements in the New Testament preaching. The preachers preach the Kingdom of God or the things about it (Acts 1:3; 8:12; 20:25; 28:23, 31). The term "Kingdom of God" appears from almost the first verse to the last verse in the book. "Kingdom of God" constitutes a formula apparently parallel to the writer's more characteristic single verb "evangelize."[15]

Summary

A world of information is involved in the Christian Gospel of the Kingdom. The genius of Christianity is concentrated in the word "Kingdom." This essential saving information is often withheld from the public, though they are deluged with appeals to accept the "gospel." Centuries of tradition have contrived to convince Bible readers and churchgoers that the Kingdom of God is mainly an abstract rule of God in the heart of the believer. This is in flat contradiction to the New Testament. Though the Christian documents recognize that the power of the future Kingdom has already intruded into the present evil world system (the Kingdom has "come upon" individuals when they are freed from demon oppression, Matt. 12:28; Luke 11:20), the Kingdom of God is *firstly and predominantly the New World Order which cannot and will not arise on earth until Christ returns to inaugurate it.* This fact is revolutionary in its implications for the understanding and practice of the Christian faith, indeed the Christian Gospel.

It means that the whole concept of the Christian future as a departure of the believer at death "to heaven" is a misrepresentation of the biblical teaching. The Bible views the future in terms of hope for rulership with Christ on earth at the Second Coming. Attempts to move the millennial Kingdom of Christ and the saints (Rev. 20:1-6) into the present ("amillennialism") are symptomatic of the complete dislocation of the biblical scheme which has occurred through a fundamental misunderstanding about the Kingdom. This affects the Gospel and

---

[15] H.J. Cadbury, *Acts and Eschatology.*

every facet of New Testament teaching. Our whole traditional structure is colored by Augustinian Platonism, which continues to receive uncritical acceptance by whole denominations claiming to base their faith solely on the Bible.

Underlying the rejection of the biblical view of the future is an anti-Jewish and anti-Messianic tendency. Churches have fallen under the spell of the notion that what is "spiritual" cannot be related to a new political order on earth. Theology therefore constantly suppresses or ignores the obvious Messianic themes of both Testaments or tries to "reinterpret" them and make them fit its own Platonized version of the faith. This continuing "soft-pedaling" of the plain teaching of the Apostles about the future prevents whole sections of the Bible from having their intended impact as a stimulus to hope and persistence in view of the glorious future of our world. A whole dimension of the New Testament is, in varying degrees, missing from contemporary theology and preaching. In biblical Christianity the future is so much more sharply defined, making a correspondingly greater impact on life now. Recovery of the New Testament dynamic will go hand in hand with a clarification of the Good News about the Kingdom of God.

> *Old Testament prophecy teaches that the Kingdom of God will be ushered in by a divine intervention rather than through the natural processes of history, and it is this viewpoint which is indispensable to apocalyptic eschatology. Jesus shared this outlook.*[16]

---

[16] Desmond Ford, *The Abomination of Desolation in Biblical Prophecy*, p. 14.

Lesson 7
God's Great Kingdom Plan Through Jesus: How to Live Forever

Master Texts:

"All Scripture [the Bible] is breathed out by God and is useful for teaching, reproof, correction and training in righteousness" (2 Tim. 3:16)

"How blessed are the meek; they are going to have the earth as their inheritance" (Matt. 5:5)

"Anyone who goes too far and does not remain in the teaching of the Messiah has no relation with the Father, and the one who remains in that teaching has a relationship with both the Father and the Son" (2 John 9).

Wisdom speaks: "I will pour out my spirit upon you; I will make my words known to you" (Prov. 1:23).

"Not everyone who says to me [Jesus] 'Lord, Lord' will enter the Kingdom but only those who do the will of my Father in heaven. Many will say to me in that [future] day, 'Lord, Lord, we preached in your name, didn't we? We did many amazing miracles in your name, didn't we? We cast out demons in your name, didn't we?' Then I will declare to them: 'Depart from me, you who work iniquity. I never recognized you'" (Matt. 7:21-23).

"The power of the spirit will come over you [Mary] and for that reason precisely the one to be begotten [brought into existence] will be called the Son of God" (Luke 1:35).

The Gospel is the all-important Message of the Bible. Its design is to inform us human beings about what God is planning for us and the world. It reveals to us the purpose of existence. It presents us with an amazing destiny.

It was delivered to us by God's miraculously begotten Son, who, as he said "came to preach the Gospel of the Kingdom: that is the reason why God commissioned me" (Luke 4:43; Mark 1:38). Paul and the other Apostles taught the same Kingdom Gospel as Jesus had. They were obediently following Jesus by promoting the Gospel as Jesus had preached it. There is thus one Gospel for everyone, of every nation. Jesus had given his marching orders for the Church until he comes back (Matt. 28:19, 20). He commanded that the same Gospel as he had preached be announced to all the nations. Jesus also commanded that converts be discipled in the teachings of the Christian faith and that they be baptized in water.

Water baptism is not an "optional extra." It remains, as it always was, a direct command of Jesus until the end of the age. Jesus warned that saying "Lord" to him is inadequate if we are not willing to do what he says: "Why do you call me lord, and you will not do what I say?" (Luke 6:46). It is an empty pretense to claim Christ as Master, and then to oppose his simple, basic teachings, such as belief in the Gospel of the Kingdom, water baptism and of course a persistent Christian lifestyle until the end.

The Christian world is now fragmented into thousands of differing groups. Something has happened to confuse the united faith of the New Testament writers. Among these were people who had known Jesus personally, spent hours with him and listened day after day to his teachings. They well know his amazing aims and claims. In addition they knew that three days after being killed by crucifixion, he reappeared alive and immortal. They "ate and drank with him after he came back from death" (Acts 10:41).

The testimony of Jesus' Apostles and followers to his resurrection deserves our full confidence. There is every reason to believe them. They saw Jesus die. "And all his acquaintances and the women who accompanied him from Galilee were standing at a distance, seeing these things" (Luke 23:49). They knew that he had been cruelly executed; the women saw him buried and the Apostles and others saw him alive again. They had no reason at all to lie. Nor were they hallucinating! They simply knew what had happened, and they were naturally compelled to share the glorious hope of immortality, through following and obeying Jesus, with us all.

Some absurd objections have been raised against the Apostles. No one saw Jesus leave the tomb, it is said. Therefore the resurrection is only a guess. If you saw someone at home and healthy who you knew had been in the hospital, would you immediately doubt that he had left the hospital because no one saw him leave?

God does not expect us to guess, or just "have blind faith." Faith is believing and believing is based on solid evidence, the evidence of credible witnesses. Anyone who knows the New Testament documents well, works with the original languages perhaps or reads the Bible in many versions, knows that these are not fraudulent writings. Their authors would have gained nothing by lying and they were not insane. Insane people cannot produce writings of the supremely high quality of the New Testament.

The Apostles risked life and limb and the furious opposition of some Jews and Gentiles as they made the Good News of the Kingdom known in the Roman Empire. Some of them died for the Message they preached so tirelessly. To imagine they died for what they knew to be untrue is absurd! These men were honest and courageous. They were eyewitnesses of the events of Jesus' life, death and resurrection. It is the greatest presumption and arrogance for anyone two thousand years later to say he or she knows better. You were not there. They were.

Jesus and the Quest for Immortality in the Kingdom

Jesus' aim was to show the public how to live forever. How to have indestructible life. How to be beyond the power of death. How to have perfect health for all eternity.

Jesus offered the secret of immortality, by inviting men and women everywhere to believe what he taught. He himself claimed to be the one and only perfect agent and Son of God. Jesus was uniquely the Son of God as a direct result of the miracle of new creation by which God his Father, the God of Israel and of the Bible, brought him into existence,

Jesus taught the Gospel of the Kingdom as the key to immortality. He taught the great Good News about the Kingdom for years before adding to the message the facts about his impending death and resurrection. The Kingdom Gospel, including the death and resurrection of the Savior, contains the conditions of the New Covenant.

Just as Moses had given the people of Israel the terms and stipulations of the Old Covenant (Exod. 24) and had then poured blood over the people as well as the book containing the words of the covenant, so Jesus as the final prophet (Deut. 18:15-18; Acts

3:22; 7:37) did the same. He first gave all the words of the New Covenant in five blocks of teaching in Matthew, and in Mark, Luke and John's reports. Then Jesus announced his death. Blood is necessary for the inauguration of God's principal covenants in the Bible. Jesus then gave his own precious blood to inaugurate officially the New Covenant based not only on his death but on the tremendously important words of the covenant, his own teachings.

At the last supper held with his Apostles, the night before he went to his torturous death on the cross, Jesus spoke of his future reunion with the Apostles and of course all his subsequent brothers and sisters in the faith. He discussed the coming Kingdom with them by promising them a thoroughly political future with him in the Kingdom which would come to power worldwide at his return. Luke 22:29-30 contains a magnificent encapsulation of the New Covenant. "Just as my Father has covenanted with me to give me a Kingdom, so I now covenant with you to give you the Kingdom. You will be promoted to sit on twelve thrones to administer the [regathered] tribes of Israel." This is a summary of the Kingdom Gospel. It was Jesus' final promise to his disciples.

The promise of a place in the future Kingdom was a privilege and a challenge. Jesus knew that as Messiah he was going to solve the international and personal problems of the world and he invited his followers to take part with him in this venture. Like him, his followers were to become servant-administrators in the Kingdom. They were to endure various trials in the present chaotic age (Satan is said to be the god of the present nations, 2 Cor. 4:4). Then, after maintaining their faith steadily until the end of their lives or until Christ comes, they would be brought back to life, given immortality and the joy of sharing in the worldwide Kingdom government with its headquarters in a renewed Jerusalem.

This plan gave and gives the greatest possible meaning to life now, and it enables those involved in it to endure suffering and setbacks knowing that God "works together in all things, for those who are called according to His purpose" (Rom. 8:28).

The Loss of the Identity of Jesus

Fragmentation in the Church and the loss of the simple immortality program of God through Jesus is due to a huge shift away from the teachings of Jesus, which started soon after the death of the Apostles. The teaching of Jesus and his Apostles was gradually corrupted under the influence of Greek, pagan philosophy, which interfered with the basic tenets of the Bible.

The God of both Testaments is the One God of Israel. The creed of Israel requires belief in one Person who is "the only true God" (John 17:3). This creed was designed to be a shield against any departure from the knowledge of the true God. Jesus himself in a final, memorable prayer in the presence of his disciples spoke of the essence of the immortality program as believing in the Father as "the only one who is truly God" and in himself, Jesus, as the Messiah whom that One God commissioned (see John 17:3).

There is nothing complex about that creed. Had it remained intact, the history of the Church would have been quite different.

However, the Gentile mind of some early converts, after the death of the Apostles, eventually misunderstood the fact that the Son of God, Jesus, began to exist when God generated him in Mary (Luke 1:35). Based on a pagan view of the cosmos, these Gentiles finally contradicted the creed of Israel, which Jesus had confirmed as the Christian creed and the most important of all beliefs in Mark 12:28-34.

These wrongly instructed converts gave to Jesus, no doubt in the name of "progress," a pre-history which made him essentially non-human. From the second century, the loss of Jesus, the human being, the Son of God, began. Jesus was eventually turned into the Creator of the Genesis creation. He thus displaced his own Father, who had constantly insisted in the Old Testament Scriptures that He, alone and unaccompanied, was the actual Creator of all things (Isa. 44:24).

This first stage in the loss of the true identity of Jesus made him a created Person, *but created before Genesis.* This drastic shift was enough to deprive Jesus of his actual status as a real human being beginning in the womb of his mother, as all humans do. The promised Messiah is the son of David, not a prehistoric person arriving from heaven!

Confusion over the Messiah Jesus and his identity was compounded by a subsequent revision by "church fathers" of the fourth century. It was then claimed that the Son of God was in fact an *uncreated* second member of the eternal Godhead. With this new twist,[1] the unitarian creed of Israel and of Jesus (Mark 12:28-34) was again threatened and perverted. It was necessary now to explain the inexplicable: how the One God could really be both Father and Son; how two (and later three, when the Holy Spirit was wrongly defined as a third Person) could really be One.

Using terminology borrowed from the world of pagan philosophy, it was now held, and enforced by a series of Church councils, that the Son of God had no beginning; that he was really God, and that he took on "impersonal human nature" in the womb of his mother. At this point, the Son was deprived of his human status. He was turned into God. Though lip service was paid to the Messianic Son of God, there was really no biological son of David who *came into existence* in Mary. That lineal descendant of David, the promised Messiah, was replaced by an eternally existing Son of God, second member of a Triune God. Mary, under the new scheme, bore "human nature," which is vastly different from the son of David!

To counteract the very obvious objection that the Church now believed in *two* who were both "eternal God," the Church declared that God is one in "essence," no longer, as the creed of the Bible had taught, one in Person.

This abandonment of the Jewish-Christian unitarian creed of Jesus led to untold confusion over terminology and resulted, after centuries of dispute, in an inscrutable "mystery" known as the doctrine of the Trinity. This new dogma, unknown to Jesus and the New Testament, and yet proclaimed in Jesus' name, was enforced on pain of excommunication. It has remained the hallmark of what is supposed to be genuine or "orthodox" Christianity. However, as many scholars know, it is highly improbable that Jesus would have recognized the Trinity as a creed faithful to the words of God in Scripture.

---

[1]Tertullian (as well as Arius, later) said that there was a time when the Son did not exist (*Ad Hermogenes*, 3) and can hardly count as a Trinitarian. Origen introduced the idea of the "eternal begetting" of the Son, but thought of the Son as subordinate to the Father. The history of this whole unfortunate development is very well analyzed and criticized in Karl-Heinz Ohlig's *One or Three? From the Father of Jesus to the Trinity* (Lang, 2002). See also our *The Doctrine of the Trinity: Christianity's Self-Inflicted Wound* (International Scholars Publications, 1998).

An effective propaganda campaign has convinced unsuspecting church members that only those who are prepared to believe in the post-biblical revised creed, the Trinity, and that Jesus is fully God and fully man, can be accepted as Christian. Unfortunately, not only is this creed then forced into the Bible, sometimes even by mistranslation in some versions,[2] but the Bible itself becomes very difficult to read intelligently, since Jesus and the Apostles did not believe in the Trinity. Jesus never claimed to *be God.* He always expressed his subordination to God, his Creator and Father. He did, of course, claim a unique status which God had conferred on him, and he constantly expressed his complete dependence on the One God, his Father, for everything that he was able to achieve in pursuit of the will of God.

It has been Satan's aim to oppose the will of God by denigrating the dignity of the human beings whom God has created. Satan mounts his opposition to the potential of man in the service of God. The falsehood has been promulgated that Jesus, as Son of God, is "too good" to be a human being! His miracles, his extraordinary life and teaching are far beyond what any "mere" human person can achieve. God's appointed human and sinless Savior has been judged insufficient to achieve our salvation. Jesus, in view of what he did and said, must be God!

This argument makes an appeal to the religious imagination, no doubt, but it does not represent biblical teaching. The Bible is a unitarian document from cover to cover. It celebrates the fact that "salvation is from the Jews" (John 4:22) and the Jews, as everyone ought to know, believed that God was a single, undivided divine Person. Jews were urged for their whole history under God never to depart from this cardinal belief that God is one, not two or three.

The God of the Jews is also the God of the Gentiles. Paul stated this fact clearly in Romans 3:29-30. Not once did he ever hint at a revision of the biblical creed.

The doctrine of the Trinity also antagonizes a billion Muslims who have likewise been schooled for centuries never to depart

---

[2]The NIV mistranslates John 16:28 and 20:17 to give the impression that Jesus went *back* to the Father and Phil. 2:6 to say that Jesus is God ("being in very nature God") when Paul wrote that Messiah Jesus "was in the form of God."

from belief in God as a single divine Person. Both Jews and Muslims can correctly appeal to the Hebrew Bible, which with its thousands of singular personal pronouns describing God, informs us all that God is a single Person! To make this claim is simply to assert that one of the most fundamental laws of communication — that single personal pronouns describe single persons — applies to the Bible as to all literature.

The post-biblical departure from the fundamental framework of the Bible which recognizes Jesus as the human Messiah and God as one Person was a disaster for the original Christian faith. With that early loss of Jesus' identity as the Jewish Messiah of biblical prediction went also the loss of the Kingdom of God Gospel.

Again, under the influence of pagan philosophy, the goal of the Christians was shifted. A fundamental falsehood overcame the basic biblical truth that man is born a mortal being, subject to inevitable death. The falsehood was introduced from Platonic philosophy that man is innately immortal!

This false teaching about the nature of us humans confused Jesus' teaching about immortality. While the Church took on the pagan notion of inherent immortality, Jesus labored to instruct the public on how to achieve immortality, the immortality which none of us has by nature.

Jesus' whole point, repeated constantly, was that we must "be born again" in order to achieve immortality in the future Kingdom of God on earth. Rebirth is achieved, Jesus taught everywhere, by our intelligent reception of his Kingdom Gospel message. In the parable of the sower, Jesus pictured himself as sowing the essential seed of immortality, the secret of life forever.

Jesus was active in the fulfillment of the command originally given to man to "be fruitful and multiply." By sowing the seed of immortality he produced others as *spiritual* brothers and sisters. He expected those who had received the secret of immortality to share it with others and thus continue the process of multiplication. The seed Gospel of the Kingdom would be the instrument of multitudes of candidates for immortality. Paul referred to the Christian's union with Christ. It is for the purpose of bearing fruit (Rom. 7:4), which surely must include the "reproduction" of other believers as heirs to the Kingdom.

The Gospel of the Kingdom is defined as the "word" or message of God and it is also described as "the seed." When that seed message of the Kingdom of God is planted in the hearts of receptive hearers and acted upon, the germ of life forever is placed within the believer. His eyes are opened by the divine program contained in the teaching of Jesus. He becomes aware of his destiny as a candidate for life in the future Kingdom. The spirit of God and of Jesus is transmitted by that seed message. It is the spirit, mind and character of God, and it transmits a downpayment of the immortality which the Christian will gain fully in the resurrection when Jesus comes back.

The New Testament teaches that belief in Jesus and the Kingdom must be maintained until the end. There is no such doctrine as "once saved, always saved." Salvation is a process beginning now and continuing to the end. "Salvation," Paul said, "is now nearer to us than when we first believed" (Rom. 13:11). He warned converted Christians that if they did not remain in the faith, they would be "cut off" (Rom. 11:22). "Some believe for a while," Jesus had warned (Luke 8:13), but only those who persist to the end will be saved (Matt. 24:13).

A number of traps await the young believer in our present confused religious world. Firstly the threat of confusing the terms of the New Covenant taught by Jesus with the Old Covenant Law of Moses. Paul did not require his converts to observe Saturday as the Sabbath nor the feasts of the Hebrew calendar, nor the new moons. A major thrust of Paul's teaching was that the dividing wall which had separated Jew from Gentile was abolished in Christ (Eph. 2:15). Food laws given to Israel in Leviticus 11 are no longer valid (Rom. 14:14, 20, where Paul uses the very opposite word from that found in Lev. 11: "clean" as opposed to "unclean"). As a Jew and Christian Paul was convinced that "all things are clean"; "nothing is unclean of itself, unless you think it is." Paul could hardly with these words have been upholding the kosher laws of Leviticus 11!

Sunday is not a new Sabbath day, but it is entirely appropriate for Christians to meet on that day in celebration of the resurrection. Acts 20:7 speaks of just such a meeting of believers on "the first day of the week." To avoid collections when Paul visited church members were asked to lay up money every Sunday (1 Cor. 16:2). Jews in the synagogue met on the Sabbath and Paul attended such gatherings for the purpose of evangelizing. Synagogue meetings were not Christian gatherings, of course. The synagogue, as a whole, did not accept Jesus as the Messiah.[3] The New Testament Scriptures have been given us in the Greek language. Arguments about an original Aramaic version can divert us from the important business of understanding Scripture as we have it, in Greek. We have no original texts (autographs), but a large number of copies in Greek. Where corruptions have occurred the evidence usually remains. Arguments about the use of the divine name Yahweh, or how it was pronounced, are not useful. The exact pronunciation is not known, and the New Testament makes no special point about the importance of pronouncing God's name in Hebrew (or the name of Jesus). The inspired Greek manuscripts show that names may be legitimately transliterated into other languages.

Another pressing danger for the new convert is pressure to "speak in tongues." In Acts the miracle of "tongues," which means languages, not a series of meaningless syllables, involved a supernatural ability by the Apostles and those with them to speak languages they had never learned. The miracle was one of speaking, certainly not a miracle of hearing in the minds of the yet unconverted. It was the Apostles who spoke miraculously to the crowd who recognized their own various dialects being spoken by those who had never learned them. The miracle was a demonstrable evidence that God was at work and it identified the Apostles as the accredited agents of Jesus.

The "tongues" was certainly not a "practical" miracle to overcome the language barriers. When Peter preached to the same crowd (Acts 2) he spoke in Aramaic or Greek and was understood by all.

The language gift in 1 Corinthians 12-14 is listed as the least important and it was positively never intended for every believer. "Do all speak in tongues?" Paul asked. "By no means" (see 1 Cor. 12:30). Attempts to produce these gifts today are unconvincing.

---

[3]Much good literature has been written on the contrast between the two covenants. The thrust of Paul's ministry was to facilitate fellowship between Jewish and Gentile Christians. Our book *The Law, the Sabbath and New Covenant Christianity* describes our own journey from legalism to freedom and presents the case for this from Scripture.

They are not recognized consistently and reliably as real languages. Tongues speakers often do not know what they are saying. By contrast, under Paul's supervision, the gifts were unambiguous. "Tongues" should be verified as real languages as they clearly were in Acts 2. And the one who claims the ability to speak in tongues is exhorted to translate the "tongue" so that all may be benefited (1 Cor. 14:13). There is no such thing in 1 Corinthians 12-14 as a "tongue" which is supposed to remain *always* in private.

Thousands of tape recordings of "tongues" today do not produce evidence of real languages being spoken supernaturally. Rather, many have been convinced to imitate the practice of others, and pagan religions have evidence of "tongues," showing that its source is not necessarily from God. In 1 Corinthians 13:8-12 Paul made no certain statement about whether those particular gifts would continue for the whole period until Jesus returns. He did observe that the supernatural utterances in tongues and prophecies of his own time provided knowledge which would be superseded at the return of Jesus. He did not say that the utterances and prophecies themselves would continue *to be given* beyond the close of the canon of Scripture. Certainly the knowledge revealed in prophecy (and tongues translated is a form of prophecy, 1 Cor. 14:5) was supernaturally given and Paul concluded that "tongues are a sign [a demonstrable miracle] for unbelievers" (1 Cor. 14:22).

There are no Apostles among us today, at the level of Peter or the twelve or Paul. There is nothing in the New Testament about ordaining any successors to the Apostles. Apostles are those who had personally seen the risen Jesus, and Paul claimed his apostleship on the basis of his ability to do "the signs and wonders of an Apostle" (2 Cor. 12:12; Rom. 15:19) and of having seen Jesus personally (1 Cor. 9:1). The Apostles were the foundation of the New Testament church, appointed by Jesus, and the foundation cannot be re-laid. We should of course all be disciples of the Apostles who faithfully represented the faith as taught by Jesus.

None of this means that God does not intervene as He desires. His presence with the believer to guide and instruct is promised until the coming of Jesus. "God works in all things for good to those who love Him" (see Rom. 8:28).

A further trap awaits the new believer. It is the theory that there are no supernatural evil personalities in Scripture, that Satan or the Devil is simply a metaphor for the evil which resides in human nature. The New Testament speaks with complete clarity of demons as non-human, supernatural intelligent beings. Jesus spoke to them and they spoke to him. They are always distinct from the unfortunate human persons whom they influence. To deny the existence of Satan as a fallen supernatural being is to erase a whole dimension of reality from the sacred text. It amounts to a refusal to believe in a major element of divine revelation in the Bible.

The word "demon" has a perfectly clear basic meaning in Greek and we may not rewrite the lexicons and dictionaries to support our own theories. If the New Testament writers did not believe in the existence of demons, the one thing they could never have done was to lace their accounts with the words and activities of demons or evil spirits. There are perfectly good words in Greek to describe "madness" and "disease," but the writers report for our instruction that demons are intelligent, evil, supernatural personalities, working for the Devil who is equally a personal being.

Jesus recognized their existence, and so should his followers. Not to do so would be a form of unbelief. Explaining away supernatural evil challenges the authenticity of the biblical text and forces its exponents to impose a theory on the Bible which implies that Jesus was an ignorant victim of an "unscientific age." The existence of demons as demons has been obvious to millions of readers of the sacred text.

Perhaps most problematic for a clear understanding of the Bible is any theory of the Kingdom of God which defines it against the evidence of the New Testament. If the Kingdom is misunderstood, so automatically is the Gospel, which is the Gospel *about the Kingdom.* One large denomination, the Church of Christ, equates the Kingdom with the Church and creates a very large confusion over the Gospel. They propose even that the Lord's prayer "May Your Kingdom come!" is no longer valid for us, since the Kingdom arrived at Pentecost when Jesus was seated with God in heaven.

The confusion of the Church with the Kingdom obscures the future Kingdom of God as seen by all the prophets. No text says that Christians have already inherited the Kingdom. Since the dead are now dead and not ruling with Christ, it is logically impossible for the Kingdom of God as the joint rule of Jesus with the faithful to be a fact of the present. The vast majority of Kingdom verses in the New Testament refer to the Kingdom which will be inaugurated at the return of Jesus and the resurrection of the dead. Revelation 11:15-18 is a golden text to preserve clarity on the Kingdom. Its arrival is at the seventh trumpet when the nations of the present system become the Kingdom of God. Certainly the Church is to be training now in readiness for the Kingdom of God when it comes. But the Kingdom in its proper sense remains future, although its blessings can be enjoyed in part now through the spirit of God and of Jesus which is said to be a "downpayment" of future immortality in the Kingdom.

Acts 1:5-7 provides a crystal clear testimony against the idea that the Kingdom of God was initiated when Jesus went to sit at the right hand of the Father in heaven. In Acts 1:5 after Jesus had given a six-week seminar on his favorite subject, the Kingdom (Acts 1:3) the disciples, who had already been preaching the Gospel of the Kingdom under Jesus' supervision, asked the obvious question. Hearing that the spirit was to be poured out from heaven, they supposed not unreasonably that the Kingdom of God was going to appear at the same time. They defined the Kingdom as Jesus had taught them. They thought of it as involving the restored tribes of Israel in the land. "Is it at this the time," they asked, "that you are going to restore the Kingdom to Israel?" (Acts 1:6).

Jesus did not in any way rebuke them for their good question. He simply informed them that the time for the coming of the Kingdom could not be known. The restoration of the Kingdom to Israel is taken for granted. The time which has to elapse before the Kingdom comes cannot be known. Note, however, this essential point which settles any question about the Kingdom in relation to the coming of the Spirit. The spirit was to come "in a few days time." But the Kingdom was to arrive at a time unknown. This proves obviously that the coming of the spirit at Pentecost is not the same event as the coming of the Kingdom.

More devastating in its effect on the Gospel is a theory known as Dispensationalism, or in its extreme form "ultra-dispensationalism." These theories effectively divorce Jesus from the Gospel which he preached. They propose that Jesus, when he preached the Kingdom as Gospel, was talking to Jews under the Old Covenant and was not preaching the saving Gospel for us all!

Thus a leading exponent of the Dispensationalist school wrote, "The Sermon on the Mount is not church truth precisely." The Sermon on the Mount is in fact the essential heart of the ethics of the New Covenant and thus directly and urgently applicable to all believers in Christ.

Unger's Bible Dictionary in its entry "Gospel" speaks ambiguously of "two forms of the Gospel." These turn out to be two Gospels. The Gospel of the Kingdom, it is maintained, was meant by Jesus to be for Jews only. Paul, on the other hand, introduced the Gospel of grace which is for everyone now. But when the time of the future great tribulation comes, the Kingdom of God Gospel will be reinstated for people undergoing that period of unprecedented trouble.

The "ultra" form of this mistaken theory of the Gospel asks us to believe that the Kingdom was preached until either Acts 13, even by Paul, or according to a variation on the same theory, until Acts 28. Subsequently, so says this amazing theory, Paul was given a final "sacred secret" revelation which provided the Gospel for those who happened to encounter Paul after this new revelation. This then would be the Gospel for us today.

Both forms of Dispensationalism are destructive of the New Testament Gospel. They strike at the heart of the New Testament which proposes that the words of Jesus are the key to the Christian faith. Paul would have been under his own curse for destroying the Gospel (Gal. 1:6-9) if he had disobeyed the Great Commission by not preaching the same Gospel of the Kingdom which Jesus had authorized until he returns at the end of the age (Matt. 28:19, 20). Paul always preached the Gospel of the Kingdom as is seen by Acts 19:8; 20:24, 25; and 28:23, 31. He preached the same Kingdom Gospel to everyone. Acts 20:24, 25 settles once and for all (though the fact is obvious from the rest of the New Testament) that the Gospel of grace is identical with the Gospel of the Kingdom.

Finally it is absurd to imagine that Paul was given late in his life a special Gospel which superseded previous versions of the Gospel. Presumably he would have had to retrace his steps and teach the converts a new form of Christianity which he knew nothing about when he had been with them earlier!

Paul did not say that there was a Gospel revealed only to him. He said that the Gospel was revealed to the Apostles, in the plural (Eph. 3:5). Happily, there is only one Gospel. Jesus was its first preacher (Heb. 2:3). It is the testimony of Jesus himself. That "testimony of Jesus" is the mark of the true believers according to Revelation 19:10. The testimony of Jesus is the Gospel of the Kingdom preached by Jesus and commanded by him as the saving Gospel for all nations.

Another massively influential teaching of Dispensationalism is a theory which invents an additional resurrection event not found in Scripture. According to the widely publicized opinions of Tim Lahaye and Jerry Jenkins (authors of the *Left Behind* books), Jesus will come back secretly *seven years before* he comes back publicly to inaugurate the Kingdom on earth. The so-called "secret rapture" theory refers to 1 Thessalonians 4:13-18. It maintains that the moment when the faithful dead are resurrected and living Christians "raptured" or caught up to meet the Lord in the air can occur at any moment. Suddenly millions will disappear and for seven years those faithful will be in heaven with Jesus. After that the public appearance of Jesus will occur.

This "pre-tribulation" rapture-resurrection is a pleasant illusion, promising an escape to heaven for all believers, prior to the time of great tribulation. The Bible does indeed speak of a future great tribulation just before the coming of Jesus to inaugurate the Kingdom (Matt. 24:21 = Dan. 12:1). But Scripture says no word at all about an arrival of Jesus to resurrect the dead *before* the great tribulation.

Jesus' account of the future flatly contradicts the "Left Behind" theory. Jesus expressly said that "immediately following the great tribulation...the sun will be darkened and the moon will not give its light, and the Son of Man will appear and gather his elect from the four corners of the world" (see Matt. 24:29-31). This is a "post" (=after) tribulation gathering of the faithful. Paul affirmed Jesus' understanding by urging his converts to expect release and relief from present sufferings "when the Lord Jesus Christ will be revealed from heaven in flaming fire taking vengeance on his enemies" (2 Thess. 1:7-8). Paul clearly did not expect release from or an end to Christian suffering seven years earlier!

The Dispensationalist attempt to insert a "coming" of Jesus in secret does violence to Jesus' clear statement that he intends to gather the Christian "elect" after the great tribulation (Matt. 24:29-31). To say that the elect in Matthew 24:31 are not Christians is a symptom of the failure of the Dispensationalist system! They forget that the teaching of Jesus in Matthew 24 is for Christians. Any system which divorces Jesus from his own teaching stands self-condemned. Jesus taught the New Covenant and Christianity is based on Jesus and his teachings.

There is a simplicity to the New Testament message. The Christian life is one of sexual purity, lack of hate, and service to God and man, a service characterized by the presentation of the Gospel of immortality in the Kingdom. It is a life of faith in dependence daily on God and His Son. There is One God, the Father, and Jesus is the Son of God, the Messiah, who is entitled to the unique status as "God's own Son," *the* Son of God, because of his miraculous beginning in the womb of Mary.

The Kingdom of God offers immortality to those who believe it and live for it in anticipation of its arrival at the return of Jesus to reign with the saints of all the ages on a renewed earth (Rev. 5:9, 10; Matt. 5:5).

Our basic premise, submitted to the public for examination, is that the churches have long lost much of the simplicity of the New Testament scheme of teaching. This has been the complaint also of countless scholars, past and present, of church history and of the Bible. We conclude with a valuable comment from a leading scholar of the Church of England:

"When the Greek and Roman mind came to dominate the Church, there occurred a disaster from which we have never recovered, neither in belief nor in practice."[4]

---

[4] H.L. Goudge, D.D.

Appendix 1
The Various New Testament Titles of the Gospel about the Kingdom

The following list of expressions provides first the "master definition" of the Gospel and then gives the equivalent Gospel titles found throughout the New Testament. All evangelism in the Bible is evangelism about the Kingdom of God as Jesus preached it. All invitations to salvation are invitations not "to go to heaven," but *to inherit the Kingdom of God.* Following Jesus involves using his terminology, not our own. To speak like Jesus (allowing, of course, for translation into our mother tongues!) means to think as he did and does.

If one combines references to "the Gospel of the Kingdom," "the Gospel" and "preaching" or "proclaiming," there are some 325 references to the Gospel of the Kingdom. "Believing" in the New Testament means believing in "the Gospel about the Kingdom and in the name of Jesus Christ" (Acts 8:12). The next verse (Acts 8:13) says that Simon "believed," i.e., believed in the Gospel of the Kingdom and the Name of Jesus. That is the meaning of Christian faith (in Simon's case belief did not last).

In Acts 28:24 some were persuaded by the Gospel of the Kingdom (v. 23) and some did not believe. To believe, therefore, in the New Testament is to be persuaded about the Kingdom of God and Jesus.

The Kingdom of God is the key which unlocks the secret to the teaching of Jesus and gives us knowledge of God's Plan for ourselves, the whole of the human race and the future of this earth.

The "parent definition" of the Gospel comes from Jesus himself, as the model exponent of the Gospel (Heb. 2:3). Jesus was the original herald of the Message of the Kingdom (introduced briefly by John the Baptist, Matt. 3:2). The Gospel comes with a specific definition. Its primary and fundamental title appears 18 times:

The Gospel about the Kingdom of God (Matt. 3:2; 4:17, 23; 24:14; 9:35; Luke 4:43; 8:1; 9:2, 6, 11, 60; 10:9; 16:16; Acts 8:12; 19:8; 20:25; 28:23, 31)

A variety of interchangeable phrases describe the same Gospel about the Kingdom:

= THE **WORD** ABOUT THE KINGDOM (Matt. 13:19; see 2 Tim. 4:1, 2; Rev. 1:9)

= **THE GOSPEL OF GOD** (Mark 1:14 = "Believe in the Kingdom," v. 15; Rom. 1:1; 15:16; 2 Cor. 11:7; 1 Thess. 2:2, 8, 9; 1 Pet. 4:17)

= **THE GOSPEL** (Matt. 11:5; Mark 13:10; 14:9; 16:15; Luke 3:18; 4:18; 7:22; 9:6; + 80 times)

= **THIS GOSPEL ABOUT THE KINGDOM** (Matt. 24:14)

= **THIS GOSPEL** (Matt. 26:13)

= **THE GOSPEL OF THE GRACE OF GOD** (Acts 20:24)

= **PROCLAIMING THE GOSPEL OF THE KINGDOM** (Acts 20:25)

= DECLARING THE WHOLE COUNSEL OF GOD (Acts 20:27)

= THE GOSPEL OF SALVATION (Eph. 1:13; Rom. 1:16)

= **THE GOSPEL OF JESUS CHRIST** (Mark 1:1)

= THE GOSPEL OF CHRIST (2 Cor. 9:13)

= THE GOSPEL OF THE GLORY OF CHRIST (2 Cor. 4:4)

= THE GOSPEL OF THE BLESSED GOD (1 Tim. 1:11)

= THE MYSTERY OF THE GOSPEL (Eph. 6:19; see Rom. 16:25)

= YOUR (GOD'S) WORD(S) (John 17:6; 17:8: "Receive words")

= **THE WORD OF GOD** (37 TIMES) = **HIS WORD** (Tit. 1:3; 1 John 2:5)

= **THE WORD** (46 times)

= THE WORD OF TRUTH (2 Cor. 6:7; Eph. 1:13; Col. 1:5; 2 Tim. 2:15; James 1:18)

= THE KNOWLEDGE OF THE TRUTH (1 Tim. 2:4; 2 Tim. 2:25; 3:7; Tit. 1:1; Heb. 10:26)

= THE TRUTH (50 times)

= REPENTANCE AND FORGIVENESS OF SINS IN JESUS' NAME (Luke 24:47)

= THE WORD OF THE LORD (Acts 8:25; 12:24; 13:44, 48, 49; 15:35, 36; 16:32; 19:10; 19:20; 1 Thess. 1:8; 4:15; 2 Thess. 3:1; 1 Pet. 1:25)

= THE WORD OF THE GOSPEL (Acts 15:7)

= OUR GOSPEL (1 Thess. 1:5; 2 Thess. 2:14; 2 Cor. 4:3)

= THE GOSPEL OF OUR LORD JESUS (2 Thess. 1:8)
= THE WORD OF HIS GRACE (Acts 14:3; 20:32)
= GRACE AND TRUTH (John 1:14, 17)
= THE WORD OF THE CROSS (1 Cor. 1:18)
= THE WORDS OF GOD (John 3:34; 8:47; Rev. 17:17; 19:9)
= THE WORDS OF THE LIFE OF THE COMING AGE
(John 6:68)
= MY (JESUS') WORD (John 5:24; 8:31, 37, 43, 51, 52;
14:23, 24; 15:20; Rev. 3:8)
= MY (JESUS') WORDS (Matt. 24:35; Mark 8:38; 13:31;
Luke 6:47; 9:26; 21:33; John 5:47; 14:10, 24; 15:7)
= MY TEACHING (John 7:16; 2 Tim. 3:10)
= THESE WORDS OF MINE (Matt. 7:24, 26)
= MY SAYINGS (John 12:47, 48)
= MY (PAUL'S) GOSPEL (Rom. 16:25)
= MY (PAUL'S) WORDS (Acts 26:25)
= MY (PAUL'S) MESSAGE (1 Cor. 2:4)
= MY (PAUL'S) PREACHING (1 Cor. 2:4)
= **THE MYSTERY(IES) OF THE KINGDOM OF GOD**
(Matt. 13:11; Mark 4:11; Luke 8:10)
= THE PREACHING OF JESUS CHRIST (Rom. 16:25)
= THE MYSTERY OF CHRIST (Col. 4:3; Eph. 3:4; Col.
1:27)
= THE MYSTERY (Rom. 16:25; Eph. 1:9)
= THE MYSTERY OF THE FAITH (1 Tim. 3:9)
= THE MYSTERY OF GODLINESS (1 Tim. 3:16)
= THE WORD OF LIFE (Phil. 2:16; 1 John 1:1)
= THE MYSTERY OF GOD (Rev. 10:7)
= THE WORD OF FAITH (Rom. 10:8)
= THE WORD OF CHRIST (Acts 10:36; Rom. 10:17; Col.
3:16)
= THE ABIDING WORD OF GOD (1 Pet. 1:23)
= THE IMPLANTED WORD OF GOD (James 1:21)
= OUR REPORT ("the word of hearing") (John 12:38; Rom.
10:16)
= THE FAITH (32 times)
= THE WORD OF THIS SALVATION (Acts 13:26)
= THIS SALVATION (1 Pet. 1:10)
= THIS SALVATION OF GOD (Acts 28:28)
= OUR COMMON SALVATION (Jude 1:3)

= THE FAITH ONCE AND FOR ALL DELIVERED TO
THE SAINTS (Jude 3)
= THE MANIFESTATION OF TRUTH (2 Cor. 4:2)
= THE WORD OF RECONCILIATION (2 Cor. 5:19)
= THE SWORD OF THE SPIRIT (Eph. 6:17)
= THE WORD OF RIGHTEOUSNESS (Heb. 5:13)
= THE WORD OF MY PERSEVERANCE (Rev. 3:10)
= THE WORD OF THEIR TESTIMONY (Rev. 12:11)
= THE TESTIMONY OF JESUS (Rev. 1:2, 9; 12:17; 19:10;
20:4)
= THE GOSPEL ABOUT THE COMING AGE (Rev. 14:6)[1]

For evidence of the Gospel deprived of the Kingdom see the
New Scofield Reference Bible on Revelation 14:6 and the article
"Gospel" in *Unger's Bible Dictionary.*

---

[1] "Eternal Gospel" is a mistranslation. The Gospel is not eternal; it is
Good News of the Coming Age of the Kingdom. "*Aionios*" in Greek
means "to do with the coming age." "The *aionios* Gospel is not in
Christian language the 'everlasting Gospel,' but 'the Gospel concerning
the Kingdom age'" (Nigel Turner, Ph.D., *Christian Words,* p. 456).
"Eternal" ("everlasting") is thus in many passages equivalent to
"millennial" or "having to do with the age to come of the Kingdom."

Appendix 2
What Is Death and Where Are the Dead?

What impression do you gain from these verses, drawn from a range of Scriptures?

Where are the dead and in what condition? When does release from death happen?

God said to Adam: "You are dust and you are going to return to the dust" (Gen. 3:19).

"The soul which sins will *die*" (Ezek. 18:4). (Can the soul mean an immortal soul? Obviously not.)

"The Lord kills and makes alive, the Lord brings down to SHEOL/HADES [the realm of the dead] and raises up" (1 Sam. 2:6-8; making alive = raising up = resurrection).

"Man dies and lies prostrate...Man lies down and does not rise: until the heavens be no more he will not be awakened nor roused from his sleep...Hide me in SHEOL...If a man dies, will he live again?" (Job 14:10-14).

"Will my hope go down into SHEOL? Will we together go down into the dust?" (Job 17:16).

"Enlighten my eyes lest I **sleep the sleep of death**" (Ps. 13:3).

"My soul has had enough troubles; my life has drawn near to SHEOL. I am reckoned like those who go down to the pit...Forsaken among the dead, like the slain who lie in the grave, whom you remember no more, in dark places, and they are cut off from your hand" (Ps. 88:3-5).

"Will you perform wonders for the dead? Will the shades rise and praise you? Will your lovingkindness be declared in the grave? Your faithfulness in Abaddon? Will your wonders be made known in the darkness? And your righteousness in the land of forgetfulness?" (Ps. 88:10-12).

"For SHEOL cannot thank Thee, death cannot praise Thee; those who go down to the pit cannot hope for Thy faithfulness" (Isa. 38:18).

"It is the living who give thanks to Thee, as I do today; a father tells his sons about Thy faithfulness" (Isa. 38:19).

"Why then do You not pardon my transgression and take away my iniquity? For now I will **lie down** in the dust; and You will seek me, but I will not be" (Job 7:21).

"What profit is there in my blood, if I go **down to the pit**? Will the dust praise You? Will it declare Your faithfulness?" (Ps. 30:9).

"The dead do not praise the Lord, nor do any who go down into **silence**" (Ps. 115:17).

"Return, O Lord, rescue my soul; save me because of Thy lovingkindness. For there is **no mention of You in death**; in SHEOL who will give You thanks?" (Psalm 6:4, 5).

"For there is hope for a tree, when it is cut down, that it will sprout again, and its shoots will not fail. Though its roots grow old in the ground and its stump dies in the dry soil, at the scent of water it will flourish and put forth sprigs like a plant. But man dies and lies prostrate. **Man expires, and where is he**? As water evaporates from the sea, and a river becomes parched and dried up, so man lies down and does not rise. Until the heavens are no longer, he will not awake nor be aroused out of **his sleep**" (Job 14:7-12).

"If I look for SHEOL as my home, **I make my bed in the darkness**; if I call to the pit, 'You are my father'; to the worm, 'my mother and my sister'; where now is my hope? And who regards my hope? Will it go down with me to SHEOL? Will we together go down into the dust?" (Job 17:13-16).

"But man in his pomp will not endure; **he is like the beasts that perish**" (Psalm 49:12).

"As sheep they are appointed for SHEOL; death will be their shepherd; and the upright will rule over them in the morning, and their form will be for SHEOL to consume so that they have no habitation" (Psalm 49:14).

"Do not trust in princes, in mortal man in whom there is no salvation. Man's spirit departs; he returns to the earth [to dust you will return]. In that very day his thoughts perish" (Ps. 146:3, 4).

"The living know that they will die, **but the dead do not know anything**; nor have they any reward, for their memory is forgotten...There is no activity or planning or knowledge in SHEOL where you are going" (Ecc. 9:5, 10).

"For the fate of the sons of men and the fate of beast is the same. As one dies, so dies the other. All have the same breath and there is no advantage for man over beast...All go to the same place. All came from the dust and all go to the dust" (Ecc. 3:19, 20, cp. "To dust you will return," Gen. 3:19).

A prophecy for the future: "Many of those **who are sleeping** in the dust of the earth will awake, some to everlasting life...Go your way to the end of your life. You will enter into rest and **rise again** at the end of the age, for your allotted portion." (What are the dead doing and where are they?) (Dan. 12:2, 13).

Jesus said:

"Do not marvel at this: An hour is coming when **all those who are in the tombs** [cp. 'sleeping in the dust of the earth'] will hear his voice and come forth: those who did the good deeds to a resurrection of life, those who committed the evil deeds to a resurrection of judgment" (John 5:28, 29).

"You will be rewarded at the resurrection of the just" (Luke 14:14).

"Jesus raised Lazarus from the dead" (John 12:17). How does resurrection happen? John 11:11, 14: "Our friend Lazarus **has fallen asleep [and remains in sleep, as implied by the Greek perfect tense]**. I am going to wake him **out of his sleep**...Lazarus is dead" (cp. the sleep of death, Ps. 13:3). Lazarus came forth from the tomb (John 11:43). Jesus "called Lazarus out of the tomb and raised him from the dead" (John 12:17).

Paul said:

"God has not only raised the Lord, but **will also raise us up** [=wake us up] through his power" (1 Cor. 6:14).

"He who raised the Lord will also raise us [wake us up] with Jesus and present us to him with you" (2 Cor. 4:14).

After the resurrection of Jesus, Peter said:

"The patriarch David died and was buried and his tomb is with us until this day...David *did not go to heaven*...David, after he had served the purpose of God in his own generation, fell asleep and was laid among his fathers [who were also asleep!] and underwent decay. But he whom God raised did not undergo decay" (Acts 2:29, 34; 13:36, 37).

Those who belong to Christ *will be raised* (woken up) at his coming (1 Cor. 15:23). The trumpet will sound and the dead will be raised (woken up) to immortality (see 1 Cor. 15:50-55). At the sound of the last trumpet (cp. Rev. 11:15-18: the 7th trumpet) the dead will be raised and given immortality and it is only then (and not a moment earlier!) that Hades is overcome. Thus Paul quotes Hosea 13:14: "I will deliver them from the power of SHEOL; I will redeem them from death. O death, where are your thorns? O SHEOL, where is your sting?" Paul sees this verse about the liberation of SHEOL as the event of the resurrection which he everywhere says will happen when Jesus comes back (1 Cor. 15:23).

Any theory which says that HADES/SHEOL was liberated by Jesus *already*, collides head on with this statement in 1 Corinthians 15:55: Hades is overcome *only in the future*. Even when the book of Revelation was written in 96 AD Jesus is the one who has the keys to Death and Hades. He has not used them yet. Later in Revelation 20:13-15 Death and Hades give up the dead who are in them. Jesus liberates the faithful dead from Hades in Revelation 11:15-18; 20:1-4.

So also in 1 Thessalonians 5:10 Paul expects the Christians, when Jesus returns, to be either asleep in death or surviving awake on earth: "Whether we are awake **or asleep** we may live together with him." The condition before all the Christians come to life together in the resurrection is called "sleeping" — exactly the same as Daniel 12:2: "Many who are **sleeping in the dust of the ground** will awake, some to everlasting life…"

"The Lord *will descend* from heaven with the shout of the angel and the sound of the trumpet, and the dead in Christ *will rise* first" (1 Thess. 4:16).

The condition of Christians before the resurrection is either sleeping in death or awake, alive. Both groups will live with Christ in the future resurrection (1 Thess. 5:10).

"I want to know Christ and the power of his resurrection…in order that I may attain to the resurrection from the dead" (Phil. 3:10, 11). "We are eagerly *awaiting the Savior from heaven* who will transform our humble state into conformity with the body of his glory" (Phil. 3:20, 21).

Writing late in the first century the writer of Hebrews said: "These [all the patriarchs, Abraham, Isaac, Jacob, and the prophets, including Enoch and Elijah the prophet] **died in faith not having received the promises**" (Heb. 11:13, 39).

Did he really believe they were *already* in heaven, in bliss, in joy? Or are they all waiting for the resurrection, when the dead are going to be made alive? (1 Cor. 15:22, 23). How can you be "made alive" if you are already alive?! How can you be made alive and become immortal if you are already alive and immortal? Note the warning against saying that the resurrection/immortalization has *already* happened:

"Be diligent to present yourself approved to God as a workman who does not need to be ashamed [cp. Mark 8:38]. Handle the word of Truth accurately. But avoid empty chatter, for it will lead to further ungodliness and their word will spread like gangrene. Hymenaeus and Philetus have departed from the Truth [the Gospel as Jesus and the Apostles preached it] saying that **the resurrection has *already* taken place**, and thus they upset the faith of some" (2 Tim. 2:15-18)

Saying that the dead are actually alive now violates an important warning from the Old Testament: "There will not be found among you anyone who makes his son or his daughter pass through the fire, one who uses divination, one who practices witchcraft, or one who interprets omens, or a sorcerer, or one who casts a spell, or a medium, or a spiritist, or **one who calls up the dead**" (Deut. 18:10, 11).[1]

---

[1] See further my booklet *What Happens When We Die?*

Appendix 3
W.C. Allen, Professor of Old Testament at Oxford, and Other Leading Authorities on the Kingdom of God

The objective analysis of the Kingdom of God in Matthew, provided by the *Dictionary of Christ and the Gospels*, ought to serve as a much-needed guide to all our thinking about the Kingdom. The Kingdom is the heart of the Christian Gospel:

"The Kingdom — **the central subject** of Christ's doctrine. With this he began his ministry (Matt. 4:17) and wherever he went he taught it as Good News [Gospel] (4:23). The Kingdom he taught was coming, but not in his lifetime. After his ascension he would come as Son of Man on the clouds of heaven (16:17, 19:28, 24:30) and would sit on the throne of his glory...Then the twelve Apostles should sit on twelve thrones judging the twelve tribes of Israel (19:28). In the meantime he himself must suffer and die and be raised from the dead. How else could he come on the clouds of heaven? And the disciples were to **preach the Good News of the coming Kingdom** (10:7, 24:14) among all nations making disciples by baptism (28:18). The body of disciples thus gained would naturally form a society bound by common aims. Hence the disciples of the Kingdom would form a new spiritual Israel (21:43)."[1]

The same authority goes on to say:

"In view of the needs of this new Israel of Christ's disciples, who were to await his coming on the clouds of heaven, it is natural that a large part of the teaching recorded in the Gospel should concern **the qualifications required in those who hoped to enter the Kingdom when it came**...Thus the parables convey some lesson about the nature of the Kingdom and the period of **preparation for it**. It should be sufficiently obvious that if we ask what meaning the parables had for the editor of the first Gospel, the answer must be that he chose them because...they taught lessons about the Kingdom of God *in the sense in which that phrase is used everywhere in the Gospel of the Kingdom which was to come, when the Son of Man came upon the clouds of*

---

[1] *Dictionary of Christ and the Gospels*, Vol. II, p. 145.

heaven. Thus the Parable of the Sower illustrates the varying **reception met with by the Good News [Gospel] of the Kingdom as it is preached amongst men.** That of the tares also deals not with the Kingdom itself, but with **the period of preparation for it.** At the end of the age, the Son of Man will come **to inaugurate his Kingdom**...There is nothing here nor elsewhere in this Gospel to suggest that **the scene of the Kingdom is other than the present world renewed**, restored and purified."[2]

My comment: The last sentence of our quotation makes the excellent point that Matthew does not expect believers to "go to heaven" but that Jesus will come back to rule with them on a renewed earth. The perceptive reader of the New Testament will note the striking difference between the biblical view of the Kingdom and what in post-biblical times was substituted for it: a departure of the faithful at death to a realm removed from the earth. "The Kingdom he taught was coming, but not in his lifetime." "In Matthew [and in the New Testament] the Kingdom of God is conceived, **first of all**, as something **in the future**" (cited below). So say leading analysts of the Gospel records. We may add a further statement from a recognized authority on Luke:

"It cannot really be disputed that Luke means by the Kingdom **a future** entity. The spiritualizing interpretation according to which the Kingdom is present in the Spirit and in the Church is completely misleading...It is *the message* of the Kingdom that is present, which in Luke is distinguished from the Kingdom itself. He knows nothing of an immanent [i.e., already present] development on the basis of the preaching of the Kingdom."[3]

The International Standard Bible Encyclopedia gets the emphasis on the future right:

"'The Kingdom of God is at hand' had the inseparable connotation 'judgment is at hand' and in this context, 'Repent,' in Mark 1:14, 15 must mean 'to avoid being judged.' Hence our Lord's teaching about salvation **had primarily a future content: positively admission into the Kingdom of God and negatively,**

---

[2] *Ibid.,* emphasis added. The same view of the Kingdom is expressed by the author of this article on Matthew in his commentary on Matthew (W.C. Allen, *The International Critical Commentary, St. Matthew*, T & T Clark, 1907, pp. lxvii-lxxi).

[3] Hans Conzelmann, *The Theology of St. Luke*, p. 122.

deliverance from the preceding judgment. So the Kingdom of God is the highest good of Christ's teaching...Man's nature is to be perfectly adapted to his spiritual environment and man is to be 'with Christ' (Luke 22:30) and with the patriarchs (Matt. 8:11). Whatever[?!] the Kingdom is, it is most certainly not exhausted by a mere reformation of the present order of material things."[4]

"Mark 1:14, 15: Mark gives a brief summary of the preaching of Jesus. Preaching and Good News are Mark's favorite expressions. The call of Jesus is accurately summed up in 1:15, where the association of repentance and faith reveals the language of the church (Acts 5:31; 11:18; 20:21). Mark's concern is to make clear that in this preaching Jesus continues to go forth into the world and this call, therefore, is being directed also to the one who reads this Gospel today. Consequently this section serves as a caption to the whole gospel.

"The Kingdom of God. When Jesus proclaims that the Kingdom of God is near, he is adopting a concept which was coined in the Old Testament. Although it denotes God's sovereignty over creation (Ps 103:19; 145:11ff) it refers *primarily* to God's unchallenged sovereignty *in the end time* (Isa. 52:7)...Judaism spoke of the reign of God which comes *after the annihilation of every foe* and the end of all suffering...In the New Testament the Kingdom of God is conceived *first of all* as something in the future (Mark 9:1, 47; 14:25; Matt. 13:41-43; 20:21; Luke 22:16, 18; 1 Cor. 15:50 et al) which comes from God (Mark 9:1; Matt. 6:10; Luke 17:20; 19:11). Therefore it is something man can only *wait for* (Mark 15:43), seek (Matt. 6:33); receive (Mark 10:15; cp. Luke 12:32) and inherit (1 Cor 6:9ff; Gal. 5:21; James 2:5), but is not able to create it by himself...In the acts and words of Jesus the future Kingdom has come upon him already. It is decided at that very moment whether or not he will ever be in the Kingdom...Repentance is nothing less than a wholehearted commitment to the Good News."[5]

Ernest Scott, D.D., Professor of New Testament at Union Theological Seminary, makes good points but seems uncertain about the Gospel:

---

[4] *The International Standard Bible Encyclopedia,* 1929, Vol. 4, p. 2667.

[5] *Good News According to Mark,* Eduard Schweizer, pp. 45, 46, 47.

"It seems almost impossible to define the Christian 'Gospel.' Sometimes it is identified with our religion as a whole, sometimes with some element in it which is regarded as central. To accept the Gospel is to believe in the atonement or the love of God, or the revelation in Christ or the fact of human brotherhood.

"Yet it is well to remember that the word which is now used so loosely had **at the outset a meaning which was clearly understood.** 'Jesus came into Galilee, preaching the Gospel of the Kingdom of God and saying, "The time is fulfilled and the Kingdom of God is at hand."' The Gospel underwent a marvelous development…**but the Good News has always been essentially what it was at the first — the announcement of the Kingdom.** It is evident from the manner in which Jesus made the announcement that he took up an idea which was already familiar. **He did not explain what he meant by the Kingdom, for he could assume that all his hearers were looking forward to it.** Their hope for it had been newly stimulated by John the Baptist…They had long been thinking of the Kingdom and wondering when it would come and a prophet had now arisen who declared that it was close at hand…In the religion of Israel we must seek for the immediate origin of the Kingdom idea of Jesus…The idea persisted long after the royal house was firmly established that the reigning king was only the vice-regent of the invisible King…Israel had been chosen by a unique God who was known as yet only by His own people, but was nonetheless King of the whole earth. The day was coming when all nations would own His sovereignty…On the higher levels of prophecy the purified Israel of the future is conceived as attracting all nations by its high example, to the service of the One God. More often it is assumed that Israel when fully disciplined will be restored to God's favor and advanced by Him to the sovereign place. As King of this preeminent people God will reign at last over the world…On the one hand God is already King. On the other hand it is recognized that the Kingship lies in the future…**They look for a coming day when He will overcome all usurping powers and assert Himself as King.** So the prophets keep before them the vision of a new age when the Kingdom of God will be fully manifested. In that happy time Israel will be exalted, the cause of justice will be established, the earth full of the glory of the Lord. Nature in that day will be restored to its pristine glory and the wolf will lie down with the lamb and cattle will feed in large pastures; the light of the moon will be as the light of the sun. He [and His Messiah] will reign from Mount Zion and all nations will serve Him. King over a righteous nation He will extend His dominion over the whole earth."[6]

The New Testament is based on the Old. Jesus came to:

1) Proclaim the Kingdom of God (Luke 4:43)

2) Confirm the promises made to the fathers (Rom. 15:8)

3) Give us **an understanding** that we might know God (1 John 5:20)

4) Make people righteous not only by his death but by his knowledge (Isa. 53:11).

In post-biblical times the original faith in the Gospel of the Kingdom suffered massive alteration, turning the Gospel into something quite different. Greeks rather than Jews became leaders in the church and they imported alien Greek philosophy into the Church's teachings.

This alteration of the original faith led finally in the 1500s to the Reformation which was a plea to go back to the Bible. But these reformers did not fully recapture the Gospel of the Kingdom. The process of restoration is furthered when people earnestly seek the original meaning of the Kingdom of God as preached by the original Jesus. The Gospel itself is all about the Kingdom of God and "Gospel" should never be divorced from the Kingdom.

"The Gospel is the proclamation of the Kingdom announced by Jesus (Mark 1:14, 15) and now proclaimed by the Church."[7]

"The Gospel as most of my church friends and I have known it in the past is so small a part of the whole deal, that it is hard to call it an accurate Gospel at all. Perhaps this limited Gospel message as proclaimed by modern Christians explains the limited impact it is having on America today."[8]

"Stanley Grenz has reviewed the failed attempts of evangelical theology to fire the imagination of the modern world. He argues for the Kingdom of God as the new organizing center of what we say and do."[9]

---

[6] 1931, pp. 11-21.

[7] *Harper Collins Bible Dictionary.*

[8] Gary Burge, *NIV Application Commentary.*

[9] *Revisioning Evangelical Theology.*

"Over the course of the past year, faculty from each of Fuller's three schools have met together to discuss the question: What is the Gospel? A dozen years ago, the late Robert Guelich made the question the topic of his inaugural address, noting that years of professional work has returned him again and again to this fundamental subject. Guelich told the story of an encounter with the founder Charles Fuller after a seminary forum, with the 'inspiration of Scripture' as its topic. Fuller commented that he longed for the day when the seminary would host a forum on the question: 'What is the Gospel?'"[10]

My comment: This is an amazing admission. The fact is that they really are not sure what the Gospel is, and yet they say they are saving people by preaching "it." The plain fact is that the Gospel of the Kingdom including of course the ratifying blood of Jesus and his resurrection is the Gospel. Until the "heaven" at death teaching, which is Plato's and not Jesus', is dropped, how can progress be made? And how can we be sure that anyone is saved by believing the teaching of Plato and calling it the teaching of Jesus? Is God as sloppy as we are with our thinking?! Is He so indulgent that He really does not care as long as we are sincere, although ignorant of the nature of man, his destiny, the identity of God and Jesus?

"It is a serious error to hold that the Kingdom of God plays no important role in apostolic Christianity. Such a view both lacks historical perspective and is at variance with the entire thought of the literature of apostolic Christianity. The very name of the new movement, *Christ*ianity, would suggest the contrary opinion. So far from the eschatological Kingdom of God being a secondary element in the early church, *it is its great conditioning belief.* The preaching of the first evangelists was not a call to ethical ideals or an argument as to certain truths. Rather it was the proclamation of a Message...As regards the person of the Messiah, there is of course no question that the early church believed that Jesus was the Christ who had gone to heaven, whence he would come to introduce the new age and the new Kingdom. This was the very core of the entire Christian movement. **To think of Jesus as deliberately using a term with a meaning different from what it**

---

[10] *Theology, News and Notes*, Fuller Theological Seminary, spring 2004.

would have been for others is not only to raise a question as to his morals, but as to his capacity as a teacher."[11]

Advice to evangelists!

Winston Churchill said: "If you have an important point to make, don't try to be subtle or clever. Use a pile driver. Hit the point once. Then come back and hit it again. Then hit it a third time — a tremendous whack."

---

[11] Shailer Matthews, D.D., Professor of Theology, Chicago Seminary, *The Messianic Hope in the New Testament*, University of Chicago Press, pp. 144, 155.

Appendix 4
The State of the Dead According to Leading Authorities

The celebrated *Interpreter's Dictionary of the Bible*: "No biblical text authorizes the statement that the soul is separated from the body at the moment of death."[1]

The Distinctive Ideas of the Old Testament, by Norman Snaith: "No passage [in the Old Testament] speaks of any immortality of the soul, which is not a biblical idea at all."[2]

Note that the Evangelical Alliance, meeting in 1846, listed in its faith statement belief "in the immortality of the soul."

Christian Words and Christian Meanings, by John Burnaby: "Greek philosophers had argued that the dissolution which we call death happens to nothing but bodies, and that the souls of men are by their native constitution immortal. The Greek word for immortality occurs only once in the New Testament, and there it belongs to none but the King of Kings...*The immortality of the soul is no part of the Christian creed*, just as it is no part of Christian anthropology to divide soul and body and confine the real man, the essence of personality, to supposedly separable soul for which embodiment is imprisonment...*Jesus taught no doctrine of everlasting life for disembodied souls*, such as no Jew loyal to the faith of his fathers could have accepted or even understood. But Jewish belief was in the raising of the dead at the Last Day."[3]

Why then do churches constantly say that disembodied souls have gone to heaven or hell?

Companion Bible by E.W. Bullinger, on 2 Corinthians 5:8: "It is little less than a crime for anyone to pick out certain words and frame them into a sentence, not only disregarding the scope and context, but ignoring the other words in the verse, and quote the words *'absent from the body, present with the Lord'* with the view of dispensing with the hope of the resurrection (which is the subject of the whole passage, 2 Cor. 4:14) as though it were unnecessary; and as though *'present with the Lord'* is obtainable

---

[1] Vol. 1, p. 802.
[2] p. 89.
[3] pp. 148, 149.

without it." (In other words, Paul is discussing here obtaining the new body at the resurrection and being present with the Lord via that resurrection. One can only be "with the Lord" at the Second Coming, not before. 1 Thess 4:17: "thus we will be always with the Lord.")

Law and Grace, by Professor A.F. Knight: "In the Old Testament man is never considered to be a soul dwelling in a body, a soul that will one day be set free from the oppression of the body, at the death of that body, like a bird released from a cage. The Hebrews were not dualists in their understanding of God's world."[4]

Families at the Crossroads, by Rodney Clapp: "Following Greek and medieval Christian thought, we often sharply separate the soul and body, and emphasize that the individual soul survives death. What's more we tend to believe the disembodied soul has escaped to heaven, to a more pleasant and fully alive existence. [Cp. the popular phrase 'he has gone to a better place.'] We mistakenly envision the Christian hope as an individual affair, a matter of separate souls taking flight to heaven. But none of this was the case for the ancient Israelites."[5]

Martin Luther: "I think that there is not a place in Scripture of more force for the dead who have fallen asleep, than Ecclesiastes 9:5 ("the dead know nothing at all"), understanding nothing of our state and condition — against the invocation of saints and the fiction of Purgatory."

John Wesley, founder of the Methodist Church, *Sermon on the Parable of Lazarus*: "It is, indeed, very generally supposed that the souls of good men, as soon as they are discharged from the body, go directly to heaven; but this opinion has not the least foundation in the oracles of God. On the contrary our Lord says to Mary, after the resurrection, 'Touch me not; for I have not yet ascended to my Father.'"

"Heaven in the Bible is nowhere the destination of the dying."[6]

Shirley Guthrie, *Christian Doctrine.* (Dr. Guthrie was Professor of Systematic Theology at Columbia Theological Seminary in Decatur, Georgia. He is author also of *Diversity in*

---

[4] p. 79.
[5] pp. 95, 97.
[6] J.A.T. Robinson, *In the End God,* p. 104.

Faith — Unity in Christ. His book from which the following is quoted is known as a "classic text.")

"We have to talk about a point of view that from the perspective of Christian faith is falsely optimistic because it does not take death seriously enough...Because the position we are about to criticize and reject is just what many believe is the foundation of the Christian hope for the future...we reject it not to destroy hope for eternal life, but to defend an authentically biblical Christian hope...*We refer to belief in the immortality of the soul.* This doctrine was not taught by the biblical writers themselves, but was common in the [pagan] Greek and oriental religions of the ancient world in which the Christian church was born. Some of the earliest Christian theologians were influenced by it, read the Bible in the light of it, and introduced it into the thinking of the church. It has been with us ever since. Calvin accepted it and so did the classical confession of the Reformed Churches, the Westminster Confession. According to this doctrine, my body will die but *I myself will not really die*...What happens to me at death, then, is that my immortal soul escapes from my mortal body. My body dies but *I myself live on* and return to the spiritual realm from which I came and to which I really belong. If we follow the Protestant Reformation in seeking to ground our faith on 'Scripture alone,' we must reject this traditional hope for the future based on the immortality of the soul...[Death] does not mean that the immortal divine part of us has departed to live on somewhere else. It means that life has left us, that our lives have come to an end, that we are 'dead and gone.' According to Scripture...my soul is just as human, creaturely, finite — and *mortal* — as my body. It is simply the life of my body...We have no hope at all if our hope is in our own in-built immortality."[7]

Robert Capon, *Parables of Judgment*: "One last theological point while we are on the subject of resurrection and judgment. Perhaps the biggest obstacle to our seeing the judgment of Jesus as the grand sacrament of vindication is our unfortunate preoccupation with the notion of the immortality of the soul. The doctrine is a piece of non-Hebraic philosophical baggage with which we have been stuck ever since the church got out into the wide world of Greek thought. Along with the concomitant idea of

---

[7] p. 378.

[immediate] 'life after death,' it has given us almost nothing but trouble: both concepts militate against a serious acceptance of the resurrection of the dead that is the sole basis of judgment."[8]

Archbishop William Temple, in the Drew Lecture for 1931: "That Conditional Immortality is the prevailing doctrine of the New Testament seems to me beyond question as soon as we approach its books free from the Hellenistic assumption that each soul is inherently immortal. There is (however)...no necessary contradiction in principle between asserting the full measure of human freedom and believing that in the end the grace of God will win its way with every (or most) human heart(s)." (The latter statement is open to some question, but he is certainly right about the pernicious effects of believing in the natural immortality of the soul.)

Professor Earle Ellis, *Christ and the Future in New Testament History*: "The Platonic view that the essential person (soul/spirit) survives physical death has serious implications for Luke's Christology and for his theology of salvation in history...For eschatology it represents a Platonizing of the Christian hope, a redemption *from* time and matter. Luke, on the contrary, places individual salvation (and loss) at the resurrection *in* time and matter at the last day. He underscores that Jesus was resurrected in 'the flesh' and makes him 'the first to rise from the dead,' the model on which all 'entering into glory' is to be understood.

"An anthropological dualism did enter the thought of the Patristic church, chiefly, I suppose, with *the grandiose synthesis of Christianity and Greek philosophy* made by Clement and Origen. It brought into eclipse the early Christian hope of the return of Christ and the resurrection of the dead [and the Kingdom of God on earth]. But it did not characterize the Christianity of the New Testament, and can be found in Luke only if one reads the texts, as those Christian fathers did, with lenses ground in Athens.[9]

"While death is not an individual fulfillment of salvation, during death one remains under Christ's Lordship and in his care...(but) while the Christian dead remain in time, they do not count time. The hiatus in their individual being between their death and their resurrection at the last day of this age is, in their

---

[8] Eerdmans, 1989, p. 71.
[9] Brill, 2000, p 127.

consciousness, a tick of the clock. For them the great and glorious day of Christ's Parousia is only a moment into the future. The 'intermediate state' is something that the living experience with respect to the dead, not something the dead experience with respect to the living or to Christ.

"Those with lenses ground in Athens, numerous in Christian tradition, see a *quite different picture*. They posit that a part of the person, the soul, is not subject to a cessation of being (and thus is not an element of the natural world) but that at the death of the body it is 'separated' to bodiless bliss or, in a variation on the theme, that there is a resurrection at death in which the physical body is exchanged for a spirit body already being formed within. [This would destroy the program and timetable given in 1 Cor. 15 and many other places.]

"Although they have many traditional roots and attachments, such theologies have, I think, seriously misunderstood Paul's salvation-in-history eschatology. It is because Paul regards the body as the person and the person as the physical body that he insists on the resurrection of the body, placing it at the Parousia of Christ in which personal redemption is coupled to and is part of the redemption-by-transfiguration of the whole physical cosmos. The transformed physical body of the believer will be called forth from the earth by God's almighty creative word [at the Second Coming], no less than were the transformed physical body of Christ and the originally lifeless body of the Genesis creation."[10]

---

[10] pp. 177, 178.

Appendix 5
DO SOULS GO TO HEAVEN?
The Witness of the Early Church to the State of the Dead and the Kingdom

While the Jehovah's Witnesses and others are labeled cultists because they say that the "soul" does not go to heaven when a person dies, the records of early church history are testimony to the fact that "orthodoxy" is the real culprit.

Did the early church teach the separation of a conscious soul from its body at the moment of death *and its immediate departure to heaven*? (I am not here discussing the *condition* of the soul as church fathers understood it, but the question of its *immediate location* at death.)

Here are the words of **Irenaeus** of the mid-second century. Irenaeus complains that some are distorting the biblical program of resurrection.

"Some who are reckoned among the orthodox go beyond the prearranged plan for the exaltation of the just, and are ignorant of the methods by which they are disciplined beforehand for incorruption. They thus entertain *heretical opinions*. For the heretics, not admitting the salvation of their flesh, **affirm that immediately upon their death they will pass above the heavens**. [*Note that it is the "heretics" who teach that the soul goes immediately to heaven at death. Today, according to present orthodoxy, it is the heretics who teach that souls do* **not** *go immediately to heaven or hell. This makes Irenaeus a heretic!*] Those persons, therefore, who *reject a resurrection affecting the whole man*, and do their best to remove it from the Christian scheme, know nothing as to the plan of resurrection. For they do not choose to understand that, if these things are as they say, the Lord himself, in whom they profess to believe, did not rise again on the third day, but *immediately upon his expiring departed on high*, leaving his body in the earth. But the facts are that *for three days*, **the Lord dwelt in the place where the dead were**, as Jonas remained three days and three nights in the whale's belly (Matt. 12:40)...David says, when prophesying of him: 'Thou hast delivered my soul from the nethermost **hell** (grave).' And on rising the third day, he said to Mary, 'Touch me not, for I have not yet ascended to my Father' (John 20:17)...How then must not these men be put to confusion who allege...that their inner man [soul], leaving the body here, ascends into the super-celestial place? [*Irenaeus thus reckons today's teaching as shameful!*] For as the Lord 'went away in the midst of the shadow of death' (Ps. 23:4), *where the souls of the dead were*, and **afterwards** arose in the body, and *after the resurrection* was taken up into heaven, **it is obvious that the souls of his disciples also...will go away into the invisible place [Hades]**...*and there remain until the resurrection*, awaiting that event. Then receiving their bodies, and rising *in their entirety*, bodily, just as the Lord rose, they will come *thus into the presence of God*. **As our Master did not at once take flight to heaven, but awaited the time of his resurrection...so we ought also to await the time of our resurrection**.

"Inasmuch, therefore, as the opinions of certain orthodox persons are derived from **heretical** discourses, they are both ignorant of God's dispensations, of the mystery of the resurrection of the just, and of the earthly **Kingdom** which is the *beginning of incorruption*; by means of this **Kingdom** those who will be worthy are accustomed gradually to partake of the divine nature."[1]

(Irenaeus thus condemns the whole "orthodox" tradition about what happens at death, the tradition, that is, which eventually swamped the biblical teaching, from the third century onwards.)

The protest of Justin Martyr against what later became orthodoxy, and remains so to this day, is no less incisive: "They who maintain the wrong opinion say that there is no resurrection of the flesh...As in the case of a yoke of oxen, if one or other is loosed from the yoke, neither of them can plough alone; so *neither can soul or body alone effect anything, if they be unyoked from their communion* [i.e. the soul can have no separate, active existence]. For what is man but the reasonable animal composed of body and soul? *Is the soul by itself man? No*; but the soul of man. Would the body be called man? No; but it is called the body of man. If then neither of these is by itself man, but that which is *made up of the two together is called man*, and God has called *man* to life and resurrection, he has called not a part, but the whole, which is the

---

[1] *Against Heresies*, Bk. 5.

soul and body...Well, **they say, the soul is incorruptible**, being a part of God and inspired by Him...Then what thanks are due to Him, and what manifestation of His power and goodness is it, *if He purposed to save what is by nature saved*...but no thanks are due to one who saves what is his own; for this is to save himself...How then did Christ raise the dead? Their souls or their bodies? *Manifestly both*. If the resurrection *were only spiritual*, it was requisite that he, in raising the dead, should show the body lying apart by itself, *and the soul living apart by itself*. But now he did not do so, but raised the body...Why do we any longer endure those unbelieving arguments and fail to see that we are retrograding when we listen to such an argument as this: **That the soul is immortal**, but the body mortal, and incapable of being revived. For this we used to hear from Plato, even before we **learned the truth**. If then the Savior said this and proclaimed salvation to the soul alone, what new thing beyond what we heard from Plato did he bring us?"[2]

Justin thus implies that teaching an immediate survival of the soul in heaven or hell is Platonism, not Christianity.

Justin is here refuting the arguments of Gnosticism which denied the resurrection of the flesh. Traditional Christianity has taken a similar, but slightly different tack by including in the creed a belief in the resurrection of the body, while also teaching an immediate salvation of the soul alone in a conscious, disembodied state. This is said to be the real person, albeit disembodied. Such an idea is flatly contradicted by Justin and Irenaeus and is identified by them as pagan. Present-day "orthodoxy" is thus partly Gnostic and pagan.

Justin Martyr: *Dialogue with Trypho on the Millennium:*

Trypho: "Do you really admit that this place Jerusalem will be rebuilt? And do you expect your people to be gathered together, and made joyful with Christ and the patriarchs?"

Justin: "I and many others are of that opinion, and believe that this will take place, as you are assuredly aware; but on the other

---

[2] *Dialogue with Trypho*, ch. 80.

hand, I signified to you that many who belong[3] to the pure and pious faith think otherwise. Moreover I pointed out to you that some who are called Christians, but are godless, **impious heretics**, teach doctrines that are in every way blasphemous, atheistical and foolish...I choose to follow not men or men's teachings, but God and the doctrines delivered by Him. For if you have fallen with some who are called Christians, but who do not admit the truth of the resurrection...who say that there is no resurrection of the dead, and *that their souls when they die are taken to heaven*, do not imagine that they are Christians...But I and others who are *right-minded Christians on all points* are assured that there will be a resurrection of the dead, and a thousand years in Jerusalem, which will then be built, adorned and enlarged, as the prophets Ezekiel, Isaiah and others declare...We have perceived, moreover, that the expression 'The Day of the Lord' is connected with this subject. And further, there was a certain man with us, whose name was John, one of the Apostles of Christ, who prophesied by a revelation that was made to him that those who believed in our Christ would dwell a thousand years in Jerusalem; and that thereafter the general and the eternal resurrection of all men would take place."

Justin's Statement on the Intermediate State (in full, ca 150 AD)

"For if you have fallen in with some who are called Christians, but who do not admit the truth of the resurrection and venture to blaspheme the God of Abraham, Isaac and Jacob; **who say that there is no resurrection of the dead, and that their souls when they die are taken to heaven: do not imagine that they are Christians**; just as one, if he would rightly consider it would not admit that the Sadducees, or similar sects of the Genistae, Meristae, Galileans, Hellenists, Pharisees, Baptists, are Jews, but are only *called* Jews, worshipping God with the lips, as God declared, but the heart was far from Him. But I and others, *who are right-minded Christians on all points*, are assured that there will be a resurrection of the dead, and a thousand years in Jerusalem,

---

[3] A number of commentators believe that the text has been corrupted here and that Justin wrote "who do *not* belong..." The alteration was made to make Justin less condemning of amillennialism.

which will then be built, adorned and enlarged, as the prophets Ezekiel and Isaiah and others declare."[4]

The Latin church father **Tertullian** (often known as the father of Western Christianity) is another who would disagree strongly with modern "orthodoxy" about what happens to the soul at death. He protested against the idea that the soul leaves the body at death and goes to heaven:

"**Plato**...*dispatches at once to heaven such souls as he pleases*...To the question whither the soul is withdrawn [at death] we now give the answer...The Stoics place only their own souls, that is, the souls of the wise, **in the mansions above**. Plato, it is true, does not allow this destination to all the souls, indiscriminately, of even all the philosophers, but *only those who have cultivated their philosophy out of love to boys* [homosexuals]...In this system, then, the souls of the wise are carried up on high into the ether...All other souls they thrust down to **Hades**.

"By ourselves the lower regions of **Hades** are not supposed to be a bare cavity, nor some subterranean sewer of the world, but a vast deep space in the interior of the earth, and a concealed recess in its very bowels; inasmuch as we read that **Christ in his death spent three days in the heart of the earth**, that is, in the secret inner recess which is hidden in the earth, and enclosed by the earth, and superimposed on the abysmal depths which lie still lower down. Now although Christ is God, yet, being also man, 'He died according to the Scriptures' (1 Cor. 15:3) and 'according to the same Scriptures was buried.' With the same law of his being he fully complied, **by remaining in Hades in the form and condition of a dead man; nor did he ascend into the heights of heaven before descending into the lower parts of the earth**, that he might there make the patriarchs and prophets partakers of himself. [*Nothing is said in the Bible about Jesus altering the condition of the patriarchs while he was in Hades.*] This being the case you must suppose **Hades** to be a subterranean region and *keep at arm's length those who are too proud to believe that the souls of the faithful deserve a place in the lower regions*. These persons who are 'servants above their Lord, and disciples above their

---

[4] *Dialogue with Trypho*, ch. 80, *Ante-Nicene Fathers*, Eerdmans, Vol. 1, p. 239.

Master,' would no doubt spurn to receive the comfort of the resurrection, if they must expect it in Abraham's bosom. But it was for this purpose, say they, that Christ descended into **hell**, that we might **not** ourselves have to descend thither. Well, then [they say], what difference is there between heathens and Christians, if the same prison awaits them all when dead? [But I say] **How, indeed, will the soul mount up to heaven, where Christ is already sitting at the Father's right hand, when as yet the archangel's trumpet has not been heard by the command of God?** When as yet those whom the coming of the Lord is to find on the earth, have not been caught up into the air to meet him at his coming, in company with the dead in Christ, who will be the first to arise? [1 Thess. 4:13-18] **To no one is heaven opened.** When the world, indeed, will pass away, *then the kingdom of heaven will be opened.*"[5]

Another "Church Father," Hippolytus (ca 170-236), certainly did not think that souls were in heaven:

"But now we must speak of **Hades**, in which the souls both of the righteous and the unrighteous **are detained**...[he apparently knew nothing of the **liberation of Hades**]. The righteous will obtain the incorruptible and unfading Kingdom, **who indeed are at present detained in Hades,** but not in the same place with the unrighteous...Thus far, then, on the subject of Hades, **in which the souls of all are detained** until the time God has determined; and then He will accomplish a resurrection of all, **not by transferring souls into other bodies**, but by raising the bodies themselves."[6]

Modern scholars realize that the view of death which has prevailed (and is now promoted in church constantly) is not biblical. Far from it, it is, amazingly, actually "pagan" and "Gnostic." Moreover, as the above quotations from the early apologists for Christianity show, the idea of going to heaven or hellfire immediately at death was a novel, heretical doctrine not taught by the Church for some 300 years after Christ. In a standard modern text of Christian dogmatics we read:

"The hellenization process by which Christianity adopted many Greek [pagan] thought patterns led in a different direction as the eschatological hope came to be expressed in Hellenistic

---

[5] Treatise on the Soul, ch. 55.

[6] *Against Plato, on the Cause of the Universe*, 1, 2.

categories. Irenaeus said: 'It is manifest that the souls of his disciples also, upon whose account the Lord underwent these things, will go away **in the invisible place** allotted to them by God, and *there remain until the resurrection*, awaiting that event. Then receiving their bodies and rising in their entirety, that is bodily, just as the Lord arose, they will come into the presence of God.' Irenaeus' statement contains the concept of an abode or purgatory in which the soul of the dead **remains until the universal resurrection.** We should not denounce this as a deviation from biblical teaching, since the point of the assertion is anti-gnostic. **Irenaeus wanted to reject the Gnostic idea that at the end of this earthly life the soul immediately ascends to its heavenly abode. As the early fathers fought the pagan idea that a part of the human person is simply immortal, it was important for them to assert that there is no rectilinear ascent to God. Once we die, life is over.**"[7]

There is a further impressive protest against the popular idea that the dead survive as conscious "souls" in heaven. One might expect that such protest would initiate a wide-scale reform amongst the clergy. Alan Richardson, D.D. writes in *A Theological Word Book of the Bible*:

"**The Bible writers**, holding fast to the conviction that the created order owes its existence to the wisdom and love of God and is therefore essentially good, **could not conceive of life after death as a disembodied existence** [as millions of sincere believers are now taught in church to think of it!] ('we will not be found naked,' 2 Cor. 5:3), but as a renewal under conditions of the intimate unity of body and soul which was human life as they knew it. Hence *death was thought of as the death of the whole man*, and such phrases as 'freedom from death,' imperishability or immortality could only properly be used to describe what is meant by the phrase eternal or living God 'who only has immortality' (1 Tim. 6:16). **Man does not possess within himself the quality of deathlessness**, but must, if he is to overcome the destructive power of death, receive it as the gift of God who 'raised Christ from the dead,' and put death aside like a covering garment (1 Cor. 15:53,

---

[7] Braaten/Jenson, *Christian Dogmatics*, Vol. 2, p. 503, section written by Hans Schwartz, Professor of Protestant Theology, University of Regensburg, Germany.

54). It is through the death and resurrection of Jesus Christ that this possibility for man (2 Tim. 1:10) has been brought to life and the hope confirmed that the corruption (Rom. 11:7) which is a universal feature of human life will be effectively overcome."[8]

The fundamental confusion about life after death which has so permeated traditional Christianity is brilliantly described by Dr. Paul Althaus in his book *The Theology of Martin Luther*:

"The hope of the early church centered on the resurrection of the Last Day. It is this which *first* calls the dead into eternal life (1 Cor. 15; Phil. 3:21). **This resurrection happens to the man and not only to the body.** Paul speaks of the resurrection not 'of the body' but 'of the dead.' This understanding of the resurrection implicitly understands death as also affecting the whole man...**Thus [in traditional orthodoxy] the original Biblical concepts have been replaced by ideas from Hellenistic, Gnostic dualism.** The New Testament idea of the resurrection which affects *the whole man* has had to *give way to the immortality of the soul.* The Last Day also loses its significance, for souls have received all that is decisively important long before this. Eschatological tension is no longer strongly directed to the day of Jesus' coming. *The difference between this and the hope of the New Testament is very great.*"[9]

That difference may be witnessed in contemporary preaching at funerals which, though claiming the Bible as its source, reflects a pagan Platonism which the New Testament, the early church fathers and modern informed scholars reject.

Can belief in pagan ideas, promoted in the name of Jesus, result in a knowledge of Truth which leads to salvation? Is not this obvious paganism of Christianity a cause for alarm and a reason for returning to the Truth of the Bible?

We conclude with the following comments of the well-known German theologian Jürgen Moltmann:

"In the degree to which Christianity *cut itself off from its Hebrew roots* and acquired Hellenistic and Roman form, it:

1) Lost its eschatological [that is, future Kingdom on earth] hope.

---

[8] pp. 111, 112.
[9] Fortress Press, 1966, pp. 413, 414.

2) Gave up its apocalyptic solution for 'this world' of violence and death.

3) Merged into late antiquity's **Gnostic religion** of salvation.

From Justin (150 AD) onward:

1) Most of the 'fathers' revered Plato as 'a Christian before Christ.'

2) God's eternity now took the place of God's future. Incarnation made everyone look back into eternity instead of forward to the creation of the Son of God at his begetting by the Father in Mary, his resurrection and future coming to rule in the Kingdom.]

3) **'Heaven' replaced the coming Kingdom.**

4) The [pagan] idea of redemption of the soul from the body replaced the spirit as the source of life.

5) The immortality of the soul displaced the resurrection of the body.

6) People hoped for the soul's escape from the body."[10]

---

[10] *The Spirit of Life*, 2001.